The Library

Nazareth College of Rochester, N. Y.

OUR AMERICAN HUMORISTS

OUR AMERICAN HUMORISTS

BY

THOMAS L. MASSON

NEW AND ENLARGED EDITION

Essay Index Reprint Series

 BOOKS FOR LIBRARIES PRESS
FREEPORT, NEW YORK

New & enlarged edition first published 1931
First Reprinting in this Series 1966
Second Reprinting 1969

112494

STANDARD BOOK NUMBER:
8369-0692-6

LIBRARY OF CONGRESS CATALOG CARD NUMBER:
67-23245

PRINTED IN THE UNITED STATES OF AMERICA

FOREWORD

This book is intensely personal.

I have known and suffered with most of the men who are unfolded in these pages. I say that I *have* known them, because, after this book is issued, I may not know them again. They may not want me to.

I have suffered with them when we were discussing the humor of those who were not present at the time. Occasionally I have laughed at them, and with them.

For twenty-eight years I was the literary and managing editor of *Life*. During this short and eventful and melancholy period of American history, all of the humorists of the day, incipient or otherwise, passed before me in review.

During the first five years I read so many jokes that I rapidly fell into a hopeless decline; I was given up by seven doctors, the majority of whom have since passed away—and they sent me off to a sanitarium. By careful nursing for a year, however, I came back. After having lived in an American sanitarium, even for a few months, you become so hardened to all other forms of suffering, that nothing else matters. From then on, until the past few months, I have read jokes unceasingly, and risen above them so far that I can still smile. This shows what heights of endurance a human being can attain, when he abandons his conscience and his moral courage.

FOREWORD

The humorists I have met and still know, in spite of what the future holds forth, are many and numerous. Some of them are still very young, emerging, so to speak, from the parent egg only within the past year. Others are old and hardened—like myself. Some of them, in spite of their occupation, manage to be occasionally cheerful; others, with naturally cheerful dispositions, are afraid to show them for fear that they will lose their gift of humor. Still others have become successful playwrights, and from their lofty financial heights can afford to look down with pity and sympathy upon the poor devils who still struggle to give others a little laughter.

Now you, gentle—and like myself, frequently misguided—reader, may think that you have a sense of humor. Maybe you have. You couldn't make me laugh anyway, but that would not be a fair test. One thing is quite certain: if you have not a sense of humor, nobody will ever be able to convince you that you haven't. You will never know. You will always think you have, and perhaps that is the one thing necessary.

But here is a fair test—which you probably will not agree to. (In these days, never agree to any test: it's the only safe way; otherwise they will have you locked up in a nut-factory inside of twenty-four hours—you will be convicted of being so hopelessly unintelligent that even people from whom you have borrowed money will cross over when they see you coming.) And this is it: If you are now beginning to wonder what this is all about, if you are beginning to ask yourself the question, "What is this fellow driving at anyway?" then you must have a sense of humor, because a sense of humor is nothing if not practical. It has no use for the superfluous. It insists, not only upon results, but upon the right kind of results; and of this I shall now hope to convince you in a few simple words, without that excessive ornamentation with which—if I cared to use it—I might easily convince you that I was a genuine highbrow.

There is no other country in the world that can boast of an actual race of professional humorists, such as we have here in America. And yet the word "professional" does not seem quite to cover the case. It conveys a wrong idea. I suppose the reason is that humor is assumed to be a spontaneous affair, something that springs up quite by accident, and therefore must always be non-professional. As a matter of fact, the direct contrary is the truth. Instead of being spontaneous, humor is either long premeditated, or else it is the result of a background of such solemnity and gloom that the flashes of humor that come out of it only seem to be spontaneous by contrast. Let us take Dickens—perhaps the supreme humorist of England—as an example. His boyhood was steeped in sadness. Sensitive almost beyond words, he was thrown into an atmosphere of such intense gloom as to have his soul seared with it. The misery of London sank into the very depths of his consciousness. And it was from this drab background that his humor came, that wonderful racial humor that grows right up from the soil, that smells of the soil. We see the same law working in Lincoln. Out of his melancholy youth, out of his tragic love affair, out of his efforts to adjust his great mind to the homely conditions of his environment came the sympathy and sense of contrast that enabled him to call up from his own vivid experience all those incidents that illuminate his thought in such a marvelous way. Mark Twain, in perhaps different manner, is another example. These men were intense individualists; the genuine humorist always is. He *feels* himself. With the sense of a great finality, he recognizes the utter hopelessness of circumventing Fate. This being so, he takes the only course possible for anyone who has any sort of backbone—he resolves to laugh it off. It is the very depth of melancholy in the genuine humorist that compels him to take this course —otherwise he would go mad. Thus he becomes the passionate advocate of brevity; anything long or dull infuriates him; and it is through this gift that he renders his greatest service to humanity. Think of what would happen to us here in America if there were no humorists—life would be one long Congressional Record.

I want to press on this point a little harder because it is desirable for you to see that this book is unique. Defective as it may be—and I offer no hopes that it is near perfect—at least it is the first attempt here on this continent to set right the race of humorists, to show definitely what they are here for, to make it plain that they are here for a great purpose, and that, without them, we should already have been wrecked. There is no hope for this present world of ours without humor. In the long process of time it may indeed vanish; we may ultimately reach a stage where we shall all be utterly passive and humorless in our serenity. But finally, to reach this Nirvana, we must

be steered right by humor. Humor is a constant corrective; it is a kind of ballast. You would be surprised
if you knew how it is forever reaching up into high
places and setting men right; setting them right silently,
making them pause. For nothing is more effective
than ridicule. An epigram may make an exile of a
man. We have only to think of some of the instances
of the past. Think of James G. Blaine as The Tat-
tooed Man! Do you remember Mark Hanna's dollar-
mark suit? Are you aware that one of the causes
that influenced his managers not to run Mr. McAdoo
for president was because they feared the rush of
ridicule about his name? Once fasten upon any man
a thing ever so slight that makes him an object of
laughter and his cause is lost. That is one of the
reasons, of course, why all popular leaders have to be
so careful not to convey the impression that they are
humorists; that is one of the reasons why Lincoln was
so great—he is almost the only man in history who was
able to rise above this.

And, owing to numerous conditions that lie deep
in our Colonial history—one of them being the sense
of intimacy that we were able to generate out of our
adventure on this Continent- we Americans have
raised up this set of humorists, who are in a class by
themselves. Or, perhaps I should say, who are in a
group by themselves—this group being divided into
sections or classes, but all having the same general
purpose, which is to make proper fun of everything
in sight. The object of this book is to make you see
them all in this light—is to make you understand them,
and to realize their great service. It is more than this:

FOREWORD

it is to make them see themselves. Most of them haven't realized what they are here for, and perhaps, at the time, this was a blessing, because a humorist who has an avowed mission in life may, after all, become only a nuisance. It is his very innocence that makes him effective. When he gets to be self-conscious he is lost. They tell us that was what was the matter with Mark Twain. He was quite all right until he came to wear white flannel suits. And I must interrupt the proceedings to tell a story about him. I hope it is true. You know that, at one of the most distressing periods of his life—when he had financially failed—his friend Rogers came to his rescue, straightened out his accounts and put him on his feet generally. Both Mr. and Mrs. Rogers naturally came to be very fond of Mark. He visited them in their Adirondack Camp. On one occasion he dolled himself up in a white flannel suit. Mrs. Rogers, seeing him thus accoutered for the first time, complimented him on his appearance. Mark was very vain.

"You like me in it?" he asked.

"You never looked better."

"Then I shall always wear it." And so his white flannels became historic.

Another: At a Turkish bath place in New York to which I once became addicted, one of the rubbers told me that, some years before, Mark Twain came down from Hartford one day and, upon the recommendation of a friend, went there to take a Turkish bath. And he was so overjoyed by the experience that he did not come out of it for a week!

Let me now indicate briefly some of the classes into

FOREWORD

which our American humorists fall. First there are the columnists, with whom all American newspaper readers are so familiar, and who form such an important part of our daily newspaper pabulum. Where did they originally come from? Personally, I think that Ben Franklin is responsible for them. This great man started more things on this continent than anyone else that has ever lived here. And among other things, his *Poor Richard's Almanac* is the North American progenitor of the column. The wonder of it is that nobody has yet been able to exceed him in wit and fertility of resource. Go back to his time, study his period, and then read what he has written, and you will be astonished at his genius. His enormous influence over his period, indeed, his enormous influence over the men that made the Constitution, can scarcely be measured. What was it that impelled him, then an aged man, to write his great letter of compromise about the Constitution at the most critical moment of our history? A divine sense of humor, which is always founded on a sense of justice. He said there were things in the Constitution of which he did not approve, but, after all, it was the spirit of concession that must be exercised. When we look back upon this creating of an immortal document that has carried us along such a distance in good faith and prosperity, we must pause and give a large part of the credit to Ben Franklin, our first great humorist, who also, with Lincoln, was great enough to rise above his reputation for being only a maker of fun.

From Ben Franklin's time, the columnist has always flourished in American newspapers. Artemus Ward

FOREWORD

might be called a sort of traveling columnist. He exhibited on his own account. His column was a separate affair, conducted by himself independently. Bill Nye started on a paper called the *Laramie Boomerang* —and a remarkable personage he was. He was quite "unrefined," but that is of small consequence, because it was a part of the picture. He had small education from the academic standpoint, none of that literary sense which we have come to term *precious*, and of which Henry James stands as the chief representative. But he was very funny, and in a large sense he was intensely wholesome. Latterly, he traveled about the country, writing his weekly letters for *The New York World*, and other papers. An artist friend drew weekly caricatures of him that appeared with his contributions. He received two hundred dollars a week for these letters. I happen to know this, for, at that time, I was a young cub editor, and his beautifully written copy passed through my hands and thence on to the syndicate of papers. And I cannot help but contrast this with the lordly sums later received by Mr. Finley Peter Dunne for his Dooley letters which, I believe, at their height, brought Dunne well over a thousand dollars a week.

Somewhat later came the delightful and poetic Eugene Field, whose column on *The Chicago News* was so remarkable for its high literary standard. Gene Field had all the qualities of a columnist, and more. He had genuine pathos and genuine humor. And, in addition, he had a touch of genuine comedy, which is, I think, the rarest trait in the world. At least, we are entitled to think so when we consider how few, in all

FOREWORD

the history of the world, have possessed it. You ask we what comedy is, in contrast to humor, and my reply is that it would take too long to explain, and, even then, my explanation would be mysterious and probably inadequate. I can only refer you to George Meredith's essay on the subject. Comedy, to my mind, is essentially Greek in its origin: it is paganism with an aura. Whatever it is, Gene Field undoubtedly had it. His verses—many of them exquisite in their admirable fooling—still linger with us. And it is only recently that Bert Leston Taylor, perhaps his ablest successor in Chicago—who was the columnist for *The Chicago Tribune*—passed away, lamented by a great public and mourned by his loyal circle of friends. I knew Mr. Taylor when he began so many years ago, on *Puck,* and followed him through his career with constant admiration. Just before he died, when I was engaged in compiling this book, he took the trouble to write out for me a short biography of himself—with the brevity of a modest reluctance—and it was only a few days after receiving it that I was shocked to hear the news of his death. The great pity of a life like his is that, because of the fugitive quality of his work, so much of it disappears. Since his death in 1921 two posthumous books of his, "The Penny Whistle" (with a foreword by Franklin P. Adams), "Cliff Dwellers" (in memory of B. L. T.) and the "So-Called Human Race" have been published. As for all our living columnists of to-day, they abound and seem to be a growing and prosperous race. And, in this book, they are to receive fair and, I hope, decent treatment. I merely wish now to emphasize the fact that they are a family by themselves. One of the marks of success in any local American paper is to be able to maintain its own columnist.

The other species of humorists peculiar to this country comprises the joke-writers, who do so many of the dialogues appearing under drawings in the comic papers; the writers of humorous short stories, whose number is constantly, although slowly, increasing; the satirists, a small and rather exclusive body; the humorous essayists, also quite small and select; the big bow-wow humorists, such as George Ade, Ring Lardner and Irvin Cobb; the after-dinner speakers, whose work is not generally original; the special newspaper reporters, called at one time "Bright young men" (a term originating in the old *New York Sun* under Mr. Dana), the humorous verse writers, and those geniuses who, day after day, in pictures, delight thousands by their comic strips, and the burlesquers.

All of these different species are working very hard —for what purpose? To maintain themselves? Certainly, but in reality for something much more important. In reality, they are stemming the tide of dullness, of utter stupidity, of horrible uniformity that would otherwise engulf us. We have only to think of the fate awaiting us, if we were enslaved wholly by the theologians, the philosophers, the solemn historians, the reformers, all the alleged deep thinkers, to render up thanks daily and hourly for the noble band of humorous martyrs who stand between us and unutterable boredom.

Looking back over the history of this country from

FOREWORD

the time the Puritans landed, it is almost impossible to overestimate the service rendered to us, and to humanity generally, by our humorists. It may be said that they have been unfair—that they have made a laughing-stock out of many estimable people. That is pure nonsense. And even if they have, what of it? Anything is better than not to have them around. Besides, it is fact that when any one of them gets a wrong slant, he is immediately set upon by all of the others. And it is astonishing how conscientious they are, how hard they work to get at the truth. But more astonishing still is the way they work to help one another. While the competition among them is fierce, I know of no body of men working at one trade that will do more for one another than these same humorists. It is a singular fact that, among themselves, they are always looking for new talent. When some kid comes along who shows any talent, the rest of the gang, instead of pouncing upon him and throttling him, as would be (alas!) quite human, make all kinds of sacrifices to give him a start. And so far as I can remember, I have never seen the slightest envy expressed over some youngster who has shown talent enough to forge himself ahead. But God help him if he does not make good!

I must admit that this spirit has, and does lead to some logrolling. That, however, is due to other causes than mere commercialism. It is due, in some cases, to bad manners. In others, it is due to plain ignorance. It is not always easy for a writer whose work is read daily by hundreds of thousands of people to keep his perspective. It is quite natural for him, when he be-

FOREWORD

gins to write of himself, and finds that nothing happens, to come to depend upon that sort of thing too much. I am doing it now, in the sense that I am playing up my own relationship to many of these friends because I sincerely desire to sell this book. But I do not altogether desire to sell this book for mercenary reasons. On the contrary, I think I have an idea that has never been put forward before, so far as I know, in just this way. It is a perfectly homely idea. What I desire to show is that there is no other class of writers in America that is actually doing more for the country than the humorists. I defy anybody to prove that this is otherwise. I put this on a broad plane. I am not discussing literature, but life. The moment that one gets into any discussion about art or beauty he is —as Thomas Huxley once put it—up against the ultimate problems of existence. What so many specialists, either in painting or music or literature, do not understand is, that the art of living is the supreme art of all. God knows that we have room for improvement in the art of living. God knows that, when we consider the hopeless welter of slums and bad finance, and utterly banal patter wasted upon our outstanding problems, such as education, one could cry aloud for some new satirist to arise who, with a truly illuminated pen, would show us the utter folly of so much that we accede to—for example, the frightful stupidities of prohibition, the deliberate atrocities forced upon us by so many anti-Christs of all the arts. But, certainly, the salvation of the world cannot be worked out in a day. And the real point is that we are beginning to get glimmerings of some kind of a national spirit. And

FOREWORD

the humorists are working like nailors, constantly trying to correct the things that they see are wrong—oftentimes weakly, oftentimes in error, sometimes foolishly, frequently vulgar, but practically always sincere.

What interests me more personally than anything else is the humor of crowds, when crowds get together continually in a common spectacle, as for instance, baseball crowds. The astonishing variety of the vocabulary of Americans under these conditions is a constant object of admiration. It is exceeded by no other race on earth. It is a combination of good nature and satire perfectly inimitable. Precious people no doubt shudder at it, but real people understand it. The most intelligent Englishmen almost always refer to it with great respect.

This book is by no means complete. There is no order, no system about it. It is largely a labor of love. Begun first as a kind of perfunctory attempt to group some of our most prominent humorists, the effort at formal biography so saddened and disheartened me that I threw aside the whole work, and made up my mind that, never again, would I attempt to write of human beings as if they were so many harvesting machines. Then, my own utter inadequacy to show them as they are throttled still another attempt. Then, their own messages began flowing in upon me; it was as if they themselves had all come to my rescue. I made up my mind that we would all help together. I began to see that, each in his own star, we were actually working together. I recalled the keen joy I had felt so many times in the past when some new youngster came

FOREWORD

to the front and took his place in the ranks, and then I tried to visualize the great mass of Americans stretching over this vast country, most of them smiling once a day at some clever bit of satire, some philosophical comment on our national life that exposed in a sentence the whole frailty, or some joyous yawp that just made one feel good without knowing why; and of all these same Americans who didn't know what humor is (which I don't myself), and didn't realize what it meant, and was meaning daily to them. And so it seemed to me that, after all, even the lamest kind of an attempt to put our humorists on, at least, a basis of common understanding with the whole country ought to be made. That is why I have done this book, and if anyone has inadvertently been omitted, or aught set down in malice, I ask to be forgiven.

CONTENTS

CONTENTS

CONTENTS

OUR AMERICAN HUMORISTS

CHAPTER I

GEORGE ADE

IN the introduction to Ivanhoe, Sir Walter Scott, with the genial candor that was one of his most charming traits, laments that hitherto he has been unable to break away from the uninterrupted course of the Waverley novels. "It was plain, however," says Sir Walter, "that the frequent publication must finally wear out the public favor, unless some mode could be devised to give an appearance of novelty to subsequent productions. Scottish manners, Scottish dialect, and Scottish characters of note, being those with which the author was most intimately and familiarly acquainted, were the groundwork upon which he had hitherto relied for giving effect to his narrative." He then adds: "Nothing can be more dangerous for the fame of a professor of the fine arts than to permit (if he can possibly prevent it) the character of a mannerist to be attached to him, or that he should be supposed capable of success only in a particular and limited style."

Indeed, Sir Walter was so much impressed by the truth of his observation, that he insisted upon publishing "Ivanhoe" anonymously, and it was only upon the assurance of its success from his publishers that he consented to the use of his name.

This danger has long been recognized by authors, and during the last half century—inspired quite possibly by the example of Sir Walter,—British writers have quite largely succeeded in overcoming the handicap. We have Mr. Kipling starting out as a writer of short sketches from India, creating a new vein of Anglo-Indian literature, but shortly breaking away from his environment and becoming a short-story writer of universal appeal, then a first rank novelist, and the only poet of his generation who has voiced in rugged song the heart and soul of Imperial England. We have Jerome K. Jerome, whose "Three Men in a Boat" and whose housemaid's knee fastened upon him the reputation of a professional humorist, suddenly becoming a dramatist of high order. There was Thackeray of Punch, likewise a professional humorist and satirist, breaking bounds and becoming the author of "Vanity Fair": and, after him, Du Maurier, who used to write his own jokes to his own drawings and, leaving the conference table (they say in a fit of pique) built forthwith his "Trilby"—surely a work of literary art of the first magnitude. Still more recently we have Mr. A. A. Milne, who, from being in the beginning a chance contributor to Punch, is rapidly achieving a reputation not only as a humorist and dramatist of the first rank, but as a writer whose breadth of vision is constantly increasing. There are numerous other examples in Great Britain of authors that have risen above their first reputations: Mr. Wells is a notable instance, for it would be difficult to say whether he is more preëminent as a novelist, a historian, or a sociological psychologist: and whether Thomas Hardy is greater as a poet or a novelist is a question upon which his staunchest adherents are divided.

The literature of this country is, quite inevitably, built upon smaller lines than that of Great Britain, but the same struggle of our authors to rise above their first limitation has been going on here, as there, though with less success. Mark Twain tried to rise above it in "Joan of Arc," which he published anonymously because he feared that his reputation as a humorist would detract from the dignity of his effort. The problem appears to be more difficult in America than elsewhere.

All things considered, by right of achievement and what one may term "intrinsic merit," our two leading humorists are George Ade and Finley Peter Dunne: yet neither of them has fully succeeded in breaking away from his single reputation. Mr. Dunne became widely known as the author of the inimitable Mr. Dooley: and henceforth nothing else but the observations of Mr. Dooley would satisfy an eager public. Mr. Ade became known as the author of "Fables in Slang": and Mr. Ade is still known as the author of "Fables in Slang," although it must be said that as the creator of the comic opera "The Sultan of Sulu," the comedy, "The College Widow" and others meritorious, his fame as a dramatist is closely allied to his fame as a fablist. Yet here the observation may be made, let me hope without offense, that if Æsop had not written his fables, it is probable that George Ade's reputation as an American humorist would have been none the less, but his reputation as a dramatist might easily have been less if Gilbert and Sullivan's operas had not been written. Of this, Mr. Ade says himself: "I wanted to do something on the order of 'The Mikado' or 'Patience,' but all the plans and specifications handed to me called for 'Chimme Fadden' minus the dialect." Nevertheless, and in spite of his modesty, Mr. Ade did succeed. He produced rollicking operas with true American tang, influenced largely in his form by Gilbert. And so his fables are American fables; and the form in this instance does not particularly matter: the form, granted, is very old—like hexameter verse, or the ballade, or the sonnet. The point is that Ade is an American, which—in an American —gives one a great advantage. Ade was born in the middle of America: not exactly in the middle, but enough to insure his being an American. He wasn't born near enough to the Atlantic coast to become an Anglomaniac, or to take on too much Eastern education to obscure his racial traits. It is probable that the mud of Indiana stuck to him long enough to charm him against foreign influences. Along somewhere in the middle of his life, after he had achieved fame, he traveled abroad: he went to Egypt. But it was then too late to spoil his jokes: their racial quality had become fixed.

George Ade, born in Kentland, Indiana, February 9, 1866, was educated at Purdue University. It probably did him less harm than might have been done to him anywhere else he might have gone. He succeeded in preserving his Americanism: he stuck to Indiana more or less, and learned to write at first in a very practical school—a Lafayette, Indiana, newspaper office. Then, still an American, he flew to Chicago, and consorted with high and low spirits; plied his trade as a reporter and writer, and served his apprenticeship. This leads me to observe that there would be nothing the matter with American literature if it were only permitted to grow up. If a man has native talent—a gift—he needs to have it protected from foreign influences long enough for it to stand upon its own legs! Otherwise it is crowded out and becomes merely an echo. That is so often the trouble with our most energetic writers.

George Ade practiced on his slang for a long time. It was something that came out of the American Middle West soil, and to which he gave his genius, molding it to his purpose and producing things that, as finished products, could scarcely have been produced anywhere else. That is what constitutes his merit, his claim to be an American humorist of the first rank.

Of course, no writer can produce things like that without having qualities. Mr. Theodore Dreiser, for example, is, in my opinion, a great novelist—another American—but when Mr. Dreiser writes essays attacking his own country—its vulgarity, its crudeness, its banality, etc., he charms me not nearly—no, not fractionally as much as Mr. Ade, who arrives at the same result (and so much more effectively) in his Fables. Mr. Sinclair Lewis in "Main Street" has written a long novel to prove that the people who live on Main Street are drab and uninteresting—at least so I am told by those that have read it. Personally, I do not care for Mr. Lewis's opinion of the people that live on Main Street, because I sense his book as an echo: and besides, George Ade supplies me with what I want to know about these folks in Main Street: he has them all down: he hits them off—and he doesn't waste a lot of time over them either.

At this point it is perhaps as well to make a pertinent observation about humor. It is probable that this book, if it is not classed as a regular text book, will be read quite largely by University students. Therefore, you may put it down here, as a mental note, that the right kind of humor is always in sympathy with the people it "takes off." George Ade does not hate the people he writes his fables about. He doesn't stand off and fire poisoned arrows into them, and snarl at them, and hold them up to ridicule by showing you how much he resents them. He doesn't resent them. He doesn't even go so far as to *tolerate* them. He likes them. He is one of them himself. They are his crowd. George Ade, born in Indiana, went to Chicago and learned the mechanics of his art. He went to Egypt, and looked it over, and left it where it was and came back to Indiana, bought a farm there, and he lives there. In other words, George Ade is a plain American, a man of genius, living among his own people, putting on no frills, and if you want information about what has really been going on in America since, say 1900, get his Fables and read them, and you will come nearer to the truth than you will find in all the books on sociology and history that have been written during this period.

I have stated that he began his trade in Chicago.

Let him here tell the story for himself, in his own inimitable manner, from a personal narrative he wrote for the *American Magazine*. "They Simply Wouldn't Let Me Be a Highbrow" he declares in his title, thus revealing the limitations the American public fastens upon its geniuses.

Away back in the year when the Infanta Eulalia came to Chicago, and Lake Shore Drive put on its evening clothes in the afternoon, I began to write a daily column for a Chicago newspaper. John McCutcheon drew the pictures interrupting my text, and only a thin vertical line divided us from Eugene Field and his delightful, whimsical, inimitable "Sharps and Flats."

Now this column-conducting, back there in the nineties, was not all lavender.

We had not discovered the latter-day secret, so nobly promoted by B. L. T. and F. P. A., of permitting the contributors to shoulder the bulk of the toil.

And this column, undertaken by McCutcheon and the author of this article was not a column, when you come right down to it. It was *two* columns.

And the daily grind, allowing for the breaks on account of cuts, had to be anywhere from fifteen hundred to eighteen hundred words in order that the stuff would get well below the fold on the second column.

He goes on to explain his difficulties with the night editor and his feverish associates to whom the news that "a guy over on the West Side beat his wife's head all to a pulp" was more important than anything else:

You can imagine what happened to my placid little yarns about shopgirls and stray dogs and cable-car conductors.

. . .

Fortunately, there was a friend at court. The high chief of the paper could not stay up every night in order to protect my fragile output, so he gave me a "department," and surrounded it with "Hands off!" signs, and told me to go ahead and revel in the inconsequential.

So I started on a seven-year Marathon.

In a little while we discovered that readers became more interested in our "Stories of the Streets and of the Town" if they could find familiar characters recurring in the yarns. The first to bob up about once a week was a brash young office employee named "Artie" Blanchard, a very usual specimen of the period. Then "Pink" Marsh, a city negro of the sophisticated kind, became a regular visitor. He was followed by "Doc" Horne, an amiable old falsifier, not unlike "Lightnin'," so delightfully played by Bacon.

In 1898 these very bourgeois "types" had found their way into books. I had clipped out the reviews, which proved that I was almost an author. Henry B. Fuller and Hamlin Garland had spoken words of encouragement, and there was a letter from William Dean Howells which gold could not have purchased.

The publishers kept dinging at me to stop trifling with the fragmentary sketches, and to write a regular full-book story, a novel—possibly the great American novel. Why not? Everybody else was getting ready to do it.

But there was no time to write his novel. He couldn't do it with a department going. And so:

One morning I sat at the desk and gazed at the
empty soft paper, and realized the necessity of concocting something different.   The changes had been
rung through weary months and years on blank verse,
catechism, rhyme, broken prose, the drama form of
dialogue, and staccato paragraphs.

Why not a fable for a change?   And instead of
slavishly copying Æsop and La Fontaine, why not
retain the archaic form and the stilted manner of composition and, for purposes of novelty, permit the language to be "fly," modern, undignified, quite up-to-
the-moment?

Also, in order to take the curse off the performance
and so that no one might accept the article under a
misapprehension, and, further, lest the critical-minded
might suspect that the colloquialisms were used
through a vulgar ignorance of proper speech and not
in a mere cut-up spirit, it seemed advisable that the
thing should be called a "Fable in Slang."

Now, up to this time I had gone fairly straight.   My
ambition was to be known as a realist with a compact
style and a clean Anglo-Saxon vocabulary and the
courage to observe human virtues and frailties as they
showed on the lens.   I had written slang, but always
in the third person.   People in my stories had talked
slang, but only when they had to do so in order to
be plausible and probable.   If I used a word or a
phrase which was reasonably under suspicion, I would
hang up the quotation marks so that the reader might
know that I was not approving the language, but
merely utilizing it for picturesque effect.

Of course, I had been tempted a million times to
use the new idioms and the current catch phrases, because they were the salt needed for the proper savoring.
But I didn't want to fly-speck my compositions with

quotation marks, and I had a real fear of the law against dealing in contraband.

But after affixing the "Poison" label I could put in anything.

And it was a real lark to write in slang—just like gorging on forbidden fruit. The bridle was off and all rules had been abolished.

Still, there are niceties of distinction even when out on a slang debauch.

I never referred to a policeman as a "bull," because that word belongs in the criminal vocabulary, and Mother and the girls are not supposed to be familiar with the cryptic terms of yeggmen.

I never referred to a young girl as a "chicken." The word originated in the deepest pits of white slavery, and it always gave me the creeps. A young girl may be a flapper, a bud, a peach, a pippin, a lollypaloozer, a nectarine, a cutie, a queen, the one best bet, a daisy, or even a baby doll, without being insulted; but never a "chicken," unless one is writing a treatise on social problems.

There are words of popular circulation which don't sound well in the mouth or look pretty in type. "Slob" has always been in the *Index Expurgatorius*. Our fellow citizen may be a dub or even a lobster, and possibly a mutt, but let us draw the line on "slob."

Besides, this so-called "slang" that romps so gayly into the homes and offices of the socially important is not slang at all. It is not the argot of a criminal element, and more of it is hatched on the university campus than in the red parlors of the underworld. It is highly figurative speech, tinctured with the American spirit of playfulness, bantering, unconventional.

Take the first fable I ever wrote—the one that started

me upward on my dissolute career until I landed in the gutter of notoriety.

It was about Sister Mae, who did as well as could be expected. Mae was a sister of Luella, whose Features did not seem to know the value of Team Work. Her clothes were an intermittent Fit. She was a lumpy Dresser.

Luella worked in a Factory, and every Saturday the Boss crowded Three Dollars on her.

Sister Mae was short on Intellect but long on Shape. She became Cashier in a Lunch Room and was a Strong Card.

She married a Bucket-Shop Man who was not Handsome, but was awful Generous.

They went to live in a Flat with a quarter-sawed Oak Chiffonier and Pink Rugs.

Mae bought a Thumb Ring, and the Smell of Cooking made her Faint.

After she had broken into Society and was in the Heyday of Prosperity, did she forget Luella? No, indeed. She gave Lu a Position as Assistant Cook at Five a Week.

And the Moral was that Industry and Perseverance bring a sure Reward.

That's only a rough idea, but you get the whole plot. Just a piece of Cold Truth told jocosely in large type and trimmed up with colored phraseology.

It was a specimen of willful freakishness rather than an exposition of slang, but it was called slang so as to have an alibi in case of barbarisms, Americanisms, colloquialisms, provincialisms, or any "ism" that stood on the doubtful list.

It was simply a gleeful little experiment in outlawry, and was not intended to corrupt the morals of

Methodist families and teach babes in arms to grow up to be poker players.

It went into the grist as a thousand other items had gone before, and little did I suspect that it was the beginning of the end of a serious-minded young novelist.

Next day the score-keepers told me I had knocked a home run.

The young women on the staff told me the piece was "just killing."

I found the head editor giggling over the darn fool thing.

"You've struck a lead," he said. "Follow it up."

Then I heard from the publisher.

"Write a lot more of those fables for the paper," he said. "Because of the bold type, they are filling; and in a little while we can get out a book and substitute it for 'The College Widow.'"

"The College Widow" as a novel never got beyond the "dummy" stage. Five years later it appeared as a play, and later it was a movie, and only yesterday it bobbed up as a musical comedy.

Closed in upon by frantic advisers, the harried author began to write fables in slang with both hands.

In vain did he protest that he was not a specialist in the easy-going vernacular, and that he wanted to deal with life as it is instead of verbal buck-dancing and a bizarre costuming of capital letters.

The friends told him to take the gifts that were falling into his lap, and not crave the golden persimmons that grow on the hill tops.

So the crazy fables became a glaring feature of our newspaper department, and McCutcheon did most amusing imitations of the old-style woodcuts.

When the first volume called "Fables in Slang" appeared in the shop windows (impudently bound in yellow and black) I began to get messages of commendation from nearly every one except Mr. Howells.

I seemed to have tickled the orthodox citizen's sneaking fondness for the unconventional.

Also I learned that, in the writing game, if you have for sale an article that is a variation on the standardized ingredients of a six-and-seven-eighths, cutaway-coat newspaper, you can sell it to a great many different people and draw many salaries.

After ten years of clanking toil on a daily paper and being heralded as the author of several books, and finally earning the sacred privilege of signing my initials, I commanded a salary of sixty dollars a week.

Soon after backing out of the newspaper office and falling into the arms of the wizard who sold syndicate features to the daily press, I was getting eight hundred dollars a week as my share of the conspiracy, and later on, the nuggets became larger and we passed the thousand mark.

My father was cashier of a modest county-seat bank down in Indiana, and I sent him all my checks, so that he could show them to the loyal townspeople, well-wishers, and members of the Helping Hand who had told him in 1883 that it was a mistake to send me to college.

Father read the fables, and several times he wrote and asked if I had concealed from him any of my sources of revenue.

One short story a week instead of six long ones!

Checks that looked like three-sheet posters fluttering out of the large square envelopes used by the generous Robin Hood who was taking it away from the newspaper owners and sending it on to me!

Publishers setting traps for me and baiting them with lumps of sugar!

Could anything be more salubrious? Apparently not.

In those first breathless days of purple prosperity, when the whole world seemed to be slapping me in the face with twenty-dollar bills, I had not fully encompassed the fact that the net result of all this Barnum and Bailey presswork would be to make me a Professional Slangster for the rest of my life, even if I lived to be a thousand years old.

The idea was to grab a lot of careless money before the reading public recovered its equilibrium, and then, later on, with bags of gold piled in the doorway to keep the wolf out, return to the consecrated job of writing long and photographic reports of life in the Middle West.

Man proposes, and a triumvirate composed of the tired business man, the lady in the morning wrapper, and the human mechanism that sits at a roll-top desk do the subsequent disposing.

So the twentieth century opened up, and I learned from the clipping agencies that I was a "humorist." I went around denying it, but the newspapers had more circulation than I had.

Of course Mr. Ade is a humorist, and a first-class one at that, not essentially because he is a member of the National Institute of Arts and Letters, as because he has sounded a genuine American note in a manner of his own. The real trouble with the majority of people who read him is that they don't take him seriously enough: that is, they don't study him: they don't realize, as I have already hinted, that if you want real information about America, real insight into American character snapshots at the American animal in his haunts, so to speak, here is where to get it.

The "highbrows" are doubtless fooled because the fable is short, because it is offhand and slangy and because it isn't always so funny as it might be. All that comes from a mistaken idea about the nature and quality of humor. Some people should never attempt to read anything humorous. It cannot possibly do them any good: it only makes them worse. It is amazing indeed to see how little attention is paid to understanding or reading of humor in our public schools. I venture the assertion that a really good piece of literary prose humor or humorous verse—a classic if you will—would meet with scarcely any appreciation by an average class of high-school students. I know this because I have tried it.

It has been my experience that George Ade's "Fables" are hard to read aloud to a group of average people (if there be such a thing). The reason is perfectly plain. These Fables are high literary art, but not dramatic art, because the impact of the slang word is often just too late to produce the instantaneous effect necessary to the listener. This of course is not always so: but it is so often enough to make the reading of these fables anything but a certainty: occasionally a clear-cut phrase will go home with telling effect: but, generally speaking, Ade's Fables need to be lingered over in silence: they are concentrated food; to be taken as a tonic, say one or two after a meal. It is quite natural also that they should not all be good: or that some of them should be better than others. But, in this respect, be not deceived. Your personal knowledge means much: you are sure to respond more to those things which reveal your own experience: so that if a certain fable appears to fall flat, it may easily be because that part of life has not particularly touched you.

They are, in quite a large sense, allegorical. You have to rise to the bait yourself. This is the beginning of one of Ade's "Fables":

> Once there was an Indian who had
> a Way of putting on all his Feathers
> and breaking out of the Reservation.

Think of reading that aloud to a committee of eight or ten—say a Board of Education or a Board of Health. You would have to explain at once that Ade in reality was not talking about an Indian at all: that he might indeed be talking about the Chairman of the Committee himself. You would then have to make a personal appeal to the Chairman, and ask him if he ever felt like an Indian, felt like putting on his store clothes, and sneaking out of the side door for the purpose of raising Cain. By this time you would be engaged in a controversy—which proves certain things that those who understand will already know, and those who do not understand can never be taught.

Personally, I haven't read Ade's "Fable of the two Mandolin Players" for some years: but I know precisely what kind of "birds" they are, and I like to think about them. He did not make me hate or despise them—he only made me laugh at them. There are certain things inside of me that are just like the things inside of those two Mandolin Players of Ade's. I know they are there because I have been reminded of them: and I know there are also other things in other people in the other fables of Ade's that are like the other things I have inside of me, and somehow I am not so ashamed of them as I was before I read the Ade "Fables," because it has made me feel after all, that we are all of us, East and West and North and South, a great deal alike: made up of about the same parts, in various combinations.

George Ade united with the late Henry James the distinction of having achieved literary fame without benefit of clergy: that is to say, without matrimonial aid. This is the only respect, however, in which they appear to have anything in common. Henry James scorned his native land—George Ade revels in his Indiana farm. Henry James took himself seriously and wrote in a language that few understand. George Ade snapped his countrymen, living among them and doing them good by his presence. His slang is almost wholly his own: you see plainly where he gets it from: but he rolls it a little and fits it in and changes it to suit his plan. It is impossible to overestimate the unconscious effect of a George Ade upon a generation: a combination of naturalness, common sense, sympathy, raillery, tolerance—this gives us glimpses of ourselves, that as a corrective, is an asset for genuine Democracy much more powerful than we have any idea of. That kind of humor which reflects American traits: rough in spots, dull in spots, but true in its essence and untainted by foreign influences—that is extremely valuable to us as a people: highly sanitary, and serves, possibly more than we realize, to keep us in control of ourselves at critical moments. This kind of raillery, of frankness, displayed in our train of humorists— Josh Billings, Artemus Ward, Mark Twain, George Ade and other natives—came out of the original town meeting—a by-product of the process of self-government. It has helped to make of the American people— climatically nervous and daring—one of the most patient and tolerant peoples in the world. Character- ized by the bluster and brag that comes as the after- math of the conquering of a new continent, with the rawness and vulgarity that jars upon Dreiser so much —all this in its full uninterrupted swing doubtless is offensive: but with it, this rough sense of humor— the capacity, so to speak, to "josh" oneself has given us something as a corrective which will be a large help as we grow up into more "cultured" ways. Besides, I am not so sure that this America of ours is so crude a thing as the critics would have. Art is not con- fined to any medium. In new forms it is misunder- stood in the beginning, and it is quite possible that in a larger sense there is an art to the living of a national life by a whole people far beyond any particu- lar form of art. The Greeks developed the highest sense of art in Architecture, Sculpture, Philosophy, Drama, but they broke down in the art of preserving themselves. It is possible that America is developing a soul—something hitherto thought superfluous in a Christian people.

It remains only to answer the question; Why is it that American writers, and in particular American

humorists, move along such restricted lines—never get
beyond a certain point—in contrast with their British
prototypes? Alexis de Tocqueville, a most acute observer, who wrote when this country was first forming,
has declared that, in a democracy, the same attention
cannot be paid to letters as in an aristocracy. "Most
of those who have some tinge of *belles-lettres* are
either engaged in politics or in a profession which only
allows them to taste occasionally and by stealth the
pleasures of the mind. . . . They prefer books which
may be easily procured, quickly read, and which require
no learned researches to be understood . . . above all,
they must have what is new and unexpected."

In short, the American audience is too heterogenous,
too mixed and scattered, too much occupied with material excitements. St. John Ervine, a more recent
observer, attributes our lack of literature to the so-
called process of standardization. "Standardization,"
he says, "means the destruction of individual preferences. . . . it is not difficult to prophesy that the outcome of it will be sterility of the soul. . . . A great
literature cannot flourish in an atmosphere of initiation
and suppressed personality, and unless America can
somehow solve this problem of making a man's in-
dividuality grow and become vivid, there is slight like-
lihood of her making credit for herself with an art
or a literature to which the world will yield respect."

From this standpoint, if you will, the fault lies not
with the individual himself, but in the nature of things.
In the case of George Ade, it is not his fault, but that
of the audience, and the audience is the country. Here
is a writer of undoubted native genius, a national

humorist who achieves celebrity as the author of "Fables in Slang," and there stops. In the midst of a world upheaval, and a silent revolution in our own country that is producing astonishing changes in our body politic, we ask ourselves why no great writer arises, why no great satirist holds over us the whip of scorn, why it is that with so much material for the universal humorists, there is no universal humorist. The answer is that we don't want him. We have no time to listen to him. And unless we cultivate within ourselves the need of him, he will not grow up out of us.

CHAPTER II

F. P. A.

I HOPE you won't quote directly," writes F. P. A. "I write so much about myself every day that I am weary of the subject."

The handling of oneself in a daily column is in itself an art so delicate that it almost requires a special explanation. As I have pointed out elsewhere, the personal pronoun, "I," enters very largely into the work of every humorist. With one or two exceptions, it is common to all American humorists. It is quite legitimate, but dangerous to an amateur. Franklin P. Adams certainly does it better than anyone I know. He could not do it unless his work was based upon the utmost sincerity.

In my opinion, he is the first columnist now writing in America. There are doubtless other men writing other columns who have qualities leading in certain directions beyond F. P. A. I should say that Don Marquis goes beyond him in the creative expression of a joyous humor, and in richness of imagination. But that is beside the mark, as I am not considering their relative merits. As an all-around columnist, with all that the word implies, I think Adams more nearly fulfills every requirement than any other writer. He has literary integrity, a sense of humor, and restraint.

He is not perfect. Nobody that I know anything about, is. His literary judgment is invariably good, but his taste is sometimes at fault, as when he prints paragraphs occasionally that hurt needlessly, and are not always in full sympathy with the subject satirized. It is a great art in itself to deal with something that you think needs correction in such a manner as to be helpful and not destructive—although, in connection with this, I may say that the word "destructive" has been sadly abused. It is much too easy, when we don't agree with somebody, to say that his work is destructive. When Adams writes down anybody, be it in a paragraph or in a single line, he never does it with evil intention; on the other hand, I think it is true that he has been a great help to letters in keeping up a certain standard. It seems to me that he must have had a great influence over a large body of chance readers.

He was born in Chicago, November 15, 1881. Armour Scientific Academy (1895-1899). University of Michigan (1899-1900). He left the University of Michigan in his freshman year and took a job as insurance supply clerk with Adolph Loeb & Son, Chicago, in June, 1900. He went into the life insurance business as solicitor in 1902 and in October, 1903, got a job conducting a column of verse and miscellany, called "A Little about Everything," in the *Chicago Journal*. The only stuff he had written was what he had contributed to Bert Leston Taylor's column, "A Line-o-Type or Two," in the *Chicago Tribune*. At the time he got the *Journal* job, Taylor had left Chicago, and was on the staff of *Puck*. Adams got $25 a week for his column and a daily weather story. Later he was advanced to $30 and allowed to sign his initials.

After a year on the *Chicago Journal* F. P. A. went to New York. Mr. T. E. Niks of the *Evening Mail* said he was willing to try him out. Thereupon he returned home and resigned from the *Chicago Journal* and moved to New York regularly in October, 1904. He conducted the column, "Always in Good Humor" —a misnomer of a title saddled on it on its first day by Mr. Henry L. Stoddard—until January 1, 1914, when he went to the *New York Tribune* to conduct "The Conning Tower." With the exception of the war's interruption, the column has been running since then. In 1922 Mr. Adams moved to the *New York World*.

He began to write by sending stuff to Taylor's column, and it was reading Eugene Field that interested him in verse. His preparation was mostly mathematical and scientific; English was almost neglected in the curriculum. But he learned to have a respect for truth and accuracy in English from the mathematics professor, Professor Victor Clifton Alderson; and a veneration for honesty and fearlessness of expression from Rabbi Emil G. Hirsch of Chicago. He says of himself that he never attained the ideals the examples of these men made him hope for, but they kept him straighter than he might otherwise have been.

"I try as hard as I can and I have entire freedom," he once told me. "Nobody ever tells me to write this, or not to write that. That is the discouraging part. A man with that leeway ought to have more to say than I have and be able to say it better than I do. You have no idea how that corrodes, that consciousness."

Mr. Adams's verse is of a high order. Along so much that is good, it is difficult to make a selection, but the lines that follow are undoubtedly among his best:

Song of Synthetic Virility

Oh, some may sing of the surging sea, or chant of the
    raging main;
Or tell of the taffrail blown away by the raging
    hurricane.
With an oh, for the feel of the salt sea spray as it
    stipples the guffy's cheek!
And oh, for the sob of the creaking mast and the hal-
    yard's aching squeak!
And some may sing of the galley-foist, and some of
    the quadrireme
And some of the day the xebec came and hit us abaft
    the beam.
Oh, some may sing of the girl in Kew that died for
    a sailor's love,
And some may sing of the surging sea, as I may have
    observed above.

Oh, some may long for the Open Road, or crave for
    the prairie breeze,
And some, o'ersick of the city's strain, may yearn for
    the whispering trees.
With an oh, for the rain to cool my face, and the wind
    to blow my hair!
And oh, for the trail to Joyous Garde, where I may
    find my fair!

And some may love to lie in the field in the stark and
    silent night,
The glistering dew for a coverlet and the moon and
    stars for light.
Let others sing of the soughing pines and the winds
    that rustle and roar,
And others long for the Open Road, as I may have
    remarked before.

Ay, some may sing of the bursting bomb and the
    screech of a screaming shell,
Or tell the tale of the cruel trench on the other side
    of hell.
And some may talk of the ten-mile hike in the dead
    of a winter night,
And others chaunt of the doughtie Kyng with mickle
    valour dight.
And some may long for the song of a child and the
    lullaby's fairy charm,
And others yearn for the crack of the bat and the
    wind of the pitcher's arm.
Oh, some have longed for this and that, and others
    have craved and yearned;
And they all may sing of whatever they like, as far
    as I'm concerned.

CHAPTER III

JOHN KENDRICK BANGS

WHILE this book was in process, there occurred the sad death of John Kendrick Bangs, who for many years has been a familiar figure on the lecture platform, where he amused and enlightened thousands of people, and whose life was more intimately connected with the history of comic journalism of the past twenty-five years than that of any other man. Mr. Bangs was one of the principal factors in the development of this journalism, which in years gone by was represented by the old *Vanity Fair,* later by *Puck* and thereafter by *Life.* Before he became the editor of *Puck,* however, Mr. Bangs was the editor of "The Drawer," in *Harper's Magazine.* At the same time he had charge of the back page of the old *Harper's Bazar.* This back page was in its day quite famous and at that time was representative of the best short humor published. The great publishing firm of Harper & Brothers had its headquarters in Franklin Square. In those days it was what may be termed the periodical center of the United States. Mr. Howells was there then, Charles Dudley Warner, and indeed a whole group of men whose names have since been

enrolled in the annals of our literature. Mr. Henry
M. Alden, whose remarkable record as the editor of
Harper's Magazine has, if I am correct, never been
exceeded in length, and certainly not in honor, was
there at that time.

I myself was one of the chance contributors to
Harper's "Drawer" and the *Bazar*. I used to hand in
my effusions once a week. On my first visit I was
personally received by Mr. Bangs, who invited me to
be seated while he read my "copy." Mr. Bangs, as
one might have said during the war, was a "cordial and
sincere" person and doubtless mitigated the effect of
his decisions as much as possible by his sympathetic
manner. Still, the ordeal was a painful one, I fancy,
for him as well as for myself. To sit in the actual
presence of an impartial but, of necessity, a ruthless
editor while he reads things of your very own which
you have fondly hoped would induce him to laugh—
to see him frown and, ever and anon, look puzzled—
and then to see him lay by the whole miserable week's
output with a sigh—all this is not conducive to the
most lasting tranquillity.

After our first melancholy interview, in which Mr.
Bangs, who did his best to work up a faint smile,
decided that one of my pieces was "good enough," we
agreed there and then that, in the future, I was to wait
outside. Thereafter I would call on a certain day,
hand my manuscript to the office boy, who would take
it through the long editorial room to Mr. Bangs's
dingy sanctum. A period of intense silent agony would
then ensue, while Bangs was engaged in his mournful
diversion. Once, in the gray distance, I heard a peal

of hearty laughter, and felt, as Oliver Wendell Holmes suggests in his delightful verses, that I had "dared" to be too funny. Alas! It was not the voice of Bangs, it was only two remote and irreverent gentlemen—I think one of them was Richard Harding Davis—telling stories.

After waiting thus in horrible suspense for what seemed an eternity, the nonchalant boy would reluctantly emerge from the Bangs's sanctum and stroll forward to where I sat, with my envelope in his hand. Bangs would indicate what he had accepted, and I would go my way joyless or rejoicing as the case might be.

Before he became the editor of *Harper's* "Drawer," Bangs was the associate editor of *Life.* In fact, as he himself states, he was Mr. Mitchell's first assistant. Mr. John Ames Mitchell (long-time editor of *Life,* author of "Amos Judd," "The Pines of Lory," etc.) founded *Life,* with Andrew Miller and Edward S. Martin, in 1883. Bangs came to assist him the following year. At this time *Puck* was the leading pictorial humorous periodical of America. I purposely avoid using the word "comic" in connection with *Puck* because *Puck* was never a comic journal in the sense in which George Meredith used the word comedy, and which I take it to be the best sense. Keppler's cartoons in *Puck* gave it a national reputation. One of its earliest literary features, however, (Fitznoodle) which attracted wide attention was, as I recollect, written by an Englishman. It was under the editorship of Mr. H. C. Bunner that *Puck* later achieved its preëminence as a purveyor of the very best American humor. Yet it cannot be said of Bunner, as it might have been said, and has indeed been said of Mitchell, that he had the spirit of comedy, although I think his occasional touches of whimsicality lend the appearance of it to his work (notably in his story "The Love Letters of Smith"). Bunner had fine literary judgment, good taste and editorial ability of a high order, and he made *Puck* an influential journal. Mitchell had within him quite strongly the spirit of true comedy. Professor Brander Matthews (as will appear later) seems to feel that Bunner also had comedy. It may be so. George Meredith in his essay on comedy and the uses of the comic spirit (which I advise everyone to read if they would know what comedy really is) writes:

Good comedies are such rare productions, that notwithstanding the wealth of our literature in the comic element, it would not occupy us long to run over the English list.

There are plain reasons why the Comic poet is not a frequent apparition; and why the great Comic poet remains without a fellow. A society of cultivated men and women is required, wherein ideas are current and the perceptions quick that he may be supplied with matter and an audience. The semi-barbarism of merely giddy communities, and feverish emotional periods, repel him: and also state of marked social inequality of the sexes: nor can he whose business is to address the mind be understood where there is not a moderate degree of intellectual activity. Moreover, to touch and kindle the mind through laughter, demands more than sprightliness, a most subtle delicacy.

And again:

The laughter of satire is a blow in the back or the face. The laughter of Comedy is impersonal and of unrivaled politeness, nearer a smile: often no more than a smile. It laughs through the mind, for the mind directs it; and it might be called the humor of the mind. One excellent test of the civilization of a country, as I have said, I take to be the flourishing of the Comic idea and Comedy: and the test of true Comedy is that it shall awaken thoughtful laughter.

In this sense then, *Life* was a more comic journal than *Puck*. Bunner had humor and sentiment. Mitchell undoubtedly had more of the comic spirit. Bangs helped Mitchell at first with *Life*. Later on, he became editor of *Harper's* "Drawer" and in 1904, became editor of *Puck*. But the moment had passed to restore its energies even by the help of such a fruitful mind as Bangs'. It descended finally into the arms of Mr. Hearst, perhaps the greatest comedian this country has produced (with the possible exception of Mr. Bryan) but who was unable to save it.

At this point it may not be out of place to quote Professor Brander Matthews, who undoubtedly knows more about our literature than any living man and who, in an article in the *Bookman* entitled "American Comic Journalism," writes:

American Comic Journalism

I

Comic papers are like two of their constant butts, the baby and the widower, in that they are difficult to carry through the second summer. In humorous journalism the percentage of infant mortality is appallingly high. Evidently the undertaking is far more hazardous than it seems at first sight. It might be said that starting a comic paper is no joke—that it is in fact a very serious enterprise not to be entered upon lightly.

Puck survived for more than forty years; it was the first American comic weekly to establish itself successfully, and it had a longer lease of life than any of its predecessors. It leaves behind it two journals which were more or less its rivals. *Judge* was set up avowedly as an opposition paper by the Blaine Republicans when *Puck* abandoned its early political independence to advocate ardently the cause of the Cleveland Democrats. *Life* was the creation of John A. Mitchell, who conducted it for thirty-five years, impressing upon it his own genial personality and winning the affectionate devotion of all his contributors, both literary and artistic.

One reason for the popularity of all three of these humorous journals is that no one of them was intended to be an imitation of *Punch,* but felt itself free always to develop as it might prefer. *Punch* is the most solidly established comic paper in the world, and it has loyally preserved its original characteristics. It is essentially and fundamentally British; and yet this comic weekly, as its title still confesses—*Punch or the*

London Charivari—was founded as an imitation of
a famous Parisian comic daily. The abiding vitality
of *Punch* is due to a variety of causes—first of all,
to the continuity of ownership; secondly to the large
staff retained year after year on satisfactory annual
salaries; and thirdly to the solidarity created and kept
alive by the weekly dinner which every contributor with
either pen or pencil is expected to attend. The tradition established four score years ago is jealously
cherished, and the torch is passed down from generation to generation with its flame ever brightly burning.

Of course, *Punch* is glad to consider the voluntary
offerings sent to it by casual correspondents scattered
throughout the British commonwealth; but it does not
rely on these volunteers. It has its tried and true bat-
talion of regulars, to be trusted to supply the comic
copy and the comic sketches which must be forthcom-
ing week after week. Now and again a free-lance
may have a happy thought; and *Punch* is unfailingly
hospitable to happy thoughts, no matter whence they
come. But the burden and heat of the day is borne
by the cautiously recruited staff, each of whom felt it
an honor to be invited to a seat at the weekly dinner
and each of whom continues to feel it to be his duty to
give to the venerable weekly the very best that he
can do.

Artemus Ward, at the height of his London success and only a few weeks before his untimely death,
was asked to contribute a few letters and he was bidden
as a guest to the dinners; and he declared that this was
the most grateful compliment that had ever been paid
to him. And Mark Twain also appreciated highly the
invitation to put his legs under Mr. Punch's mahogany.

Punch being what it is, we need not wonder that

innumerable attempts have been made to start an American *Punch;* nor need we wonder that these efforts have always been fruitless. Indeed, the very fact that the new weekly was an imitation of *Punch* seems to have been sufficient to condemn it to an early death. In Orpheus C. Kerr's parody, "The Mystery of Mr. E. Drood," the lugubrious undertaker points out the last resting-places of men foredoomed to an early death: "He patched up all these graves, as well as them in the Ritual Churchyard, and I knew them all, sir. Over there, editor of a country journal; next, stockholder in Erie; next, the gentleman who undertook to be guided in agriculture by Mr. Greeley's 'What I Know About Farming'; next, original projector of American *Punch;* next, proprietor of rural newspaper; next, another projector of American *Punch*—indeed, all the rest of that row is American *Punches.*"

Punch had been founded in 1841; and half a dozen years later *Yankee Doodle* evoked an epigrammatic couplet in Lowell's "Fable for Critics":

That American "Punch," like the English, no doubt,
Just the sugar and lemons and spirit, left out.

It may be noted that F. O. C. Darley was one of the artists who contributed to *Yankee Doodle* and Charles Fenno Hoffman was one of the literary men. A second attempt was made by John Brougham, who started *Diogenes hys Lanterne* in 1852, and who succeeded somehow in keeping it alight for eighteen months. The third effort was *Vanity Fair* which began in January, 1859, and which did not succumb until 1863, when Artemus Ward was its editor. He is said to have remarked: "They told me I could write comic copy; I wrote a lot of it—and the paper died." An

earlier editor had been Charles Godfrey Leland, the
lyrist of Hans Breitmann; and George Arnold was a
regular contributor. Its cartoonist was H. L.
Stephens, who also supplied the cartoons for *Mrs.
Grundy* which had a brief career in 1865 and which
may be regarded as an attempt to revive *Vanity
Fair.*

Thomas Nast had been one of the artists on *Mrs.
Grundy* and shortly after its demise he joined the staff
of *Harper's Weekly* where he was free to point the
finger of scorn at the Tweed ring, then engaged in
plundering New York. Tweed felt the force of Nast's
cartoons and complained that they reached his constituents, all of whom could see a picture, even if only
a few of them could read. It was probably the desire
to have an organ of their own which led Tweed and
Sweeny, Jay Gould and "Jim" Fisk to put in five
thousand dollars each, for the support of *Punchinello,*
which first appeared in April, 1870, and which emitted
its final squeak in the following December. H. L.
Stephens was again the cartoonist; and among the other
contributors of sketches were Frank Bellew and George
Bowlend. Oakey Hall, the Tammany mayor of New
York, supplied an alleged comic serial bristling with
elaborate puns. The dramatic critic was William L.
Alden and the editor was Charles Dawson Shanly,
who had been one of the conductors of *Vanity Fair*
and who wrote for *The Atlantic* an interesting essay
on the difficulties of editing an American *Punch.*

II

The solid success that *Puck* enjoyed for nearly a
quarter of a century must be ascribed to a series of
lucky accidents. Adolf Schwarzmann was a lith-

ographer in St. Louis and he joined forces with Joseph
Keppler, a lithographic draftsman, to get out a little
German weekly, illustrated in color and intended to
circulate mainly among the theater-going Germans of
St. Louis. After a while they both removed to New
York, where they revived their German weekly with
its colored cartoons drawn on stone. They had a small
staff; and they borrowed a large proportion of their
comic cuts from the German humorous papers. The
cartoons of Keppler were so effective that *Puck* was
read by many Americans; and at last Mr. Sydney
Rosenfeld was able to persuade Schwarzmann that it
would be possible to issue *Puck* also in English, so
that Keppler's drawings might profit by circulation
among Americans of other than German descent.

Rosenfeld was the first editor of *Puck* in English;
and he immediately enlisted the aid of his friend,
Henry Cuyler Bunner, who had worked with him on
an earlier and less fortunate weekly. In the beginning
the English *Puck* was simply an annex to the German
Puck. Its political and social cartoons were in accord
with German taste rather than with American; and
the paper in English was expected to make use of all
the comic cuts which had earlier appeared in the paper
in German. It was; I think, in the fall of 1876 that
this hybrid weekly began to attract attention. Those
were the doubtful days of the Hayes-Tilden disputed
election, happily decided at last by the ingeni-
ously devised Electoral Commission which ultimately
awarded the presidency to Hayes by a vote of eight to
seven; and Keppler never drew a more telling cartoon
than that which disclosed the seven Democrats in a
rat-trap the wires of which outlined the profiles of the
eight Republicans.

It was early in 1877 that I made my first contribution to *Puck* and that I accepted its editor's invitation to call on him at the office, then in a dingy old building in North William Street, soon to be torn down for the approach to the Brooklyn Bridge. On the ground floor were the lithographic presses; on the floor above was the composing room; and in a dim corner of the top loft was the editor's desk. Rosenfeld introduced me to Bunner; and then began a friendship which remained intimate as long as he lived. A few weeks later Rosenfeld had a disagreement with Schwarzmann, and as a result Bunner became editor of *Puck* which soon achieved its independence of its German half-brother—that is to say, a time came when *Puck* in English had a far larger circulation than *Puck* in German; and ultimately the weekly edited by Bunner so far outstripped its elder brother that Schwarzmann finally ceased to issue the paper in German.

III

Necessary as were the artistic facility of Keppler and the business acumen of Schwarzmann, the qualities which Bunner brought to the editorship were equally needful. Without him the *Puck* of Teutonic origin and ownership could never.have been made acceptable to the American people. He spoke German; and he knew German literature; but he was also familiar with French and his acquaintance with French literature was both wider and deeper than his knowledge of German literature. And wider and deeper than either was his intimacy with the literature of our own language, both British and American. His was the only useful cosmopolitanism, that which is rooted in a man's native soil. His reading was really remarkable in its range, when we remember that he was not twenty-three years old when he took charge of *Puck*.

Remarkable as was Bunner's equipment it was not as extraordinary as his fecundity. Into *Puck* in its struggling days he poured prose and verse of an unfaltering cleverness and of an unfailing sparkle. He was equally apt and swift in writing a column of brisk paragraphs and in rhyming a lilting lyric to justify the insertion of some German illustration. Abundant as were these contributions in quantity they were equally notable in quality. As *Puck* became more prosperous and its editor was allowed to spend money a little more freely, Bunner was able to relax his own efforts, although to the very end of his life he felt and responded to the obligation to supply his paper with the various kinds of writing that its readers expected from him.

One of the most abundant contributors to the letter-press of *Puck* was Mr. James L. Ford, who printed in its columns most of the satiric sketches afterward collected in the volume entitled "The Literary Shop," including the ever delightful story of "The Bunco-Steerer's Christmas." Another frequent contributor was the late R. K. Munkittrick, a most ingenious rhymester, who supplied to *Puck* most of the comic lyrics which he garnered later into the little book which he aptly called "The Acrobatic Muse." So long as Bunner lived the comic verse which appeared in the pages of *Puck* was kept up to a high standard of technical accomplishment. He insisted on distinctness of rhythm and on exact accuracy of rhyme. He tolerated no slovenliness in versification; and he himself set the example of strict obedience to the rules of the game. Inspired by the unfailing felicity of Austin Dobson's transference into English of the fixed forms of the French, Bunner and his associates poured into the pages of *Puck* a flowing stream of triolets, rondeaus, and ballades.

Of course, no one of these friendly rivals equaled Bunner either in facility or in range. As a comic poet he had a note of his own; but he was also a marvelous parodist, with the rare gift of capturing the spirit of the poet he was imitating, as sympathetically as he aped the outer form. It was to exhibit this power of getting into the skin of any other bard, ancient or modern, that Bunner invented the figure of V. Hugo Dusenbury, Professional Poet, ready to take a contract to deal with any theme at any time in any manner. Nor was Bunner less multifarious in his prose contributions. He early appreciated the surpassing skill of Maupassant's brief tales; and in "Made in France" he accomplished successfully the daring feat of transferring a dozen of the French plots to American surroundings. And it was more or less under the influence of Maupassant that he wrote his own very American and very original series of stories called "Short Sixes."

It may seem like a paradox to say that the influence of a comic journal depends to a certain extent upon its not being exclusively comic. On occasion *Punch* can be nobly serious, as it was when it printed Hood's "Song of the Shirt" and Tom Taylor's apologetic verses on the death of Abraham Lincoln. Bunner never liked to have *Puck* considered as merely a funny paper. His own memorial verses—on Grant and on Longfellow, for example—were dignified and lofty. And when Cleveland issued his message on the tariff, warning us that we were confronted by a condition and not by a theory, Bunner began a series of editorial articles which revealed a new aspect of his ability. He expounded the principles of protection and free trade

with the utmost lucidity and with a total absence of
heat.

Bunner was the editor of *Puck* for nearly twenty
years, during which the paper steadily expanded its
circulation and its influence.   Keppler died in 1894
and Bunner followed him in 1896, leaving Schwarzmann alone to carry on the paper.   But *Puck* had depended largely upon individuals, upon Keppler and
Bunner first of all, and then upon more or less casual
contributors.   It was edited at one time by Harry Leon
Wilson and at another by John Kendrick Bangs.   But
there was no permanent staff, no loyal organization,
no solidarity, like that which has kept alive the tradi-
tions of *Punch* for three generations.   And when
Schwarzmann died in his turn, the torch flickered and
soon went out.   There was nothing left but a name—
only an empty shell.   The paper changed owners two
or three times, passing at last into hands so unworthy
that its old friends were not sorry to learn that it had
ceased publication.

The part that Bangs played in the development of
this "comic" journalism has already been indicated.
For many years (in addition to his published books)
he poured forth a stream of remarkably sane and
highly intelligent humor.   I am inclined to credit him
with more of this true spirit of comedy than so many
of his contemporaries: His "Idiot" and "Houseboat"
are examples.   The fact is, as Meredith indicates, the
American audience is not quite up to this sort of thing.
Both Aristophanes and Molière would have a hard
time among us, although I am inclined to think
Aristophanes would fare much better.

Bangs was not only an editor and a "humorist,"

but his remarkable abilities as a lecturer must be again referred to. As an oratorical entertainer of a very high order he has few equals. During the war he threw himself with his untiring energy into the work of rehabilitating devastated France, and in this field his labors were extraordinary and highly valuable. In the following interesting paper which he wrote and sent to me before his death he gives a most modest and characteristic account of himself.

The Confession of John Kendrick Bangs

Although I was not able to prove the fact to the entire satisfaction of the Passport Division of the United States Department of State during the war, I was, like most of my contemporaries, born. I have no distinct recollection of the event, but there is credible testimony from persons in whose veracity I have had perfect confidence, notably my father, that the thing really did happen, and the fact that I undoubtedly do exist at this writing would seem to lend the color of truth to the assertion. The date of the episode has been reported to me as of May 27, 1862. Reference to the newspapers of that period fails to disclose any particular public interest in the incident. I do not find anywhere any announcement of my arrival among other prominent persons in town, but it is possible that the news of my coming was crowded out by items of possibly larger popular interest concerning a Civil War which at that time was being waged between two sections of the United States, familiarly known to students of History as the North and the South. The town of this presumed nativity was Yonkers, New York, located at that time about fifteen miles from New

York City, but now its too proximate next-door neighbor. The house overlooked the Hudson, and was shaded by noble elms, but latter-day improvements combined with the onward march of civilization have changed matters so that it now looks out upon long lines of cattle-cars stretching north and south upon the rails of the New York Central Railroad, and is sheltered from the burning rays of the afternoon sun by an eight-story sugar-refinery, whose classic lines suggest the most flourishing period of the Gothic-Vandalian Renaissance. I attribute the intense cosmopolitan quality of my nature to the fact that I was born in Yonkers, since by it I escaped the narrow provinciality of the average New Yorker, and as a commuter became at an early age a traveler by sheer compulsion. I also attribute my sturdy Americanism to my Westchester County birth, for, as I understand the situation, to be born in New York City is an almost certain indication of an alien strain whose prenatal affiliations are mainly either Slavic or Neo-Tipperarian.

The foundations of what education I have were laid in an early collection of postage-stamps, which I well remember as one of my treasured possessions at the age of five. From it I gained a considerable knowledge of geography, and of history. I learned my letters on the block system, and my first conscious reading was in a little cloth-covered volume, abundantly illustrated with rich-hued wood-cuts, entitled "Mother Goose's Melodies." I do not wish to include in this biographical sketch anything of an invidious nature, but I cannot escape the conviction that for a very real inspiration, for literary form, for nicety of touch, delicacy of feeling, and, above all, high intelligence, the contents of that volume far excelled anything that I have read in the effusions of our latter-day poets.

From nursery to school was but a step, and at the age of seven I found myself headed for omniscience in the primary school, conducted by a great human in New York City named Morris W. Lyon. He was a man of rare parts, vigorous, stern, sympathetic, and a master of all that he taught. There was more discipline in one flash of his eye than I have since been able to discover in the combined torches of any ten of our modern universities. The boy was as much his concern as the teaching of the boy, and I am inclined to think that his urge was to turn out Individuals rather than what, for want of a better term, I may call Human Flivvers, which is the tendency of our Twentieth-Century Educational Works. At any rate, whether for good or for evil, my good teacher discovered at an early period of his association with me that there was a special affinity between words and myself, and while he did his best with the poor soil at his command to make me fructify along mathematical and other necessary lines, he devoted himself to the cultivation and control of the streams of verbosity, written, spoken, whispered, and signaled, of which I appeared to be, and undoubtedly was, a fount. I was especially encouraged to write compositions, and these I produced at fortnightly intervals throughout seven joyous school-years, expressing ideas either immature or over-advanced in six or eight times as many words as the case required, with a facility which I now recognize as a weakness. At the foot, and sometimes below it, in all my other classes, I invariably led my class in composition from the beginning to the end of my school life. I mention this in no spirit of vainglory, but in an endeavor to explain what has been rather one of my faults, for it is a sad fact that one of the bases of merit in those far-off writing days of mine was *length,* fluency, always a fatal gift, rather than conciseness operating to the advantage of my standing. I had not then, any more than I have now, the slightest desire either to rank or pose as a humorist, but it so happened that my glorious father, a man of infinite wit, used always to give me for the embellishment of my effort some story inextricably interwoven with laughter which I never failed to avail myself of, with the result that when on Commencement Day I read aloud to the assembled parents of my schoolmates the chosen product of the year there was always a laughing response from the audience, so that in a way I unconsciously began to measure my little success by the amount of smiling encouragement received.

My college life at Columbia College was but an expansion of my school life. Columbia was at that time, 1897 to 1883, in a state of transition, and the liaison between the old and the new was attended by difficulties. There was no adequate course in English Letters at Columbia at that period, and what knowledge I gained of the Masters of English I gathered wholly from my own reading outside of the collegiate walls, mostly from English novelists, and American romancers—Dickens, Thackeray, Bulwer, Hawthorne, and Poe. I loved Dickens, admired Thackeray, reveled in Bulwer, rejoiced in Hawthorne, and found a certain morbid enchantment in the fancies of Poe. So much indeed was I enchanted by Poe that, for a time, had not other influences intervened I think my whole literary career, if I may so call it, would have been directed exclusively to the production of tales of weird and morbid cast. Fortunately for me the intervening influences prevailed. I became the editor of the *Acta Columbiana,* a fortnightly publication of the usual undergraduate type, wherein I was required to be sportive rather than ponderously solemn, and to this work I devoted myself so assiduously that it has now become a wonder to me that my Alma Mater was ever willing to give me the degree of Ph.B., conferred upon me at Commencement. However this may be, it is the fact that my experience as a college editor was the point of diversion which started me from what might have been to that which is, for printing-office contacts brought me into a close personal relation with my inspiring friend the late John A. Mitchell, the founder of *Life*. We used to meet in the press-room where both *Life* and the *Acta* were printed. When we first met Mitchell was a tyro at editing, and, callow youth as I was, I had become a veteran—not an expert, but an old hand at the technique of it, and the instances were many when the presuming amateur was able to render "First Aid" to the professional. Words cannot express how I felt then, or how I feel now, in regard to Mitchell. He was one of the three most lovable men I have ever known. The first was my father, and the second was my later chief, the dearest of my friends, Mr. J. Henry Harper. Mitchell was many years older than I, but he never lost the spirit of youth, and when he offered me the post of assistant editor of *Life,* the Law for which I seemed doomed, lost me forever. Aside from the rare joy of his friendship, he rendered me the inestimable service of taking me out of the clutches of the gloomster and set me upon the highways leading to more joyous prospects. I think too that from him I gained my first intimation that good humor was good-humored, and that underneath true humor must lie something in the nature of serious thinking.

Nevertheless, in spite of four very happy years as Mitchell's assistant, the earlier influences remained in modified form. I delighted in ghost stories, and in tales having to do with the vagaries of the human mind, and when I came to the writing of stories myself, those stories dealt largely with apparitions, only instead of treating them seriously I presented them in lighter vein, seeking rather the laugh than the shudder. "The Water Ghost," and "Ghosts I Have Met," speak to me now of the inner conflict between two sorts of things, to either one of which chance alone could keep me from succumbing. That the necessities of official position compelled me to take the more joyous course is a fact for which I am profoundly grateful, for, after all, we react mentally and spiritually from the things that we do, and I have been far happier personally from the choice which was really no choosing of my own.

"The House-Boat on the Styx" was nothing more than the natural outcome of my love of treating spirits lightly. From treating purely fanciful spooks lightly it is an easy step to the treating of real spirits in the same fashion, and the field is limitless. I do not myself consider the "House-Boat" a masterpiece, but it is human, and perhaps for that reason it may be called good humor. I fancy it was the novelty of the underlying idea, and the extravagant juxtapositions of historical and other figures, that accounted for its popularity. Since it is now old enough to vote I shall let it speak for itself, and neither boast that I have written it, nor apologize for having done so. That it has pleased so many thousands of people in all parts of the world is a matter of gratification to me, and even if it were infinitely worse than it is I should still be glad that it was mine to write.

Altogether I have written some sixty-odd books, several of them more popular with me than the "House-Boat," but since I seem to have shared the fate of the one-book man, I shall not refer to the others—not even to "Coffee and Repartee" and "The Idiot," in which so many of my critics seem to find something in the nature of autobiography.   Having at the request of the compiler of this volume interpreted myself up to the Stygian Climax, I feel that I have gone as far as the special occasion requires.   I would like to say in conclusion, however, that in our own day the title of *humorist* is not one to be sought, and will not be until it comes to have a more definite meaning than it has at present.   The modern conception of humor is too various to lend any distinction to the word humorist.   To some persons, a humorist is little higher than a buffoon. To others, he is a practical joker whose alleged humor is based wholly upon another's pain.   To still others, the word connotes a delicate fancy intermingled with pointed wit.   The range of humor at this hour of writing runs from the vagaries of Charlie Chaplin up through the keen satiric wit of Bernard Shaw, to the exquisite fairy-like fancies of a James M. Barrie.   If the things that Chaplin does are humor, then the things that Mark Twain, and Addison, ·and Charles Lamb have done must be something else, in view of all of which, his is indeed a strange choice who asks the world to consider him to be a humorist.   May Heaven spare me that title, or, if I have won it, which I doubt, may it be my good fortune some day to emerge from the shackles of anything so unmitigatedly nondescript.

CHAPTER IV

ROBERT C. BENCHLEY

A FTER keeping at Mr. Benchley for weeks, nay months, he finally wrote out the following authentic biography of himself:

OUTLINE OF MY LIFE. R. C. Benchley.
Born Isle of Wight, September 15, 1807.
Shipped as cabin boy on *Florence J. Marble* 1815.
Arrested for bigamy and murder in Port Said,·
 1817.
Released 1820. Wrote "Tale of Two Cities."
Married Princess Anastasie of Portugal, 1831.
Children: Prince Rupprecht and several little girls.
Wrote "Uncle Tom's Cabin" 1850.
Editor "Godey's Ladies Book" 1851-56.
Began "Les Miserables" 1870 (finished by Victor
 Hugo).
Died 1871. Buried in Westminster Abbey.

To add anything to this painstaking historical document is a crime. Yet it must be done. Mr. Benchley was originally born in Worcester, Massachusetts. He is a Harvard man. He came to New York some time or ·other and began his work on *Vanity ,Fair*. After this, he wrote book reviews for the *New York World*, and from thence went to *Life* as the dramatic critic.

He knew nothing about the drama, he declared, but his weekly observations are considered very important by a large circle of readers. Among the younger humorists of the day he ranks very high. His book "Of All Things!" is a remarkable volume of humorous essays. Benchley's humorous touch is unerring, and back of what he writes is substance. From his book I have taken the liberty of making the following extract:

The Social Life of the Newt

It is not generally known that the newt, although one of the smallest of our North American animals, has an extremely happy home-life. It is just one of those facts which never get bruited about.

I first became interested in the social phenomena of newt life early in the spring of 1913, shortly after I finished my researches in sexual differentiation among amœba. Since that time I have practically lived among newts, jotting down observations, making lantern-slides, watching them in their work and in their play (and you may rest assured that the little rogues have their play—as who does not?) until, from much lying in a research posture on my stomach, over the enclosure in which they were confined, I found myself developing what I feared might be rudimentary creepers. And so, late this autumn, I stood erect and walked into my house, where I immediately set about the compilation of the notes I had made.

So much for the non-technical introduction. The remainder of this article bids fair to be fairly scientific.

In studying the more intimate phases of newt life, one is chiefly impressed with the methods by means of which the males force their attentions upon the females, with matrimony as an object. For the newt is, after all, only a newt, and has his weaknesses just as any of the rest of us. And I, for one, would not have it different. There is little enough fun in the world as it is.

The peculiar thing about a newt's courtship is its restraint. It is carried on, at all times, with a minimum distance of fifty paces (newt measure) between the male and the female. Some of the bolder males may now and then attempt to overstep the bounds of good sportsmanship and crowd in to forty-five paces, but such tactics are frowned upon by the Rules Committee. To the eye of an uninitiated observer, the pair might be dancing a few of the more open figures of the minuet.

The means employed by the males to draw the attention and win the affection of those of the opposite sex (females) are varied and extremely strategic. Until the valuable researches by Strudlehoff in 1887 (in his *"Entwickelungsmechanik"*) no one had been able to ascertain just what it was that the male newt did to make the female see anything in him worth throwing herself away on. It had been observed that the most personally unattractive newt could advance to within fifty paces of a female of his acquaintance and, by some *coup d'oeil*, bring her to a point where she would, in no uncertain terms, indicate her willingness to go through with the marriage ceremony at an early date.

It was Strudlehoff who discovered, after watching several thousand courting newts under a magnifying lens (questionable taste on his part, without doubt, but all is fair in pathological love) that the male, during the courting season (the season opens on the tenth of March and extends through the following February, leaving about ten days for general overhauling and redecorating) gives forth a strange, phosphorescent glow from the center of his highly colored dorsal crest, somewhat similar in effect to the flash of a diamond scarf-pin in a red necktie. This glow, according to Strudlehoff, so fascinates the female with its air of elegance and indication of wealth, that she immediately falls a victim to its lure.

But the little creature, true to her sex-instinct, does not at once give evidence that her morale has been shattered. She affects a coyness and lack of interest, by hitching herself sideways along the bottom of the aquarium, with her head turned over her right shoulder away from the swain. A trained ear might even detect her whistling in an indifferent manner.

The male, in the meantime, is flashing his gleamer frantically two blocks away and is performing all sorts of attractive feats, calculated to bring the lady newt to terms. I have seen a male, in the stress of his handicap courtship, stand on his fore-feet, gesticulating in amorous fashion with his hind feet in the air. Franz Ingehalt, in his *"Ueber Weltschmerz des Newt,"* recounts having observed a distinct and deliberate undulation of the body, beginning with the shoulders and ending at the filament of the tail, which might well have been the origin of what is known to-day in scientific circles as "the shimmy." The object seems to be the same, except that in the case of the newt, it is the male who is the active agent.

In order to test the power of observation in the male during these maneuvers, I carefully removed the female, for whose benefit he was undulating, and put in her place, in slow succession, another (but less charming) female, a paper-weight of bronze shaped like a newt, and, finally, a common rubber eraser. From the distance at which the courtship was being carried on, the male (who was, it must be admitted, a bit near-sighted congenitally) was unable to detect the change in personnel, and continued, even in the presence of the rubber eraser, to gyrate and undulate in a most conscientious manner, still under the impression that he was making a conquest.

At last, worn out by his exertions, and disgusted at the meagerness of the reaction on the eraser, he gave a low cry of rage and despair and staggered to a near-by pan containing barley-water, from which he proceeded to drink himself into a gross stupor.

Thus, little creature, did your romance end, and who shall say that its ending was one whit less tragic than that of Camille?   Not I, for one. . . . In fact, the two cases are not at all analogous.

And now that we have seen how wonderfully Nature works in the fulfillment of her laws, even among her tiniest creatures, let us study for a minute a cross-section of the community-life of the newt. It is a life full of all kinds of exciting adventure, from weaving nests to crawling about in the sun and catching insect larvæ and crustaceans.   The newt's day is practically never done, largely because the insect larvæ multiply three million times as fast as the newt can possibly catch and eat them.   And it takes the closest kind of community team-work in the newt colony to get things anywhere near cleaned up by nightfall.

It is early morning, and the workers are just appearing, hurrying to the old log which is to be the scene of their labors. What a scampering! What a bustle! Ah, little scamperes! Ah, little bustlers! How lucky you are, and how wise! You work long hours, without pay, for the sheer love of working. An ideal existence, I'll tell the scientific world.

Over here on the right of the log are the Master Draggers. Of all the newt workers, they are the most futile, which is high praise indeed. Come, let us look closer and see what it is that they are doing.

The one in the lead is dragging a bit of gurry out from the water and up over the edge into the sunlight. Following him, in single file, come the rest of the Master Draggers. They are not dragging anything, but are sort of helping the leader by crowding against him and eating little pieces out of the filament of his tail.

And now they have reached the top. The leader, by dint of much leg-work, has succeeded in dragging his prize to the ridge of the log.

The little workers, reaching the goal with their precious freight, are now giving it over to the Master Pushers, who have been waiting for them in the sun all this while. The Master Pushers' work is soon accomplished, for it consists simply in pushing the piece of gurry over the other side of the log until it falls with a splash into the water, where it is lost.

This part of their day's task finished, the tiny toilers rest, clustered together in a group, waving their heads about from side to side, as who should say: "There— that's done!" And so it *is* done, my little Master Draggers and my little Master Pushers, and *well* done, too. Would that my own work were as clean-cut and as satisfying.

And so it goes. Day in and day out, the busy army of newts go on making the world a better place in which to live. They have their little trials and tragedies, it is true, but they also have their fun, as anyone can tell by looking at a log full of sleeping newts on a hot summer day.

And, after all, what more has life to offer?

CHAPTER V

GELETT BURGESS AS A HUMORIST *

BY GELETT BURGESS

I F you will clamber up almost any one of the many, many church steeples in Boston—from the New Old South to the Church-of-the-Holy-Beanblowers —you will find, near the top, a curious mark—a monogram composed of the Phoenician letters F. G. B. But Gelett Burgess, in those kidloid days, was really no Steeple Jack. His marks were scrawled inside, not outside those steeples.

And, as he had sometimes in the pursuit of this peculiar fad to break into those churches to climb up into the steeples, so he broke into Literature from the inside, and left his mark.

Noticing, even at fifteen, that most of the "Notes and Queries" in the *Boston Transcript* were requests for lost doggerels, he induced a boy friend to write to the editor and ask for the author of a poem—one of G. B.'s own private effusions. And the next week,

---

* The account of Gelett Burgess has been written by himself at the request of the author of this book. He requested, and indeed the condition of obtaining it was, that it should not be changed in any particular; and so it follows just as Mr. Burgess wrote it.

he himself sent in, and proudly he saw printed his answering letter:

Editor of the Transcript:

DEAR SIR:

The author of the poem entitled "The dismal day, &c." is Frank Gelett Burgess, and the whole poem is as follows:

> The dismal day, with dreary pace,
>   Hath dragged its tortuous length along;
> The gravestones black and funeral vase
>   Cast horrid shadows long.
>
> Oh, let me die, and never think
>   Upon the joys of long ago!
> For cankering thoughts make all the world
>   A wilderness of woe.

With this merry literary achievement he was for some years content; he made no further attempts to create a demand for his work. G. B. a civil engineer would be. In the back of his arithmetic, an illustrated problem had shown him a clever surveyor measuring across a river without crossing it. This had fired his imagination.

The Massachusetts Institute of Technology, where he became, in four years, a Bachelor of Science, had, no doubt, although indirectly, a strong influence upon his imagination. It gave him precision of thought, if not direction. It made his ideas definite. It did not, however, encourage the pursuit of letters, except perhaps the Alphas Betas and Deltas which nearly

conquered him in Stresses and Strains and the Theory
of Elasticity.

He did, though, interrupt his Calculus and Quar-
ternions occasionally, to contribute an article or poem
for the student magazine, *The Tech;* and when, later,
he was camped with an engineering outfit of the
Southern Pacific Railway in the seven-foot-high
growth of mustard where now arise the houses of
Pasadena's greatest and best, he wrote a story for
the *Boston Budget.*

Still, all the time, persistently, though secretly, G. B.
was committing light verse, mainly celebrating the
ladies of his acquaintance.   To this hard training in
versification is attributable what skill and style he has
attained.   Several thick books of unpublished *vers de
société* and fancy still exist to prove his assiduity and
his mastery of technique and condensed thought.

Alas, the fates denied the young poet's desire to
build tunnels and bridges in the fastnesses of the
Andes.   He was too good a draughtsman to be sent
into the field; and three years of office work in San
Francisco (usually with a poem or sketch concealed
under his maps) sickened him of science.

A call to the University of California as Instructor
in Topographical Drawing soon gave him the opportunity and leisure to indulge his muse.   But, ere three
years of this unseemly dignity had passed, a midnight escapade, though it endeared him to the students,
brought an intimation from the President that his
resignation from the Faculty of the U. C. would be
accepted.

It was this pulling down of the cast-iron statue of

the famous Dr. Coggswell—so long an aesthetic scandal in San Francisco—that launched G. B. into a literary career. With Bruce Porter, another of the iconoclasts, he started *The Lark*. This was to be known, during its two years' sprightly existence, as the most original magazine ever published in America.

In its initial number one nonsense rhyme achieved for G. B. a fame which he has made a lifelong attempt to surpass. This was

> I never saw a Purple Cow,
> I never Hope to See one;
> But I can Tell you, Anyhow,
> I'd rather See than Be one!

The Lark was unique in that it contained neither satire, parody, nor comment or criticism of any kind upon contemporary writers. It eschewed both local color and timeliness. Every page, in fact, was a definite contribution of appealing originality. Nonsense, serious verse, essays, fiction, drawings, inventions—*The Lark* was versatile—all had the freshness and gayety of youth. Its creed was optimism and *joie de vivre*. And most of it was written by G. B.; often the whole number, from cover design to jocose advertisements, was from his pen.

As a nonsense writer, however, he was still best known and enjoyed; and these two poems came near to rivaling his P. Cow.

> The Window has four little Panes—
> But One have I.
> The Window Panes are in its Sash—
> I Wonder Why!

The Towel hangs upon the Wall—
And Somehow, I don't Care at All.
The Door is Open. I must Say
I rather Fancy it That Way!

Amongst the many gallimaufries in *The Lark* was
an essay consisting of six paragraphs each of which
could be used in combination with any other, hap-
hazard, making an infinite number of apparently logical
permutations. If you don't believe it, try for yourself
any arrangement of these "Interchangeable Philosophical Paragraphs":

1. It may be doubted that any system of thought
arranged upon the lines herewith proposed can be a
success. The fact of its accomplishment alone, important as it must be, is no proof of method.

2. For instance, the correct relation between any
two facts is one that must be investigated along the
lines of thought most perfectly correlated to those
facts.

3. And in spite of what might at first sight be called
irrelevancy, there is this to be observed, no matter what
bearing the above may have upon the subject in hand,
that the relations of one part to another may or may
not be true.

4. And here must be noted the importance of the
demand that such types of thought do exist. This is,
no doubt, a quality of subjects, rather than of rela-
tivity between modes of expression.

5. So, too, are questions affecting the expression of
coherent symbols of equal importance with the method
by which these symbols are expressed.

6. But at the same time there must be a certain

divergence in form between the types of questions to be discussed.

Equally erudite was a short, pointed story in the key of A-sharp, by G. B. which began—and continued quite as extravagantly—with this burst of verbiage: —all words guaranteed genuine:

An autumnal sun, hanging in abditative attitude behind the atramental abysses of the wood, peered through the apertures of the adustive foliage, casting ampliated, anfractuous penumbric anamorphoses of the arbuscles in the Park. In the arbor, beneath an acacia, sat the austere Anthea, analytical, yet attrehent.

and the following attempt of a typewriting machine at automatic poetry is a patent satire upon all machine-made verse:

> Oh Phliis, "j??zVbx Aj%5 2q part,
>   So soon—1Q'k"jyx,-, 2-morrow,
> Alas, q1Q)$ 'Vmlj-; my poor heart!
>   Ah—$$,%, ws 4pdq7, Qkcd, sorrow.

> Fare"well,. .QJmdubz$ "-,never mind,
>   Sweet Phylli$, "jzf%1 ,-missing—
> Ah me,, v$%Aw"mjx . .js$. .have to find
>   Another g$irlx $993% to do $gzk kissing!

The "Burgess Nonsense Book," containing many of *The Lark's* best humorous features and other eccentricities coined by G. B.'s whimsical mind, put him in a class apart. There have been few volumes of sheer, premeditated absurdity—too few. For Wit and

Humor are more common than is generally supposed.
Parody and Burlesque, too, are easy enough.   Satire
we find in spots.   But Nonsense is a ticklish medium
to essay.   It takes a clear head to walk that narrow
steep pathway along the wall of Pomposity without
falling into the abyss of Silliness.   Could G. B. do it?
Perhaps, of such unadulterated nonsense, this is his
gem of purest ray serene:

Abstrosophy

> If echoes from the fitful past
>   Could rise to mental view,
> Would all their fancied radiance last,
> Or would some odors from the blast,
>   Untouched by Time, accrue?
>
> Is present pain a future bliss,
>   Or is it something worse?
> For instance, take a case like this:
> Is fancied kick a real kiss—
>   Or rather the reverse?
>
> Is plenitude of passion palled
>   By poverty of scorn?
> Does Fiction mend what Fact has mauled?
> Has Death its wisest victims called
>   When idiots are born?

Upon moving to New York G. B. almost came
down to earth.   But of course, not quite.   His
sophistication is evident in one of his lesser known
books (half-suppressed by his half-hearted publisher),
one of the million parodies of the immortal Fitzgerald.

"The Rubaiyat of Omar Cayenne" was a skittish skit on contemporaneous literature, so-called. A few quatrains will show G. B.'s satiric intent:

Why, if an Author can fling Art aside
And in a Book of Balderdash take Pride,
    Wer't not a Shame—wer't not a Shame for him
A Conscientious Novel to have Tried?

And though you wring your Hands and wonder Why
Such Slipshod Work the Publisher will buy,
    Don't grumble at the Editor, for he
Must serve the Public, e'en as You and I.

We are no other than a Passing Show
Of clumsy Mountebanks that Come and Go
    To please the General Public; now, who gave
To IT the right to Judge, I'd like to Know!

G. B., however, had more serious aspirations than to be a clown. A reputation for nonsense, even for humor and fancy, he knew to be dangerous. In New York, therefore, he began in the magazine fiction field. It was more dignified—people didn't, in private expect one to be funny—and one made more money.

Still, a fatal facility with rhyme, when combined with some talent as a grotesque illustrator and that cursed sense of humor to boot, was a seductive trio—almost irresistible. Luckily G. B. was able to steer these three Graces in a didactic direction, and escape motley for a while. The invention of a queer new race of beings, ill-behaved children—he called them Goops (it was a quaint word, once)—started him as a nursery Mentor. Book after book of Goops in-

culcating principles of infant etiquette in verse, and
illustrated by himself with eccentric drawings, have
made him now even better known as a juvenile writer
than as a nonsense poet.

Not a youthful fault but has not been described
and deprecated; and a sample from one of these
Manual of Manners will show how he succeeded in
teaching children manners without their suspecting it:

> The Goops, they lick their fingers,
> And the Goops, they lick their knives.
> They spill their broth on the table-cloth—
> Oh, they lead disgusting lives!
> The Goops, they talk while eating,
> And loud and fast they chew.
> So that is why I'm glad that I
> Am not a Goop—are you?

Hardly had G. B. been thus labeled, when lo, he
escaped from the juvenile pigeonhole and appeared in
a new rôle. Perhaps it was a year in London writing
for *The Sketch* that changed him, although while
there he accomplished a whole series of ultra-modern
fairy tales whose heroes and heroines were new to
fiction—such as "The House who Walked in her
Sleep," "The Locomobile in search of his Fortune,"
"The Lazy Lamp Posts," and "The Very, Very Grand
Piano."

At any rate, he returned to New York as a full-
fledged satirist to set a new word in people's mouths
from Maine to Florida. Bromide! Why, it even
got into the dictionary. Are You a Bromide? he
asked, in a most provocative social analysis that divided

the world into two classes—those who have original ideas, and those who think by syndicate. True, most readers understood and were amused only by his list of platitudes, such as "If I leave my umbrella it is sure to rain," and "the world is a very small place, after all," but the essay itself while couched in jocosity, is a searching presentation of the limitations of the "bromidic" mind.

Encouraged by the notice this booklet received, G. B. now turned his mischievous attention to Women. He put their foibles under his merry mental microscope in two books which have aroused the wrath of feminists. "The Maxims of Methuselah," giving in striking mock-biblical diction and modern slang, the result of the venerable patriarch's 969 years of experience with the woman of the Land of Nod, was followed by an even more spicily audacious set of "Maxims of Noah." Each had a sober and scholarly Introduction, into which he wove all the lore concerning the two old men embodied in the ancient legends of Hebraic literature —such as the Talmud, the Midrash, the Book of Yashar and of Enoch, etc.

The two books of Maxims are guaranteed by the impertinent author to give young man a complete course in the art of Understanding and Managing Women. G. B.'s views on this parlous topic may be illustrated by a few Maxims:

My son, many a damsel is a *kitten* with men, who is a *cat* with women.

But when thou goest amongst women, let not thy *left* girl know what thy *right* girl doeth.

As a *leaky* hot water bottle in time of need, so is a fond woman who telleth thy secrets; her folly exceedeth her comfort.

As one who seeketh to fold a newspaper in a high wind, so is he who argueth with an *angry* woman.

As a cork that hath been pushed into a bottle, so is the mind of her who nurseth her *first born;* thou canst not attain unto it.

Can one lick a frosty door knob and not lose skin? So he who kisseth a widow shall not easily escape.

Stolen kisses are sweet, and hands held in secret are pleasant; but *he knoweth not* that when he hath *gone,* then will she tell all the details to her sisters without shame.

Gum may be removed from the hair, and ink under the thumb nail will in time pass away; but she who talketh too *loudly* in the street car cannot be changed.

Yea, as fascinating as a loose tooth is a secret to a young maiden; for she knoweth not whether to spit it out, or to keep it safe; yet *she cannot forget* it.

A teasing woman is as a squeaking shoe, or as when one walketh upon spilt sugar; it annoyeth me utterly.

Testifying to G. B.'s versatility, meanwhile, several novels, a book of poems, one of essays on The Romance of the Commonplace, and a book of detective stories, appeared in his endeavor to demonstrate his sobriety to the world. It was of little use. He was compelled to milk that Purple Cow for the rest of his life.

Already the word Blurb (self-praise, to make a sound like a publisher), had been widely adopted to describe the advertised praise of books, tobaccos, break-fast foods and sundry. The success of this coinage, as well as the popularity of Bromide and Sulphite, led him to try his hand at other vivacious vocables and apt neologisms. He became, in fact, a lexicographer, and collected 100 Words You have Always Needed into a volume he unblushingly denominated "Burgess Unabridged." Each new word is not only defined, but described and illustrated elaborately in both prose and verse. They are not, on the whole, pretty words, but they bite right into every-day life. Each of them, to coin a phrase, fills a long-felt want.

How, for instance, would you describe the appearance of one who is not quite the thoroughbred—an East Orangean, for instance, or a lady from Meriden? He is apt to wear one of those mushroom-pleated shirts with a swallow-tail, and probably he carries a cane but no gloves. She wears white gloves, but badly soiled; her shoes are run over at the heels. The answer, to G. B. is easy. We have described a Bripkin.

In this lively mixture of glossolalia and satire, G. B. is at his comic best and most original. A few abbreviated citations from "Burgess Unabridged" will convince one of the paucity of the English language:

ALIBOSH—A glaringly obvious falsehood or exaggeration.

COWCAT—An unimportant guest, an insignificant personality.

DRILLIG—A tiresome lingerer, a buttonholer.

EDICLE—One who is educated beyond his intellect.

GEFOOJET—An unnecessary thing, a wedding present, curios.

GUBBLE—Society chatter, the hum of foolish conversation.

KIPE—To inspect appraisingly, as women look at each other.

MEEM—An artificial half-light beloved by women of a certain age, as of three red candles.

SPUZZ—Mental force, aggressive personality, stamina.

VARM—The quintessence of sex, a female atmosphere, as of a man entirely surrounded by women.

VORIANDER—A woman who pursues men, especially when she is unattractive. A female who demands attentions.

WOG—Food on the face, egg in the whiskers, milk on the lips, or other unconscious adornment of the person.

ZOBZIB—An amiable blunderer, one displaying misguided zeal.

And an idea of how amenable these terms are to poetry and give an intriguing flavor, G. B. gives many poems, of which the following is the most abstruse:

When vorianders seek to huzzlecoo,
    When jurpid splooch or vilpous drillig bores,
When cowcats kipe, or moobles wog, or you
    Machizzled are by yowfs or xenogores,
Remember Burgess Unabridged, and think
    How quisty is his culpid yod and yab;
No fidgeltick, with goigsome iobink,
    No varmic orobaldity, his gab!

In the realm of more conventional comedy verse also, G. B. is well known. Here as elsewhere he is essentially a satirist of manners, and as usual, ruthlessly at the expense of women's frailty. His best known poem in this line has caused much discussion amongst the literati, as to the identification of his hero. There have been many claimants to the honor. But one stanza will show the animus.

Dighton is engaged! Think of it and tremble—
Two and twenty maidens in the city must dissemble!
Two and twenty maidens in a panic must repeat,
"Dighton is a gentleman—will Dighton be discreet?"
All the merry maidens who have known him at his best,
Wonder what the girl is like, and if he has confessed.
    Dighton, the philanderer! Will he prove a slanderer?
A man gets confidential ere the honeymoon is sped.
    Dighton was a rover then; Dighton lived in clover
        then;
Dighton is a gentleman—but Dighton is to wed!

A sample from another poem (written on a bet, while making a call) will show still more plainly his tendency to make fun of the unfair sex.

Leave the lady, Willy, let the racket rip;
She is going to fool you—you have lost your grip.
Your brain is in a muddle, and your heart is in a whirl;
Come along with me, Willy—never mind the girl!
        Come and have a man-talk,
        Come with those who can talk,
Light your pipe and listen, and the boys will pull you
        through
        Love is only chatter,
        Friends are all that matter—
Come and have a man-talk—that's the cure for you!

But even G. B.'s fiction has always (though sometimes concealed slightly) the sarcastic note. His comedy is oftener a comedy of manners than of situation.   An abandoned example of this is his New York Arabian Nights Entertainment called "Find the Woman."   He does, it is true, indulge in such farce as a kidnaped hero coming out of his chloroform to find himself without trousers in a pigeon loft, to be subsequently entertained by a Club of Liars—but G. B. is more apt to laugh at the general tendency than the specific instance.   Like O. Henry, he has been remembered more for ingenious construction and knowledge of human nature, than by the creation of any popular character.   The most original—or perhaps the maddest of his *dramatis-personae* in this novel is "the President of an Anti-Profanity League," one Dr. Hopbottom; and this is the way he relieves his irate emotion:

See here, you slack-salted, transubstantiated interdigital germarium, you rantipole sacrosciatic rockbarnacle, you—if you give me any more of your caprantipolene paragastular megalopteric jacitation, I'll make a lamel-libranchiate gymnomixine lepidopteroid out of you!

Little need be said of G. B.'s more serious literary work—novels, plays, poems and essays.   But one must take its existence into consideration in appraising his work as a humorist.   For humor is a natural reflex from serious and earnest impulses.   The first arboreal anthropoid ape who, safe at the top of his tree, cackled in primitive laughter at the sight of his fellow at the bottom being attacked by a deadly enemy, felt something of what we call humor.   And it was because that ancestor of ours knew by experience the seriousness of the other's plight that he made primordial fun of him. It might be said, indeed, that not only are humorists the most sapient commentators upon life, but that no one who cannot be earnest can be really funny.

And especially is this true of that form of applied humor called satire, which is never successful unless the subject ridiculed is well understood, if not indeed beloved. G. B. is always like one who chaffs his brother or his best friend—or, so far as that goes, himself. Nowhere is this better shown than in his outrageous "Lady Mechante," which bears the pregnant sub-title, "Life as it Should Be." This novel, written, at odd moments for the mere delight of unrestraint, for his own wild pleasure, consists of four books. "The Cad and the Countess" is a satire on society boredom; "The Walking Peanut," a skit on hypnotism; "The Cult of Mars," a travesty on new occult religions; and "The Cave Man" an explosive burlesque on modern art. And in the latter it is G. B.'s own pet theories and beliefs that are most merrily attacked—his favorite schools of music, painting, architecture and literature.

Here, for instance is the Cave Man's first poem— something sacred and holy, he avers—a part of the divine mystery of his being. Like a love letter it is the sort of thing that isn't often exposed to public view. But Haulick Smagg thus displays his hidden feelings:

> My shirt is sticky. It clings to my back.
> Gawd, my gawd, but I'd like to cry!
> I got up at night and stepped on a tack—
> Gawd, but I want to die!

I got my hair all covered with glue—
I wiped my face on a towel new—
  Gawd, my gawd, but I'd like to cry!
I seen a guy with a pale blue scarf—
I heerd a gal with a horrid larff—
  Gawd, but I want to die!

Almost as extreme in its abandon is G. B.'s string of anguished tales entitled "Ain't Angie Awful!" They are vulgar, and yet charming. They are silly, yet comic. Here his style is almost legerdemain. He is atrocious. You crawl all over—but you read on. Satire, though—satire again. He hits everything within reach of city life. . . . An introduction:

In the good old days when girls wore ears, and lacquered their faces in privacy, Angela Bish held the proud position of 23rd assistant gum-chewer in a six-cent store. . . .

Angela was only sixteen. But what does that matter, when one is young! . . .

For a young girl, life in New York is so hard-boiled as to be practically indigestible. There were times when Angie didn't know where her next kiss would come from.

Ill as she could have afforded the luxury, she would have given nine dollars any day for a husband, alive or dead. If wealthy, she would have preferred him dead. But all the matrimonial agencies had given her up as too wonderfully willing. Men, they said kindly, liked to pursue an elusive woman, like a cake of wet soap in a bath tub—even men did who hated baths. . . .

G. B.'s ever-youthful play instinct, in these two books carried to its absurdest limits, has always had a way of breaking out in the most unexpected and joyful directions. He has spent a fortnight constructing a completely equipped miniature farmhouse, with mica windows, and green velvet lawns—only to set it afire for the amusement of a dinner party. He has built dozens of Nonsense Machines—most elaborate assemblies of mechanisms, whose sole object was to be busy in the most complicated possible way without doing anything useful whatever. With T. R.'s he once set out on a trip abroad to buy a foreign title— and ended by digging up first century B.C. Roman tombs in Provence. He published in San Francisco, with another madcap, Porter Garnett, a magazine of rankest nonsense, *Le Petit Journal des Refusées,* and printed every copy on a different pattern of wall paper. And he exhibited, in an exclusive gallery on Fifth Avenue, some thirty water colors ambitiously hight "Experiments in Symbolistic Psychology." With Will Irwin, too, he collaborated not only on two books, but also in the management of the San Francisco & Arcady Railroad, an 87-foot line laid all over the floor of Suicide Hall, the apartment they shared on East Twenty-third Street.

Now do not these enthusiastic avocations cast a brilliant sidelight on G. B. as a writer? It will be seen in this psychoanalysis that his mind is essentially scientific, rather than dramatic. His permutative System of Philosophy, his employment of every known French form of verse in the *Lark,* his sarcastic comments on Art, in "The Cave Man," even the mechanical accurate quality of his drawings in "The Lively City o' Ligg"—all exhibit the same ironic, accuracy-loving, but law-breaking mind. To overcome technical difficulties, and at the same time exploit a really satiric idea, is his delight.

In "Dinarzade's Three Weeks," for example, which he wrote for the *Century*, G. B. proved that brevity is the soul of wit, by having the sister of Scheherezade outdo that lady by telling twenty-one stories, each of only ten words! Here are some of them:

Yawning bride's false teeth fall out before responses at wedding.

Old maid forgets to remove cotton from ears before proposal.

Aged lady, ambitious to become Steeple Jack, practices village church.

Escaping murderess detected through characteristic drinking milk through green veil.

Animal lover spends month in stable searching for pet fly.

Mouse on platform disturbs New Thought lecturer on "Banish Fear!"

Fighting in dark, man cuts own throat, thinking it enemy's.

Spinster dreams promenading Broadway undressed, wakes to find it true.

It will be seen by this time that G. B. loves *tours-de-force*. He loves machinery, and the intricacies of technique. He loves the extravagant, the outrageous. But he uses his gift always to demonstrate the absurdities of life. He creates his characters only to destroy them. He formulates complex theories and blows them up with blasts of laughter. He is amused at everything, respects nothing. It is all he can do to be merely decorous. Surely satire, to such a nature should be as easy as sneezing.

In one of his water colors, symbolizing Fancy, G. B. showed a Liverbone (another of his whimsical creations) who has leaped from the roof of a castle, and is seated, horseback, atop the moon. That bizarre, outlandish, care-free creature might also represent G. B.'s own mind. Say, Gertie, wouldn't it be awful to be like that?

CHAPTER VI

ELLIS PARKER BUTLER

IT was a great many years ago that Ellis Parker Butler came into my office one day from Kansas City. It must have been a quarter of a century ago. He was a pleasant-looking young man at the time: he is still pleasant-looking, in spite of all the humorous things he has written since: but doubtless he is wiser. For one thing he has lived in Flushing, New York, and continuous life in a place like Flushing, which enables a man to escape from New York with great rapidity, is more or less of a cultural process. In my time I have known several creative workers who lived in Flushing, and they appeared to be no worse for it.

Mr. Butler, however, did not go to Flushing by my recommendation. He went somewhere else. He told me that he had come on to New York to make his fortune, that he wanted to become a writer, and that he expected to become a married man in due time, the sooner the better. My advice to him was to get on a Broadway car, go north until he saw green, and then inquire at the nearest drug store for a suitable boarding house. But I had forgotten about Central Park, so Butler, seeing green, got off there and wandered around for a while among the swans and policemen, until, having by this time lost all confidence in my intelligence, he struck north for himself, got his bearings, became an editor, wrote "Pigs Is Pigs," acquired twins, lived in Paris, and became famous.

Butler went to Paris after he wrote "Pigs Is Pigs." He thought a residence in Paris, as a supplement to Kansas City and Flushing, would enlarge his fount of inspiration. Alas! he told me he was not able to write a thing during his stay there, and was glad to get back to his native land. He has given various explanations of how he wrote "Pigs Is Pigs," but perhaps the best one is that his grandfather was a pork-packer. He writes:

I brushed through the first year of high school at Muscatine well enough but just after I dipped into the second year I quit to go to work, because my father had hard sledding as a low-paid bookkeeper with eight children. We were a mighty poorly financed family. My grandfather, Sage O. Butler, had been a pork-packer, Mobile, Cincinnati, St. Louis, Muscatine—following the hogs—and the big slump in provisions just after the Civil War caught him overloaded and extended, and he failed.

For a number of years, as a boy, I lived with my grandmother and aunt at Muscatine. My aunt was a spinster and one of the most genuinely cultured women I have known—a lover of good literature and good music. Chopin and Beethoven were her favorites, and the "Lake Poets," and Charles Lamb and Matthew Arnold, and the finer old Americans—Lowell, Longfellow and Emerson. She felt that good literature was something almost as holy as religion, and she made me feel that a great poet or a great writer of prose was not second to any hero.

It was this delicate and cultured aunt who taught me to read and to know my numbers. I learned to read with Sir Walter Scott's "Tales of a Grandfather" as a primer, and Shakespeare's plays as a "First Reader," and the printed word gained then has always held for me color and mystery and "alarums" and glittering panoplies and clash of arms. I remember lying on my belly on the dull red parlor carpet reading "Hamlet" while my aunt practiced a Chopin nocturne—and Chopin still means good music to me, and Shakespeare means good, healthy, vigorous English.

It was inevitable that I should write poetry first. I remember a serious parody of "Blow, Bugles, Blow" that I wrote on the theme of a cyclone that hit Muscatine. It was published in a local paper about the time I began losing my milk teeth, and I wrote many more "poems."

Recently I met Dean Jewell of the University of Arkansas and he told me something of the psychology of humorists. I had always said I became a humorist because my father was a great lover of humor. I remember I gave him, once or twice, the Christmas numbers of the humorous weeklies as my Christmas gift, and he knew and liked *Peck's Sun*, the *Burlington Hawkeye*, the *Toledo Blade* and the other weekly humor papers of a type now dead, ending with *Texas Siftings*. I had always imagined that this close association with humor publications and my father's great admiration for Bill Nye, Bob Burdette and Mark Twain was the influence that turned me to humor, but Dean Jewell says this is not so. He says the psychology of the humorist is that he is timid and thin-skinned; he has had a love of writing put into him and has written something serious and some one he loves or admires has laughed at it, and in protection of his egotistic and quivering sensibilities he turns to humor as to something that will be laughed at without causing him pain. Or words to that effect.

This seems true in my own case, and is no doubt true in most cases. Dickens, the gutter-snipe, must have feared the criticism of the snobby educated, and he turned to the laugh. Most of our own famous humorists come from small towns where the writer of serious verse or prose is considered a poor freak.

I know that even my dear aunt's gentle and kindly criticisms of my raw, youthful poems often sent me shamedly to tears of hurt self-esteem, but I do not recall that I tried to write humor while I lived with her first. She did not consider humor worthy, unless it was the refined humor of Lamb or dear Oliver Wendell Holmes, and a boy in short pants can't do that sort. If he can he ought to be shot as a little prig.

It was when I went home to my parents that I wrote my first great laughing success, a poem about our colored servant's hair "switch" which blew out of her bedroom window and became tangled in the top of a blossoming cherry tree. The family liked that poem, and I had to make several copies of it.

When I started to school, well up in the classes because of the home tutoring I had had, I began a career as a humorist that gave me great pleasure, although it was not widespread. There was a custom of giving, as a punishment for slight infractions of the school discipline, the task of writing an "essay" of five hundred or a thousand words. I loved this and I was disgustingly proud to stand before the school and read an essay

on "Trees" or "Prohibition" that made the teacher
and the scholars giggle and even laugh aloud.

I think it was inevitable that I should be a writer of
some sort because my aunt had given me such an admiration of literature. There was a time, when I was
six years old, when I longed to become a blacksmith,
because, I think, I loved the odor of hot iron against a
horse's hoofs, as I do still, and somewhat later I wanted
to become a doctor, but this was because that profession
seemed to make a college education necessary, and what
I wanted was the college education. I know I would
have made a disgusting doctor. I would have been very
popular and would have become wealthy while the
graveyards filled with my patients. I would have had
a most profitable bedside manner but I would have
given, too often, arsenic for quinine. In my heart, I
think, I never believed I would be anything but a writer.
To write and have what I wrote printed always seemed
the noblest success I could obtain, because my heroes
were the writers of books, and not preachers or soldiers or statesmen or millionaires or social successes.
I would rather be George Ade than Rockefeller, and
Napoleon has never seemed to me worth one of Bunner's short stories. I would rather see Booth Tarkington from across a wide street than spend a month with
President Harding, as a guest of honor. My first view
of the old Century building on Union Square thrilled
me ten thousand times as strongly as my first view of
Niagara Falls.

I spent ten or eleven years, after leaving high school,
in "jobs" in a spice mill, an oatmeal mill, a china store
and a wholesale grocery, doing clerical work, being a
floor salesman, selling groceries and one thing and another, but my real life was after hours when I could
take a pen and get at my writing. I sold quite a few

serious poems, but Hood's "Rhymester," which I happened to hear of as a textbook, put me in love with *vers de société* and the exact forms of verse tinged with wit, and I did a lot of that and sold it to *Life, Puck, Judge* and *Truth*. It was inevitable that in selling to these I should see a further market for my "stuff" in the form of prose-humor—paragraphs and longer skits, and I found the market a good one and managed to sell the *Century Magazine* some things—a glory indeed. I worked until twelve or one each night, after my regular work, and presently I was earning more by what I wrote than by my "job" in the wholesale grocery, and when I had an opportunity I visited New York and asked R. U. Johnson of the *Century,* Tom Masson of *Life,* and the editor of *Truth* whether it would be wise to come to New York and be the thing I wanted most to be, a literary man. They all advised me to come to New York and I did, and I have been grateful to all three for the advice.

It seems to me inevitable that a man depending on his pen for his income and not wishing his family to dwell in poverty must write much that he would not write had he an income otherwise available, but I am fairly well satisfied with what I have done thus far, and it is difficult to decide what I like best of the things I have written. "Pigs Is Pigs," with its instant success and continued popularity, is probably the "best" thing I have done or it would not have attracted such wide and continued attention. It is not a "work" however, and an author is apt to be proudest of the thing he has done more intentionally. I love "Pigs Is Pigs" and can laugh at its humor myself, even after having read it a thousand and one times, but it was an accident and not the result of a studied effort. We are prouder of the things we plan carefully and then labor over. I think "The Jack Knife Man" is the best thing I have done, judged in this way, but probably "Pigs Is Pigs," "Mrs. Dugan's Discovery," "Billy Brad and the Big, Big Lie" and other things that were merely dashed off without premeditation are the best test of whether I am a humorist or not. Being unstudied, they show I have humor in me that will come out if I let it. Things like my "Goat Feathers," "Swatty" and "In Pawn" are greater sources of pride to me because I set myself a task and accomplished it fairly well in each case.

I have had twenty books published, but some of the things I like best have not been put in book form yet, mainly because they are short and disconnected and because I have not bothered to gather them together and urge their publication.

Without meaning to be egotistic I think the humorist does more good in the world than any other writer with the exception of the true poet and the vital essayist. A great poet is the world's greatest treasure, and a great essayist is a true prose poet, but the humorist, however cheap and trashy, does something important that no other writer does—he gives the reader a laugh.

What Butler says in this charming letter about the psychology of humorists stirs me profoundly. It explains a great deal about humorists that I never before understood and confirms my own experience with these denatured human beings.

Indeed, it requires a great stock of brains to overcome being a humorist, and one's sense of humor needs to be kept in constant retirement. In this country Benjamin Franklin, perhaps the one universal genius America can boast of, made his sense of humor serve him in all of his capacities, and I fancy that Dean Jewell's remark would scarcely apply to him. But it is largely true of our present-day humorists.

As for a sense of humor, how many people do you know who have one? Scarcely anybody, you say promptly. Are you sure you have one yourself? Oh, yes, of course. You wouldn't deny that. If anyone should accuse you of not having a sense of humor, would you laugh at him? You would be secretly sore. This charge might rankle in your mind for days. What is a sense of humor anyway? Are you clear in your mind about it?

There is nothing that the average man is more sensitive about than this same sense of humor. You have it—only it is quite possible that you have never learned how to use it. How do you know that you haven't been secretly and subconsciously afraid to use it? Maybe in a rash moment you have tried it on someone and the result has been so disastrous that it cured you. The practical joker is not in good standing. If you turn the laugh on the other man the immediate result may be highly effective, but you have made an enemy. And we learn by hard experience that we cannot afford to make too many superfluous enemies.

And yet a sense of humor, if it is rightly applied, is one of the most powerful assets in the world. It not only keeps a man sweet and clean, but so far as one's opportunities are concerned, it acts upon them like a magnifying glass—brings them out, makes them larger and clearer. It all depends on how you get it and how you use it. An instance of the danger in its application is shown in the reply made by one of the officers of the Illinois Central Railroad to Abraham Lincoln when he was practicing law. He had won an important case for this railroad. He presented a bill for $2,000.

"Why," said the officer, "this is as much as a first-class lawyer would have charged."

"Lincoln," writes Miss Tarbell, "withdrew the bill, left the office and, at the first opportunity, submitted the matter to his friends. Five thousand dollars, they all agreed, was a moderate fee . . . Lincoln then sued the railroad for that amount and won his case."

In the fifth volume of the life of Benjamin Disraeli occurs a letter to Lady Bradford, of whom the foremost man of his time—seventy years old and prime minister—was violently enamored. Owing to his unconcealed ardor and Lady Bradford's divergent point of view, a slight estrangement had risen between them.

"Unfortunately for me," he goes on to say, "my imagination did not desert me with my youth. I have always felt this a great misfortune. It would have involved me in calamities, had not nature bestowed on me in a large degree another quality—the sense of the ridiculous . . . And I cannot resist certainly the conviction that much of my conduct to you, during this year, has been absurd."

This is not, of course, to be taken as a confession, coming, as it did, from one of the most remarkable men of his age—if not of all ages, but rather as a naïve explanation. As I have said, it is quite usual for most men to claim that they have a sense of the ridiculous—more commonly termed a sense of humor, and it is usual for them to believe this in all sincerity. But the rest of us are inclined to doubt it. We smile to ourselves urbanely and say "Poor fellow, he thinks he has it, but of course he hasn't; otherwise he would not take himself so seriously."

But the rest of us are wrong. Practically everybody has a sense of humor, however much this fact may be disputed. But if we exercised it right and left, where would we land? Both Benjamin Disraeli and Abraham Lincoln were exceptional men. Like Franklin, they were so big in other respects that they could display a sense of humor without disaster. Lincoln read Artemus Ward to his cabinet at a critical moment in the world's history. If a smaller man had done this, he might not have survived it. Satire and invective are one thing. Humor is another. Lincoln's perspective was so large that he could afford to be reckless about his humor. Then again—except where he needed to bring home a lesson—his humor was kindly; it usually served to illustrate some point he was making.

Mark Twain, as I have stated elsewhere, published his "Joan of Arc" anonymously because, his chief reputation being as a humorist, he believed that the public would not take his serious work seriously. He was right.

S. S. Cox ("Sunset" Cox) declared that his display of humorous proclivities undoubtedly hurt his legislative career. A public man always has to guard against getting a reputation for being a humorist.

It has been said and more than once, that Theodore Roosevelt had no sense of humor. It has been said,

however, only by a few critical people to whom humor
in any man would not be considered a damage—on the
contrary. These people were wrong. Theodore
Roosevelt did not have the same kind of sense of humor
that Lincoln had. It was not so unrestrained, so inevitable, as one might say. But, of course, he had it.
It was an essential part of his large background. An
evidence of this keen appreciation of humor is shown
in his account of an interview he had with John L.
Sullivan. Sullivan visited him once at the White
House, to enlist his help about a certain nephew who
hadn't turned out as Sullivan hoped.

"That boy," he explained to Mr. Roosevelt, "I just
cannot understand. He was my sister's favorite son,
and I always took a special interest in him myself. I
did my best to bring him up in the way he ought to go.
But there was nothing to be done with him. His tastes
were naturally low. He took to music."

The real reason why so few people develop and display their sense of humor is not because it isn't there,
but because it isn't there in proportion to the rest of
their qualities, and they think they cannot afford to
develop it. They are afraid of it. It's so powerful a
thing that it goes off in their hands and causes trouble.
They don't like to fool with it. It is a thing to be kept
under lock and key, in a secret receptacle, like Romance.

I knew a hard-headed bank president who once a
year regularly read "Little Women" and laughed and
cried to himself in his library over it. But the news
of this delightful event in his life was not chronicled
on his office bulletin board.

A sense of humor is not only dangerous, but useless in itself unless it is mixed with the man in the right proportions. Especially is this true of men with reputations for solidarity. By itself, it inspires no sort of confidence. You are not likely to trust another man with your money, your vote or your thoughts if, upon first meeting him, he laughs in your face, or "wheezes" you. In most people it is largely a case of defensive suppression.

It is my experience that judges and clergymen both have a sense of humor better developed than in other professions. But they are careful not to display too much of it outwardly. If they did, it might hurt them. Most men in settled positions of dignity and stability use it sparingly in public. That is one reason why a great man is not always understood and appreciated in his own home town. People see him with his mask off, laughing and joking and doing commonplace things in a human way. The career of many a young man has been set back or badly damaged because, at the outset, he did not know how to control his sense of humor. One of the greatest powers in the world, it must be handled correctly. Remember the story of the western cowboy, who had been delegated to break the news to the widow of a man that they had just hanged for stealing a horse, only to discover afterwards that he was innocent. He called and said: "Ma'am, we strung up your husband by mistake, and he's dead. But you certainly have got the laugh on us."

Where men are struggling for a living, they shut off any development of a sense of humor, important as it may be to the more cultivated, because they know intuitively that to be serious is to convey the idea of

reliability.   Occasionally some one among them has
it spontaneously and irresistibly.   He is tolerated by
his fellows for his "good" qualities, that are sufficiently in evidence.   They say of him, "He is a good
workman, but queer."   They do not quite understand
him, although they may enjoy his company.

All this being so, why do I say that a sense of humor
is such a big asset?   Let us look at the matter for a
moment in a large way.   Lincoln Steffens, who as a
correspondent and keen observer of social and indus-
trial conditions in many parts of the world, whose
books "The Shame of the Cities" and "The Struggle
for Self-Government" are a part of our literary and
social history, and who has frequently been called upon
to act as peacemaker between capital and labor, once
told me that if humor were applied to world conditions,
war would stop.   "Apart from its tragedy," said Mr.
Steffens, "war is ridiculous—so utterly nonsensical
that if men as a whole could be made to see it in this
light, they would be ashamed to indulge in it."

Most of us lose our perspective at critical moments.
We take ourselves too seriously.   If you doubt this,
look back upon some scene in your own past that, at
the moment, seemed utterly hopeless and tragic.   Now
that it is all over and you can look at it calmly and
impersonally, does it not strike you that your attitude
was ridiculous?   If your sense of humor could have
come into play at this moment, the whole situation
might have been relieved, and how much you might
have been saved!   This is what Disraeli meant when
he wrote of himself.   His love for Lady Bradford
had made him take himself too seriously.   But his

sense of the ridiculous kept him from going too far. Benjamin Franklin's sense of humor, which permeated his whole life, was mingled in right proportions to the rest of him, and saved him from much that otherwise would have led him astray. It gave him the power of holding two opposite things in his mind at once—the power of contrast—which is always evidence of a developed sense of humor. Thus, before the Constitution wás adopted and its fate was suspended by a hair, he was able to write that while he did not agree with all of it, he would sign it because, taken as a whole, it was best.

The passions that sweep men off their feet temporarily and lead to great tragedies might easily be prevented if humor could be brought in to clear the air. Dueling, which was once so common, has gone out because the ridiculousness of it is so apparent. Dueling is war on a small scale. Lincoln's example, in his famous duel with James Shields, had a large influence in making the duel ridiculous. Challenged by Shields, he insisted on having as weapons "broadswords of the largest size, precisely equal" and that between the principals there should be "a plank ten feet long, and from nine to twelve inches broad, to be firmly fixed on edge." A spectator who was present at this famous duel—which was adjusted without bloodshed, owing, no doubt, to the humorous twist that Lincoln had given to the affair, related the following account:

His face was grave and serious. I never knew him to go so long before without making a joke. But presently he reached over and picked up one of the swords, which he drew from its scabbard. Then he felt along the edge of the weapon with his thumb, as a barber feels of the edge of his razor, raised himself to his full height, stretched out his long arms and clipped off a twig from above his head with the sword. There wasn't another man of us who could have reached anywhere near that twig, and the absurdity of that long reaching fellow fighting with cavalry sabers with Shields, who could walk under his arm, came pretty near making me howl with laughter.

It would easily be possible for me to cite numerous examples taken from history and the private lives of illustrious men, to show not only the wonderful and direct, but the cumulative power of a sense of humor, when brought to bear at the right time. But I must pass on to its practical application to our own lives, as we live them day by day, merely expressing the hope that as individuals come to understand and realize this power, it may, in the course of time, spread to whole races who, with a national consciousness alive to the absurdity of their actions, will pause on the threshold of one more world tragedy.

A large proportion of our divorces might easily be prevented if humor were used as a sanitary measure. Women are apt to be more intense than men. They express themselves with greater freedom, and often say things on the spur of the moment that they do not really mean. In these moments they may, indeed, be reaching out for some gestures of affection. And when husbands, because of a lack of humor, allow themselves to be drawn into the same mood instead of passing over the occasion lightly, then tragedy is likely to result.

Women are entitled to their moods, and at any rate, to treat them too seriously and logically is only to increase the tension. Where a situation in so many cases is artificial, it can easily be neutralized by a little touch of humor. We can afford to be over-serious only about little things: as a rule, big things can be much better handled by treating them as incidental.

What the most of us who haven't cultivated a sense of humor don't realize is that we are all pipe-lines. We clog ourselves up with our own immediate and material concerns, and defeat the very possibilities that ought to run through us. We never see much farther than the ends of our noses. A sense of humor, therefore, is nothing but a sense of detachment. It enables a man, not only to stand off and look at himself in the right perspective, but to see everything else in the same way.

How to develop it?

First, remember that it doesn't consist in the mere saying of clever things. It isn't being merely witty. Pure wit is often caustic—and expensive. A French courtier, seating himself between Talleyrand and a lady remarked, "Now I sit between wit and beauty." To which Talleyrand replied, "And without possessing either."

And perhaps you have heard some young person say (it has so often been said to me!) "I always see the funny side of everything."

That is not quite it.

A sense of humor does not always—at least at first —consist of the mere ability to seem to be humorous. To develop it requires three things:

First, cultivate your imagination so that you will be able, not only to visualize an object, but to concentrate your mind upon it, in order to see it as if it actually stood before you, and to analyze it in its various parts, and come to value its relationship to other objects. This is the art of perspective.

Second, detach yourself from yourself. Be able to look at yourself as if you were somebody else. Say to yourself, "I am not the only pebble on the beach. I am only one, and a small one at that." When you have held this thought over a certain period, you will be surprised how it will free you from certain things that at the time seemed all important and serious, but which in reality are only incidental.

Third, practice contrast. Learn to hold two objects in your mind simultaneously, and how and why they differ from each other. By and by, when you pass judgment on any man, you will be able to take all of his contrasting qualities at once, and estimate them in their proper proportions.

From this training which, by the way, is in itself a constant revelation and delight, there will gradually come to you an accurate and powerful sense of humor. It will make you more honest, more direct, give you a proper humility and inspire the confidence of others. It will give you the trick of always putting yourself in the other fellow's place. This in itself is a great asset. Real humor is always founded on truth, which others recognize as soon as uttered.

Probably the humor of "Pigs Is Pigs" is so good because it is founded on truth. When I began this chapter, I intended to write exclusively about Butler

Instead of this I have let him tell about himself and have then done most of the talking. But never mind. This is a book about American humorists. In this place it may not have been unwise to have stated what I thought about a sense of humor. I know that Butler won't mind, for, being a married man like myself, he is uncomplaining and tolerant.

CHAPTER VII

IRVIN COBB

IRVIN COBB has written things about himself, I was about to add, "in a quite impersonal way," when I remembered that he had written about his being fat and had referred to the fact that he was homely, whereas he is nothing of the sort. Also, other people have written about him, but neither he, nor anyone else, has ever done him justice, not even Bob Davis, or Grant Overton.

Cobb is wrong about himself and others are wrong about him. I am the only one who really understands him, and yet to save me I cannot explain him in just the way that I should like.

I have said that Cobb is impersonal when writing about himself; what follows this brief introduction to him will emphasize what I mean. He does not take himself seriously but he does take his work seriously. This difference is very important, because it lies at the heart of most of our human relationships. Cobb has what I call literary integrity, but it is purely impersonal. The honesty of some people is so offensive that we wish the world were inhabited by more interesting criminals; not that the world isn't, but merely that even they try to be too honest about it.

Perhaps I can put it in another way by saying that Cobb is a natural man. And he is a natural workman. I have no doubt that he thinks he is homely. On the contrary, he is handsome. Handsome does not express just how Cobb looks, but if it did express it, that is the way Cobb would look. That is to say, he is very satisfactory to look at. I don't know of any man that I would rather look at than Irvin Cobb, and I am not joking about this. He has all the human qualities. And when he talks I could listen to him all the time. I might want to stop for meals, but if I did, I should want him sitting next to me.

The conversations of so many men have been so overrated. All through literature you read about what wonderful talkers some men were. There was Swinburne; there was Macaulay; there was Tennyson; there was Oscar Wilde. I have always believed that these men were overrated. I read once of how Swinburne (I remember now, it was in a book called "The Education of Henry Adams") kept a whole company of people up until very late talking wonderful talk and reciting poetry. I don't believe it. He must have been a deadly bore. Indeed, Max Beerbohm indicates this. Few of us are honest when it comes to our literary opinions. The memory of some evening in which we drank too much hangs over us like a beautiful rainbow; stripped of its colors it is only Scotch and soda. When I say that I would rather listen to Cobb talk than to anybody else I know, I mean it in the right sense. Cobb is human. He is not thinking about himself except in the right way. He is sympathetic. He is broad-souled. His book "Speak-

ing of Operations" is funny because, in reality—although it may seem quite the opposite—it is impersonal. I remember when it first came out in the
Saturday Evening Post. A number of people spoke
to me about it. "Have you seen that thing of Irvin
Cobb's? It's immense." And so on. You see, they
were all taking it to themselves. They thought it had
happened to them. And that, I take it, is one of the
tests of real humor.

Another test of humor is its popularity. If a lot
of people read it, that shows that it has something to
it. I heard this story, which may or not be true, but
it is such a satisfactory story that I must tell it. It
is about Mr. Cobb and Mr. Lorimer, the editor of the
Saturday Evening Post. One day Mr. Lorimer went
out to a newsdealer nearby to see how his paper was
selling. And the newsdealer said:

"They ask me if there is anything in it by Cobb. If
there is, they buy it. If there isn't, they don't."

Thereupon Mr. Lorimer said, "I must cut out Cobb."

I don't believe this story. But it is a good one. That
is the main difficulty about the best stories. They are
probably not true.

I was highly amused one day to pick up a book by
Mr. H. L. Mencken, and read what he had to say
about Cobb. He didn't like him. He said so.
Mencken, so far as I have been able to discover in his
writings, doesn't like anybody. Maybe he is right.
Not to like anybody at all may be a creditable object for
any man's ambition. It is a large undertaking. I
have tried to dislike certain people at intervals, but in
most cases have had to give it up. After pursuing

the objects of my wrath persistently, I got tired out
and ended by liking them, finding them in the long
run much like myself. Even Mr. Mencken is under
this handicap. After several pages in which he explains
at some length why Cobb is not a humorist, or at least
not a good humorist—in which he refers to the Cobb
whisker motif, the Cobb wheeze, and the Cobb publisher, he winds up with:

Nevertheless, even so laboriously flabby a *farceur*
has his moments. I turn to Frank J. Wilstach's "Dictionary of Similes" and find this credited to him "No
more privacy than a goldfish." Here, at last, is something genuinely humorous. Here, moreover, is something apparently new.

To have Mr. Mencken admit that Cobb has been
guilty of something genuinely humorous and apparently new is certainly going some. But that shows
what can happen even to a man like Mencken if he
reads Irvin Cobb.

Cobb, in common with Abraham Lincoln, was born
in Kentucky (in 1876). This—I regret to say I remember it—was the year of the great Centennial. The
Centennial, as doubtless nobody but myself remembers,
took place chiefly in Philadelphia. Cobb little knew in
that year that he was destined in time to keep Philadelphia before the people by his later contributions in the
Saturday Evening Post.

There is, however, one stain on his career—a dark
spot that I hope he will have removed as soon as
possible. He has permitted the publishers of "Who's

Who in America" to state that he was a "staff humorist." We have all of us, at one time or another, been
staff humorists. If you are any sort of a man when
your first baby is born (and also subsequently), you
become a staff humorist to that child by imitating the
ribald antics of the common or garden horse. But to
have this put down in cold print is quite another thing.
That Cobb has permitted this to be done to him is
another evidence of his humility, of the impersonal
manner in which he regards himself. That man would
let anything be said about him. After being born, he
attended private schools, from which he recovered
sufficiently to get into Dartmouth College, which
honored him with a degree in 1918. Let me now, with
the permission of the polite publishers of "Who's
Who," quote from that indispensable household
adjunct:

Shorthand reporter, contbr. to comic weeklies, reporter on local paper up to 17; editor *Paducah Daily
News* at 19; staff corr. and writer "Sour Mash" column *Louisville* (Ky.) *Evening Post* 1898-1901 . . .
represented *Saturday Evening Post* as war corr. in
Europe; lectured throughout U. S. on "What I saw at
the Front." Apptd. col. on staff gov. of Ky. 1918;
Chevalier Legion of Honor (France) 1918.

As for Cobb's books, they are quite numerous, and
many of them highly amusing. Personally, if I may
be allowed, I like "The Escape of Mr. Trimm" best.
His story of "The Belled Buzzard" is a masterpiece.
There are highly distinguished critics in England who
think he is the best short-story writer in America. As

for his work as a humorist, he has written to me by request, as follows:

Almost as far back as I distinctly can remember I tried to write funny stuff. At the grammar school I wrote alleged verses to accompany the pictures I drew. At that time my main ambition was to be a caricaturist. I had a small gift that way. My mother says I tried to draw pictures before I could walk, and, among her possessions, she treasures some drawings in color, terribly crude things, that I did before I was four years old.

The first three things of mine that were ever published in a magazine were alleged comics—pen-and-ink drawings—which I sent to *Texas Siftings* when I was about fourteen years old. *Texas Siftings* printed them but forgot to pay me for them. However, I didn't crave any pay. Merely to see them printed was reward enough for me. In a scrap-book which I compiled when I was about fifteen—the only scrap-book, by the way, I ever made, and which I still have—two of the pictures from *Texas Siftings* are pasted. The third clipping got lost and I have forgotten its subject.

I suppose, except for a bad turn in the family fortunes, I should to-day be a cartoonist, or a caricaturist, or an illustrator—probably a very bad one. I had grown through boyhood with the expectation of studying art and afterward taking it up as a profession. But, when I was sixteen years old, my father's very modest source of obtaining a livelihood failed him and it became necessary for me, a few months later, to leave school—which was no grief to me—and to go to work in order to help out with my earnings the family exchequer. I had grown up with the smell of printer's ink in my snoot. My favorite uncle, for whom I was named, was a country editor and one of the best paragraphers, I think, of the old school of Southern paragraphers founded by George D. Prentiss. My favorite play-place had been the cluttered editorial room of a little daily where this uncle of mine encouraged me to draw and try to write. A little further along I had carried papers over a route and on Saturdays I would hang about the newspaper shop and get pleasure out of the pretense that I was actually helping to get out the paper.

So it was natural, I suppose, when it became incumbent upon me to get a job, that I should seek one in a newspaper office. I became a "prentice reporter," so-called, at a salary of $1.75 a week. I expect I was about the rawest cub that ever lived, but I had my share of energy if I had no other equipment. When I wasn't hustling after local items I was working over an old-fashioned chalk-plate trying to draw illustrations for news stories, and cartoons on local topics. Presently, though, my reportorial duties so broadened that I no longer found time for the picture-making end of the game, and with a few inconspicuous exceptions I have never tried to draw for publication since. Long ago I ceased to draw for my own amusement, and, with disuse, I have almost altogether lost the knack of it and the inclination for it.

The editor of the paper on which I worked flattered my vanity and stirred my ambitions in a new direction by telling me he thought I had a turn for writing "funny stuff." Encouraged by him, I turned out bales of bum jingles and supposedly humorous comment on local subjects. And he was good enough to print the stuff; and a few subscribers were good enough to compliment it. I date the beginning of my downward career from that time.

When I was nineteen a change in ownership of the paper threw him out of a job, and for a short while I filled his place with the title of "managing editor." I had the double distinction of being the youngest managing editor of a daily paper in the United States— and the worst one. When, a few months later, the publishers of the paper found out what ailed the paper they induced the editor to come back again to his former berth and I lost my peacock feathers and became once more a plain reporter. A photograph taken of me about this time proves what a plain reporter I was.

However, I was not sorry, really, at being reduced to the ranks, because once again I had time and opportunity to write alleged funny stuff. A few of the state papers began copying my junk, and I derived considerable satisfaction thereby but no added glory, to speak of, since my copy was not signed. The paper got the credit instead.

Two or three years later I moved to Louisville and became a political reporter on the *Evening Post*. On this paper I wrote an occasional column under the title "Kentucky Sour Mash." The column was made up of paragraphs, short articles mainly containing supposedly whimsical digs at politicians and public characters, and verses. My poetry was so wooden that it fairly creaked at the joints, but I could turn it out by the yard. Here's a curious thing: For twenty years now I have done no versifying, and I find it almost impossible to frame lines that will scan and rhyme, whereas this used to be the easiest thing I did. My wits have rusted here just as my hand has lost the trick of making pictures.

From the time I was twenty-five until I was twenty-nine, past, I wrote scarcely a line that was designed to be humorous. During that time I was the managing editor, back in Paducah, of the same paper, the *News*, upon which I had made my start; only now it was the *News-Democrat,* with linotype machines and a brief telegraph service. I worked day and night on routine editorial duties, with no opportunity for the lighter side of journalistic writing. Here, for the first time in my life, I discovered I had things called nerves.

I threw up my job, sent my wife and my year-old baby down to Georgia to stay for a while as non-paying guests at my father-in-law's house, and, with a hundred dollars of borrowed money in my pocket, landed in New York in the middle of the hottest summer of the Christian Era. I spent three weeks trying unsuccessfully to get a job—any kind of a job. When my money was almost gone I had an idea; born of desperation I suppose it was. I wrote out a form letter full of josh, telling how good I was and explaining that New York journalism needed me to make it brighter and better. I sent a copy of this letter to every managing editor in town. This, I suppose, might be called my first attempt at being humorous for a metropolitan audience. Inside of two days I had replies from six managing editors, including Arthur Brisbane, either offering me work right away or promising me the first available opening on their staffs. I went to work for the *Evening Sun.* At the outset I did reportorial work. In a few months I was writing a good half of the *Evening Sun's* Saturday back page of humor and, in addition, editing the page. Howsomever, what got me a job, at better pay on the *Evening World,* was not my humorous stuff but some straight news stories which I wrote for the *Sun.*

I stayed with the *Evening World* six years. I was a reasonably busy person. I was a reporter, a rewrite man, and at intervals a staff-correspondent on out-of-town assignments. I covered the two Thaw trials and probably a dozen other big criminal cases. Between times I wrote an average of three satirical or supposedly humorous signed articles a week for the magazine page of the *Evening World* and contributed special articles to the *Sunday World*. During the last four years of the six I spent under the *World* dome I wrote a page of humor under the titles: "The Hotel Clerk Says" and "Live Talks With Dead Ones" for the magazine section of the Sunday edition. In four years and twelve weeks I did not, on a single Sunday, miss filling my page. These articles were syndicated over the country, but I then regarded my humorous work, as I still do to a greater or less extent, as a sort of side-line, for my energies were largely devoted to handling news stories, and I did the lighter stuff at odd intervals between murders and fires. There used to be a saying in the *Evening World* shop that when, in a lull in city work, I sat down at my typewriter and stuck a clean sheet of paper into the machine and looked as though I were going to burst into tears, it was a sign that I was preparing to try to write something funny. I may add that, in this regard, I have not greatly changed. I still regard humorous writing as about the most serious work a writing-man can do. I've never yet got a laugh out of anything I wrote in the line of humor. I trust that others have, occasionally, but I haven't.

My first attempt at out-and-out fiction-writing was made nine years ago at the end of a two weeks' vacation, when I was still on the *World*. It was a sort of horror story without a line in it that could be called humorous. I wrote it on a bet with my ally that I could write a straight serious fiction story and sell it to a reputable magazine. I won the bet. The *Saturday Evening Post* bought it and printed it. It was called "The Escape of Mr. Trimm." When my contract with the *World* expired I was emboldened to try magazine-writing for a means of livelihood, and I have been at it ever since. Perhaps a third of my output is what my friends are kind enough to call humor; the other two-thirds is made up of serious stuff—character yarns and descriptive articles, as when I went twice to the war for the *Post,* and straight fiction. I find that when I have written something of the humorous order it gives me an appetite, so to speak, to turn out a nice, gruesome, gory, Edgar-Allan-Poeish kind of tale, and vice versa. Personally, I would rather do the straight fiction; at the same time, I must confess that from the standpoint of popularity and financial returns in the form of book royalties, my most successful single piece of work is "Speaking of Operations," which in book form has sold upwards of 300,000 copies in five years, which still is selling at the rate of 25,000 copies a year, and which by a majority of those who read it is regarded as being humorous, although my friend Mr. H. L. Mencken does not agree with them. He thinks it's sad, not to say dreary, and perhaps he is right.

One curious thing I have discovered: A man may write serious fiction for ten years or do straight reportorial work for ten years, but let him turn out one piece of foolery that tickles the public in its short-ribs and, from that hour, he is branded as a humorist.

I have no set rule or pet formulas for writing humor. First, I get an idea. I let it churn up and down a while inside my head until the butter-fats begin to form; then I sit down and write it. Usually, but not always, I rewrite it once, touching it up and smoothing off the corners, and then I let it go. I have found that about fifty per cent, roughly, of my lines and points come to me in conversation with persons congenially inclined. The other fifty per cent, about, hop on the paper during the throes of childbirth, when I am making the first draft of the copy. I have also found out that I am decidedly a poor judge of the humor-values of my own writings. What I think is going to be funny when I set it down frequently falls flat. What I do not regard as especially funny more often goes over well with the reader.

I said just now that I had no rules in writing humor. I take that back. I have two rules which I endeavor to follow as closely as may be. In what I write with intent to be humorous I try to avoid giving offense to any individual. To my way of thinking, a joke that hurts the feelings of some one, or that leaves a sore spot on another's pelt, or that deals with the physical infirmities of men and women, is not such a very good joke after all. My other rule is this: When I write humor I seek, between the lines, to say to the reader: "Listen, old man, I'm about to poke fun at some of the foolish things you have done and said, but understand, please, that no matter how foolish you may have been in your time I'm a bigger ass than you ever can hope to be. We're both in the same boat, so bear with me while I make confession for the two of us." I am sure that if a humorous writer assumes this attitude and adheres to it the reader subconsciously falls into a state of mental sympathy with him and is more apt to like what is written.

If I may be permitted to lecture a few of my fellow-laborers, I would like to say that, in my opinion, the mistake some really humorous writers make is in assuming, wittingly or unwittingly, an air of superiority —in other words, it is as though they sat on a high pinnacle in a rarefied atmosphere of aloofness, looking down pityingly from that great height upon the foolish, futile, scrambling little human ants far beneath them, and stirring up those ants with barbed satire and clever ridicule. I am sure the reader resents this, even though he may not exactly know what it is that irritates him, and I am sure also another result is that these writers, real humorists though they may be, rarely are publicly recognized and acknowledged as humorists. The man who aspires to be known as a humorist must constantly be saying, not, "What fools *those* mortals be," but "What fools *all* mortals be—myself prominently included." To cite a few conspicuous and justly popular examples, Mark Twain and Bill Nye had this gift, and, among the living, George Ade and Don Marquis and Ring Lardner and Ellis Parker Butler and Ed Howe and Walt Mason—may their tribe increase—likewise have it.

CHAPTER VIII

HOMER CROY

I HAVE known Homer Croy intimately during the past twenty years, having seen him twice during that stretch. That is why I can write about him authoritatively. I have his secret. I got it the first time I met him; I confirmed it the second time. The reason he doesn't know his own secret is because (as you will see) he was born in Missouri. Folks born in Missouri never realize the truth about themselves. They are all people that are pursuing other occupations than those that God intended them to pursue.

The trouble with Homer Croy is that he is a humorist and not a novelist. He thinks he is a novelist first and a humorist second. He has written some very funny things, but their publication, for some reason (because he was born in Missouri), has had the opposite effect from what God intended. Just as soon as he wrote a really good piece of humor, he immediately thought he could write a novel. He is now writing novels instead of humor. Having said this much about him, I shall leave him to explain himself— which of course he doesn't:

I am glad I have so lived that I can tell people about it.

I was born in Missouri, just south of the water tank, of that popular brand of parents—poor but honest. It was early seen that I looked like my father, but the tendency to be poor I inherited from both sides of the house.

My first job was on the local paper, the *Maryville Tribune,* for which I received three dollars a week— every week, rain or shine. I was the best leg reporter the paper ever had. I could walk farther and ask more questions getting a two-line item than any other person ever employed on the paper.

The first two weeks I was on the paper about the only stories I turned in were happenings in our immediate family. One day the editor called me in and said, "I'm afraid I'll have to dispense with your services. There aren't enough Croys taking the paper to make retaining you profitable."

Taking the hint I resigned.

Some way or other I graduated from college and started out to conquer the world. I often think of this as I look at my mortgage.

Then I got a job on the *St. Louis Post Dispatch* and stayed with it as long as my friend was managing editor. Then I told the publishers they would have to shift for themselves, and I came East.

I had never had the slightest interest in baseball and had never attended a big league game, but by a twist of circumstance I became editor of the *Baseball Magazine.* A few weeks after I had been made editor I went to a game and found it much as I had expected.

Becoming interested in motion pictures, I talked one of the film companies into sending me around the world. I had a good time, but the company since has never asked me to make another trip for it. Ever since, I have been more or less interested in motion pictures and wrote some books on the subject. As far as the reviews went, they were a huge success, but as far as the royalties go, the secret is locked in the breast of myself and the publisher.

My chief interest is in novels of realism and humor, located in the Middle West. Of these I have written two or three.

I live in Forest Hills Gardens, Long Island. Just ask anybody where and they will tell you—the little house with the big mortgage.

In order, however, to make sure that nobody will think that Homer Croy is not a humorist, the following sketch, written by him, alone and unaided, is appended herewith:

Bathing in a Borrowed Suit

The desire to be seen on the beach in a borrowed bathing suit is not so strong in me as it once was. An acquaintance, under the guise of friendship, lured me out to his beach one day, saying that he had full rights to the most popular ocean in the world. I had heard his ocean spoken highly of, and I accepted.

Unfortunately I forgot to take my bathing suit, but he said that that was nothing—that he had one that would fit me as the paper on the wall. As I recall it those were his exact words.

At last he found it in the basement, where it seems that the mice, to get the salt, had helped themselves rather liberally to its none too strong fabric. From the holes in the suit it was easy to see that the party had been a merry one and had not broken up till a late hour.

The suit had never been planned for a person of my general architecture. Roughly speaking, I am fashioned along the lines of the Woolworth Building, with a slight balcony effect about the thirty-third floor. The suit had been intended for a smallish person given to bathing principally by himself. It was, in its present state, mostly a collection of holes rather insecurely held together with yarn. The waist would have been tight on a doll, while the trunks looked like a pair of pulse-warmers.

I tried to find a place to get into the suit, but it stuck together like a wet paper bag. At last I got part way in only to find that my arms were sticking through where a couple of mice had polished off a meal.

Finally I felt that I had the suit on and looked in the mirror. I drew back in startled surprise. There were two foreign marks on my body. One I recognized after a moment as being where my collar button had rubbed, but the other was larger. It was a dark splotch as if I had run into the bureau. But, on looking more closely, I saw that it was the bathing suit.

Even under the most favorable circumstances, when attired in a bathing suit, I don't live long in the memory of strangers. Rarely ever is my photograph taken by a shore photographer and put up in his exhibition case, and practically never does a cluster of people gather around me, talking excitedly with bursts of involuntary applause.

My friends were waiting on the lawn for me to join them. Taking a firm grip on my courage I walked out into the yard. The ladies were gayly chatting and smiling until they saw me, when suddenly they closed the conversation and turned to gaze far out over the blue horizon to a dim, distant sail.

The ocean looked only a couple of blocks away, but we seemed to walk miles. I was the cynosure of all eyes. I had never been a cynosure before, and in fact didn't know that I had any talent in that line, but now, as a cynosure, I was a great success. When some rude boys came up and began to make personal remarks in the tone that such remarks are usually made in, I abandoned the rest of the party and hurried for the water. I plunged in, but I plunged too hard. My suit had got past the plunging stage. When I came up there was little on me besides the sea foam and a spirit of jollity. The latter was feigned.

Something told me to keep to the deep. My friends called me and insisted that I come ashore to play in the sand with them, but I answered that I loved the ocean too well and wanted its sheltering arms around me. I had to have something around me.

I must get back to the house and into my clothes. I worked down the beach until I was out of sight, and made a break for the solace of the basement from whence the suit had come. Many people were out walking but I did not join any of them, and as they stared at me, I began to walk faster and faster. Soon I was running. A large dog that I had never seen before rushed at me. I turned around and gave him one lowering look, but he evidently did not catch it, for he came straight on. I looked around for a rock to use for something that I had in mind, but somebody had removed all the desirable ones. So I turned my back to the ill-bred creature and started on. However, this did not cut him the way I had hoped. Instead, he came on with renewed interest. I did not want him to follow me, but this seemed to be his intention, although he had received no encouragement on my part. I sped up and tried to lose him, but my efforts were fruitless, and to make it more unpleasant he kept up a loud, discordant barking which jarred on my sensitive ear.

I gained the yard and plunged against the door of the house, but some thoughtful person had closed it. I ran around to the rear, but the person had done his work well. So I ran back with some vague hope that the door would be open, although I knew quite well it wouldn't be. My surmises were right. Back the dog and I ran together, while curious passers-by began to stare. I soon found myself almost out of breath, but the dog seemed to be quite fresh. However, I ran back again. At last I came upon a basement door that was open, dived in and shut the door after me. I took particular pains to do that.

I continued to remain in the basement. Although the time hung heavily on my hands I did not stroll out to chat with the townspeople. In the course of time my friend returned and looked at me strangely.

"Aren't you feeling well?" he asked pityingly.

"No," I answered sadly. "I feel kind of run down."

"But why did you get in this basement?" he asked. "It belongs to the man next door."

Of late I get all the bathing I want with a sponge behind closed doors. I would rather have a sponge that has been in the family a long time at my back, than a strange dog similarly located, with whose habits I am not familiar.

CHAPTER IX

FINLEY PETER DUNNE was born in Chicago (in 1867), thus bearing out the contention of Mr. H. L. Mencken, that Chicago is the real literary center of the United States. Eugene Field was also evolved in Chicago, as well as George Ade, so it seems conclusively proved that as a Port of Humorists, there is none to dispute Chicago's supremacy.

Boston has produced Oliver Wendell Holmes, Samuel McChord Crothers, and latterly, Vice President Coolidge, all of whom are humorists more or less. Philadelphia has produced, or at least fostered, Benjamin Franklin and George Horace Lorimer. Other cities have produced other humorists, but Chicago appears to be the right atmosphere for a humorist to grow up in. After he has grown up, has suffered enough from his environment, so to speak, he may go elsewhere with personal safety, but it is doubtful if he will ever do anything better than what Chicago has given him to do.

Mr. Dunne began in Chicago. "Mr. Dooley," we believe, was born in Chicago. ·When Mr. Dunne brought him to New York he lasted a long time. "Mr. Dooley" is an immortal, but his voice of late has lapsed into such silence as to be a cause of lament.

There has been none quite like Mr. Dunne's "Mr. Dooley." There has been coarser and more turbulent wit. There has been more delicate literary fooling. But "Mr. Dooley," in his observations, was so unerring, so philosophical, so true, and so witty, that we seem to miss him more than ever. To have created a character like that, and to let a war go by without having the privilege of listening to him, is a crime against civilization. But so it has been. Peter Dunne, being a genius, and "Mr. Dooley," being born of Peter Dunne, there is nothing else for us to do but resign ourselves to such substitutes as we have had. Some of them have been good, but not like "Mr. Dooley."

The fact is that, before the war, "Mr. Dooley," in his friendly manner, said all there was to be said: that is, he anticipated so much that to read him over again is much like reading Aristophanes over again: we see at once that he is a genuine modern. Here is an extract from his "War Expert" which was published in 1902:

Mr. Dooley was reading the war news,—not our war news but the war news we are interested in—when Mr. Hennessy interrupted him to ask "What's a war expert?"

"A war expert," said Mr. Dooley, "is a man ye niver heerd iv befure. If ye think iv annywan whose face is onfamilyar to ye an' ye don't raymimber his name, an' he's got a job on a pa-per ye didn't know was published, he's a war expert. 'Tis a har-rd office to fill. Whin a war begins th' timptation is strong f'r ivry man to grab hold iv a gun an' go to th' fr-ront. But th' war expert has to subjoo his cravin' f'r blood. He says to himsilf, 'Lave others seek th' luxuries iv life in camp,' he says. 'F'r thim th' boat races acrost th' Tugela, th' romp over the kopje, an' th' game iv laager, laager, who's got th' laager?' He says. 'I will stand be me counthry,' he says, 'close,' he says. 'If it fails,' he says, 'it will fall on me,' he says. An' he buys himsilf a map made be a fortune teller in a dhream, a box iv pencils an' a field glass, an' goes an' looks f'r a job as a war expert. Says the editor iv th' paaper : 'I don't know ye. Ye must be a war expert,' he says. 'I am,' says th' la-ad. 'Was ye iver in a war?' says th' editor. 'I've been in nawthin' else,' says th' la-ad. 'During the Spanish-American war, I held a job as a dhramatic critic in Dedham Matsachoosets,' he says. 'Whin th' bullets flew thickest in th' Soodan I was spoortin' editor iv th' *Christyan Advocate,*' he says. 'I passed through th' Franco-Prooshan war an' held me place, an' whin th' Turks an' Rooshans was at each other's throats, I used to lay out th' campaign iviry day on a checker board,' he says. 'War,' he says, 'has no terrors f'r me,' he says. 'Ye're th' man f'r th' money,' says th' editor. An' he gets th' job.

"Thin th' war breaks out in earnest. No matther how many is kilt, annything that happens befure th' war expert gets to wurruk is on'y what we might call a prelimin'ry skirmish. He sets down an' bites th' end iv his pencil an' looks acrost th' sthreet an' watches a man paintin' a sign. Whin th' man gets through he goes to th' window an' waits to see whether th' polisman that wint into th' saloon is afther a dhrink or sarvin' a warrant. If he comes r-right out it's a warrant, thin he sets back in a chair an' figures out that th' pitchers on th' wall paaper ar-re all alike ivery third row. Whin his mind is thruly tuned up be these in-

thricate problems, he dashes to his desk an' writes what
you an' I read th' next day in th' papers."

The fact is that between 1898 and 1910 "Mr.
Dooley" anticipated about everything that was going
to happen to us.   There is scarcely a character in
American life that he did not portray.   Two thousand
years from now it would only be necessary to read
what "Mr. Dooley" has to say, in order to learn what
Americans are today.   The nearest approach to his
books in their reaction upon his age and generation I
find in the "Characters of Theophrastus," from which
(translated by Charles E. Bennett and William A.
Hammond of Cornell and published by Longman's)
I shall venture to quote.   In order to show, over a
lapse of centuries, how two satirists wrote of their
people.   Theophrastus dates from the fourth century
before Christ.

The types described by Theophrastus [writes the
introducer] are types of such intrinsic qualities, and
his pictures of ancient vices and weaknesses show men
much as we see them now.   They are not merely types
of professions or callings.   Apart from slight varia-
tions of local coloring and institutions, the descriptions
of the old Greek philosopher might apply almost as well
to the present inhabitants of London or Boston as to
the Athenians of 300 B.C.   Theophrastus, on the death
of Aristotle (322 B.C.), succeeded to the presidency of
the Lyceum, over which he continued to preside for
thirty-five years. . . . Diogenes Laertius reports that
two thousand students thronged to him. . . . He died
in 287 B.C. in the eighty-fifth year of his age. . . .
Theophrastus was one of the greatest polygraphs in

antiquity.   Two hundred and twenty-seven works are attributed to him. . . . As a local and popular force he surpassed Aristotle. . . . His estimate of oral converse at table is recorded in a rather brusque and un-Athenian remark said to have been made by him to a silent neighbor at dinner: "Sir, if you are an ignorant man, your conduct shows wisdom; but if you are a wise man, you act like a fool."

Which is not wholly unlike a remark made by Peter Dunne to the present writer.   The occasion was a dinner given to a common friend at the University Club in New York.   The present writer, upon being called upon, rose to speak, when Mr. Dunne, sitting next to him, whispered in a very loud voice:

"Sit down, Tom; you can't talk."

I have been at some pains to give this slight account of Theophrastus, because I propose to quote what he says about an avaricious man, and then to quote "Mr. Dooley" on the same.

This is Theophrastus:

The Avaricious Man

By Theophrastus, 300 B.C.

Avarice is greedy love of gain.   When the avaricious man gives a dinner, he puts scant allowances of bread on the table.   He borrows money of a stranger who is lodging with him.   When he distributes the portions at table, he says it is fair for the laborer to receive double and straightway loads his own plate.   He engages in wine traffic, and sells adulterated liquors even to his friend.   He goes to the show and takes his children with him, on the days when the spectators are admitted to the galleries free. When he is the people's delegate, he leaves at home the money provided by the city, and borrows from his fellow commissioners.

He loads more luggage on his porter than the man can carry, and provides him with the smallest rations of any man in the party. When presents are given the delegates by foreign courts, he demands his share at once, and sells it. At the bath he says the oil brought him is bad, and shouts: "Boy, the oil is rancid;" and, in its stead, takes what belongs to another. If his servants find money on the highway, he demands a share of it, saying: "Luck's gifts are common property." When he sends his cloak to be cleaned, he borrows another from an acquaintance and keeps it until it is asked for. He also does this sort of thing: he uses King Frugal's measure, with the bottom dented in, for doling out supplies to his household, and then secretly brushes off the top. He sells underweight even to his friend, who thinks he is buying according to the market standard.

When he pays a debt of thirty pounds, he does so with a discount of four shillings. When, owing to sickness, his children are not at school the entire month, he deducts a proportionate amount from the children's pay; and during the month of Anthesterion he does not send them to their studies at all, on account of their frequent shows, and so he avoids tuition fees. If he receives coppers from a slave who has been serving out, he demands in addition the exchange value of silver. When he gets a statement from the Deme's [1] administrator, he demands provision for his slaves at public cost.

He makes note of the half radishes left on the table,

[1] A county or local division.

to keep the servants from taking them. If he goes abroad with friends, he uses their servants and hires his own out; yet he does not contribute to the common fund the money thus received. When others combine with him to give a banquet at his house, he secretly includes in his account the wood, figs, vinegar, salt and lamp-oil—trifles furnished from his supplies. If a marriage is announced in a friend's family he goes away a little beforehand, to avoid sending a wedding present. He borrows of friends such articles as they would not ask to have returned, or such as, if returned, they would not readily accept.

And this from Finley Peter Dunne.

Avarice and Generosity

As reported by Mr. Dooley

I never blame a man f'r bein' avaricyous in his ol' age. Whin a fellow gits so he has nawthin else to injye, whin ivrybody calls him "sir" or "mister," an' young people dodge him an' he sleeps afther dinner, an' folks say he is an ol' fool if he wears a buttonhole bokay, an' his teeth is only tinants at will and not permanent fixtures, tis no more than nach'ral that he shud begin to look around him f'r a way iv keepin' a grip on human s'ciety. It don't take him long to see that th' on'y thing that's vin'rable in age is money, an' he pro'ceeds to acquire anything that happens to be in sight, takin' it where he can find it, not where he wants it, which is the way to accumylate a fortune. Money wont prolong life, but a few millyuns judicyously placed in good banks an' occas'nally worn on the person will rayjooce age. Poor ol' men are always older thin

poor rich men. In th' almshouse a man is decrepit an'
mournful-lookin' at sixty, but a millyonaire at sixty is
jus' in th' prime iv life to a friendly eye, an' there are
no others.

It's aisier to th' ol' to grow rich thin it is to th'
young. At makin' money a man iv sixty is miles ahead
iv a la-ad iv twinty-five. Pollytics an' bankin' is th'
on'y two games where age has th' best iv it. Youth has
betther things to attind to, an' more iv them. I dont
blame a man f'r bein' stingy anny more thin I blame
him f'r havin' a bad leg. Ye know th' doctors say
that if ye dont use wan iv ye'er limbs f'r a year or so
ye can niver use it again. So it is with gin'rosity. A
man starts arly in life not bein' gen-rous. He says to
himself "I wurruked f'r this thing an' if I give it away
I lose it." He ties up his gen'rosity in bandages so that
th' blood cant circlyate in it. It gets to be a super-
stition with him that he'll have bad luck if he iver does
annything f'r annybody. An' so he rakes in an' puts
his private mark with his teeth on all the moveable
money in th' worruld. But th' day comes whin he sees
people around him gettin' a good dale iv injyement out
iv gen'rosity, an' somewan says "Why dont ye, too be
gin'rous? Come, old green goods, unbolt, loosen up,
be gin'rous." "Gin'rous?" says he, "What's that?"
"It's the best spoort in the wurruld. Its givin' things
to people." "But I cant," he says, "I haven't annything to do it with," he says. "I dont know th' game.
I haven't anny gin'rosity," he says. "But ye have,"
says they. "Ye have as much gen'rosity as anny wan if
ye'll only use it," says they. "Take it out iv th' plasther
cast ye put it in an' 'twill look as good as new," says
they. An' he does it. He thries to use his gin'rosity,
but all th' life is out iv it. It gives way undher him
an' he falls down. He can't raise it fr'm th' groun',

It's ossyfied an' useless. I've seen manny a fellow that suffered fr'm ossyfied gen'rosity.

Whin a man begins makin' money in his youth at annything but games iv chance he niver can become gin'rous late in life. He makes a bluff at it. Some men are gin'rous with a crutch. Some men get the use iv their gen'rosity back suddenly whin they ar-re in danger. Whin Clancy the miser was caught in a fire in th' Halsted Sthreet Palace Hotel he howled fr'm a window: "I'll give twinty dollars to anny wan that'll take me down." Cap'n Minehan put up a laddher an' climbed to him an' carrid him to the sthreet. Half-way down th' laddher th' brave rayscooer was seen to be chokin' his helpless burdhen. We discovered aftherward that Clancy had thried to begin negotyations to rayjooce th' reward to five dollars. His gin'rosity had become suddenly par'lyzed again.

So if ye'd stay gin'rous to th' end, niver lave ye'er gen'rosity idle too long. Don't run it ivry hour at th' top iv it's speed, but fr'm day to day give it a little gintle exercise to keep it supple an' hearty an' in due time ye may injye it.

It is unnecessary for me to enlarge upon the delightful differences, as well as the underlying similarity of these two masterpieces of character taken from periods so wide apart in literary history.

It is given to but few men to depict the characters of their own age in such manner that for future generations they will stand out as miniature portraits. When one looks back upon the work that Peter Dunne has given us, it is so astonishing in its simplicity and accuracy, that one cannot help but wonder at the American public that permits it to be buried under so much rubbish. But then, the public that eagerly snaps at genius generally forgets it. If all the newspaper files and histories were destroyed between the years 1898 and 1910 and nothing remained but Mr. Dooley's observations, it would be enough.

I recall quite vividly when they first attracted wide attention, and how eagerly they were read every week from the Atlantic to the Pacific. I was on a westbound train one Sunday—it must have been nearly or just beyond the close of the century—and of hearing a group of men reading aloud to one another the weekly Dooley letter and chortling with glee. And I think the first Dooley book in a few months sold well over a 100,000 copies.

It may be put down as a solemn truth that any book widely read has something to it. The public indeed are not such fools as they sometimes are made to appear. There are any number of books that have sold as well if not better, than the first "Mr. Dooley," and have thereafter lapsed into obscurity.

The humor of a particular generation also has its own flavor. But allowing for all this, it does seem to me as if "Mr. Dooley" must live.

I don't think that Peter Dunne has ever appreciated how good it is. He has referred to it slightingly more than once. Dear me, how little some of us know about our own merits!

CHAPTER X

(WHAT A MODEL BIOGRAPHY THIS IS!—T. L. M.

ARTHUR FOLWELL

NOT much to tell, just one year after another of earning a living. However, since you pester me. . . .

Born in Brooklyn in 1877—if you insist—near a Long Island Railroad crossing. First defined ambition: to be a crossing gateman. Parents encouraged ambition because gateman at nearest crossing told me I must "eat all my crusts" in order to get strong. Idea of writing—except in Spencerian copy-books—first dawned when in grammar school. Started a monthly paper that lasted five years; still regard it, in all probability, as my best constructive achievement. First contribution offered: a parody on "The Charge of the Light Brigade." Offered it to *Puck*, which returned it. First job: an office boy with the Thomas Cook Tourist Agency; held job three weeks, mailing in that time at least a million letters. Next job: glorified office boy with the Pitts Agricultural Works on Park Place, near Greenwich Street, in a back-room immediately adjoining the roof of a rubber factory; rubber factory exhaust pipe the inspiration for many maiden efforts. From here, made first sale; a long bit of verse which I sent to *Collier's Weekly*. The editor, then Mr. Thomas

B. Connery, wrote: "The reader recommends the acceptance of your verses, 'The Country of Once on a Time,' for $5." That, as I now figure it, was about 5 cents a line. It looked like a mint to me. Wrote instantly of my glad acceptance, but never got any money. Finally wrote again, and then got my MSS. back with a note saying: "You have delayed so long answering our letter, we are compelled to return your poem." Not even that discouraged me, although I hated to lose all that money. After much endeavoring, got a job at nothing a week with the *Brooklyn Eagle,* and resigned my office-boy place in the road-roller business, or perhaps I should say, road-roller game. My salary office-boying road-rollers was $4 a week; figured I could make that much with the *Eagle,* writing school news for the Sunday edition, on space. Pomeroy Burton, now a very, very great man in the employ of Lord Northcliffe, permitted me to feel that I was "on the *Eagle.*" He was then city editor there, but it was Arthur M. Howe, now editor-in-chief of the *Eagle* and then (in 1895) a copy reader, who first read my stuff and had it in his power to make or break me. He let me live. Worked on the *Eagle* six years, first as a sports, then as a general work reporter. The city editor—various—let me do "the funny stories." And in my spare time, I was permitted to write verse and humorous specials for the Sunday paper without extra pay, or mention of it. The business manager, Mr. Herbert F. Gunnison, once said to me feelingly, "Folwell, you are very lucky for so young a man. See the large black type we let you sign your name in." From the *Eagle* office sent my first (accepted) contribution to a periodical; it was a burlesque bunch of country news items (old stuff now, and I guess it was then) called "This Week's Brooklyn Budget." Sent it to *Puck*. Sent everything I wrote to *Puck*. If they turned it down, threw it away or gave it to the *Eagle*. Finally, in 1902, got a letter from Harry Leon Wilson, then literary editor of *Puck*, offering me a job if I could make good. Wilson had just completed his first novel "The Spenders," and wished to quit reading jokes, writing what were undoubtedly the best editorials *Puck* ever printed, and thinking up cartoon ideas for artists. When I became house-broken, Wilson gave me the desk key—it had been Bunner's, too—and left; have seen him twice since. Subsequent history: fired by John Kendrick Bangs in 1904; rehired at less money next day; succeeded Bangs as editor of *Puck*, Bangs having offered to "come down three days a week at $5000 a year." Wrote, around this time, one-third of a book, the other fractions being done by Bangs and Bert Leston Taylor respectively. Title: "Monsieur d'en Brochette," a burlesque historical novel. Royalties, none. On *Puck* until April, 1916; left during the reign of Nathan Straus, Jr., to go to the *New York Tribune* in its Sunday department. Fired, in company with Mr. Robert C. Benchley, when the war made our frivolous viewpoints improper. Wrote a column, daily, for the *Brooklyn Times;* conducted "Film Fun" for the Leslie-Judge Company. Wrote for this, that and the other thing, from *Smart Set* to *St. Nicholas* as a free lance. On staff of Leslie publications when asked in 1921 to return to the *Tribune* as editor of Sunday magazine section. At this writing, still here. Using *Tribune* paper and typewriter to write this.

Most extraordinary experience: the fact that I could never sell *Life* anything after July, 1904, until the autumn of 1921. Sent Mr. Masson little piece in July, 1904, and received letter saying, "More; this is just the sort of thing *Life* wants." Never could sell him anything after that for seventeen years.

Subject of sketch doesn't regard himself as much of a humorist, but has had twenty years' experience watching others.

CHAPTER XI

SIMEON FORD, just because he has been for long the successful proprietor of a New York hotel, undoubtedly considers that he is immune to any highly immoral influence like mine. And so, when I wrote him, just as one Tom Sawyer to another, to write out the history of his life as a humorist, he replied as follows:

DEAR MR. MASSON:
I don't take myself seriously eno' even to think of complying with your flattering request.
Oblivious for yours sincerely,
SIMEON FORD.

I am therefore under the stern necessity of writing about him myself, digging up such information as I find available. Mr. Ford did better for "Who's Who" than he did for me. Here is what that admirable publication says about him, the proofs of which he corrected himself (for that's what they make you do):

Ford, Simeon, hotel propr.: born at Lafayette, Ind., Aug. 31, 1855. Ed. pub. schools, Propr. Grand Union Hotel. Mem. firm Ford X Shaw, Pres. Official Hotel Red Book & Directory Co. (here follows a list of the enterprises which Mr. Ford is interested in and winds up with "Well known as after-dinner speaker").

It was in 1904 that Mr. Ford published a book entitled "A Few Remarks." I happen to have the fourth edition of that book. I don't know how many editions were sold after I bought mine. I do know that nothing could induce me to part with mine. Whenever I feel particularly depressed, I get down Mr. Ford's book and read something like this:

I read that a man has just got $1,000,000 for a patent bottle which cannot be refilled and used a second time. We must get hold of that man and offer him his own price to invent a book which cannot be read by more than one person. I think my book will pretty nearly fill the bill.

He then leaves his book and goes on to the subject of travel, and particularly about sleeping cars.

I feel at liberty [he says] to make a few remarks on that branch of the railroad service, not in a carping spirit but more in sorrow than in anger. It is frequently remarked (especially in advertisements) that travel in our palace cars is the acme of comfort and luxury, and I guess they are about as perfect as they can be made and still pay dividends on diluted stock; and yet, after a night in one, I always feel as if I had been through an attack of cholera infantum. In winter, especially, the question of temperature is trying. The mercury, soon after you start, bounds up to 110° in the shade. You endure this until you melt off several pounds of hard-earned flesh and then you muster up courage and press the button.

The Ethiopian "reluctantly emerges." He is told what to do. Whereupon he "removes the roof, sides and bottom of the car and the mercury falls to three below zero, while you sit there and freeze to death, not daring to again disturb him lest you sink still further in his estimation."

Mr. Ford has a lot more to say, particularly about his experience in a Turkish bath, where the comb was chained to the wall but the brush was allowed to roam at will. He tells what the attendant did to him, he talks about patriotism and George Washington and automobiles, and no matter what he says he is very funny. And the funny part of all this is that it is just as funny when you read it as it is when he says it. The man has ideas. He is nobody's fool. He is a shrewd American citizen. He talks about clams and you laugh. He explains what, as a hotel proprietor, he is up against, and you almost believe him. You might believe him still more if you hadn't lived in New York yourself.

Mr. Ford began his career as one of the best of our American humorists (although he would disclaim this) as an after-dinner speaker. I am told that he learned all of his speeches by heart beforehand. That was what Mark Twain did in many cases. I have often thought what a pity it was that Mr. Ford should have been a hotel proprietor, instead of an editorial writer. If he had started to write humorous editorials in 1904, with his acute mind, his native shrewdness, he might have changed the entire course of our country. He doesn't know now how good he is.

CHAPTER XII

S. W. GILLILAN

I CANNOT Tell how many years ago it was, but it was I am sure somewhere in the nineties. I happened at that time to be the managing editor of *Life*. Mr. John Ames Mitchell was the proprietor and editor-in-chief. I produced the paper—that is, I selected all of the literary material, and from the pictures that Mr. Mitchell bought from numerous artists, made it up. Mr. Mitchell rarely read anything until it was set up in type. He used to glance over the dummy before it went to the printer—an affair that merely showed the arrangement of the drawings in the paper. I filled in the spaces between with literary matter, and then, when the first page-proofs came back, we would go over them carefully together. He made few changes, but the little touches he gave were invaluable. That, of course, is what makes a good editor.

I used to scan the mail very closely, looking for new material. One day I got a ragged looking manuscript from a man named Gillilan. I had never heard of him before, and indeed, his name made no impression upon me. The manuscript itself was a poem, or if you like, a doggerel verse. The title of it was "Off Agin, On Agin, Gone Agin" as I remember it.

I went off my head about the verses at once. If you haven't been an editor yourself, you will never know the joy of getting something good from a stranger. The first impulse is to suppress it. You don't want anybody to see it. You want to keep it to yourself. This is succeeded by a burning desire to spread it everywhere in big type. You cannot wait for the paper to be issued. You feel like getting out a special edition, with just this thing in it. Then these two emotions are likely to be succeeded (after a lapse of time) by a sickening sense that, after all, perhaps you are mistaken. All these things I felt about Mr. Gillilan's verses. The first thing I did was to have them set and to place them in the most prominent page of *Life*, which was the second inside page at the top of the column. When the proofs came up, I took them into Mr. Mitchell. He scanned them with his microscopic eye. When he had turned over the second page he stopped and looked at Gillilan's verses. They were reasonably long—much longer in verse than we usually ran. I am almost tempted to repeat them here, but they are now so familiar to readers and audiences all over the country that it would doubtless be superfluous. "What's this?" said Mitchell, reading first carelessly and then closely. "Don't you think they are great?" I exclaimed, my heart sinking. "Why, yes, they are pretty good," he said, "but they are not quite in our vein, do you think?" "Does that make any difference?" I faltered. He considered a moment. "No, Masson, perhaps not," he replied. "If you like them so much, run them, but put them somewhere else." And so I changed them over to the last page

at the bottom of the column. After they came out in
Life they were copied all over the country and became
a classic. Mr. Gillilan used them for years in his lectures, and I presume is doing so yet. I tell this story
not in any sense to deprecate Mr. Mitchell's judgment.
The fact is that he was exactly right. It would have
been a mistake to put the verses, which were entirely
out of *Life's* atmosphere, so conspicuously in front.
He knew, that no matter where they were in *Life,*
they would be read. Mr. Gillilan's account of himself
follows; and I hope he will not mind if I leave the
postscript in:

I worked on a farm every summer until I was
twenty-three. Winters I went to school, eventually
taught school (after 18) and went to college whenever
I could get the money. Mother knew by heart all the
poetry in the world, and Father was Irish. Surroundings gloomy. Humor was the straw to the drowning.
We had to have it in some form or die in the doldrums.
When seven years old, began keeping scrapbook of
jokes and funny stuff written by C. B. Lewis (M.
Quad), in *Detroit Free Press.* Clipped everything
funny I could find, and clung to it as to a life-raft.
Began trying to be funny. Was silly. Village cut-up.
Found it out myself. Quit it. Tried to write news
and humor for papers in Athens and Jackson, Ohio,
college and home towns. Went into straight newspaper
work at age of twenty-three—had been writing country items and squibs from "Cove Station" for the
Jackson Herald, and stuff for the Athens (Ohio)
Herald—General Charles Grosvenor's paper. Really
wanted to write dignified and tragic poetry—big, highbrow "bull" like Milton an' them! Am still occasion-

ally smitten that way. When I went to work on papers
at Richmond, Indiana, I got the real writing bug. I
began writing verses for *Sunday Indianapolis Journal,*
and prose sketches for the same paper. Prose was all
deadly serious, home, "genre" stuff, and poetry mostly
of the mother-home-and-heaven type. Still like to do
that—natural born emotional evangelist that never
evangeled, I guess. While in Richmond, wrote "Finnigin," appearing first as an attempt, in *Richmond
Palladium,* and then revamped into different form for
Life. Never wrote anything else like it or as popular.
Never will. Glad the idea came to me instead of to one
of a hundred other fellows who could have done it just
as well if not better. Preparation for writing was an
inherited literary instinct from my mother, a love of
poetry from her, also an inherent hunger for humor,
born of poverty and hard work and rather gloomy
surroundings. I learned from that experience that
humor is really one of the serious necessities of life.
I have also found out that the really funny stuff in
every generation is the "wisdom" held over from a
previous one—stuff taken seriously by folks who took
themselves that way. I learned, a long time ago (and
it has been my most saving bit of knowledge) "Blessed
is he who takes himself seriously, for he shall create
much amusement. . . ." Shortly after "Finnigin"
became a by-word and a label for me, I was coaxed to
appear publicly and recite it. I had always had a secret
scared-to-death itch for the platform, and some folk
at college had really told me I ought to do public entertaining, because I could never take elocution seriously
or the things that other folk got so worked up about.
Stress of emotion, simulated in "dramatics," was always a scream to me because it was always burlesque.
I began timidly my public work, always confessing and

intensifying my own ungainliness, and violating purposely all the tenets of the elocution teachers. The public rather liked it, for thus it was individual and "different." Then I began saying a little serious thing now and then, interspersing the laughs, and found that a good way of putting across various sorts of propaganda intended for the happifying and sanifying of mankind. I have kept this up. Since 1897 when "Finnigin" appeared, I have talked to several millions of people, face to face, and have left nearly all of them nearly as happy as they had been, and a few of them a tremendous lot happier. I believe I have helped kid a little solemn piffle off the earth, and am happy in the thought. I firmly believe the ordinary human, going along his pilgrim way, engaged daily in a desperate struggle against thinking, ready and willing to die rather than to use his mind, accepting all sorts of silly old religious formulas and political bunk because they are ready-made and save him the necessity of thinking, learning a trade because in that way he can bid his mind good-by forever—I really think that ordinary average human is something alternately to laugh and weep over. All people start life with minds, most of them end life without any, just because they never take their minds out to play or exercise. Many believe they are serious, just because they are stupid. . . . I have done many years of newspaper work, more than ten on Indiana papers, one on a Los Angeles paper, five on Baltimore papers, and if I had my way about it and could grub and garb my tribe on its income, I should still be in newspaper work. As it is, I write a little story each day for George Matthew Adams, and write steadily for ten or twelve periodicals of various classes and qualities. I have never had a sorrow that didn't eventually add to my happiness and that of other people;

I have never had any misfortune that I didn't cash in and help other people with; life has sweetened rather than embittered me—and while by no means a polly-anna idiot, I am, on the whole, far less resentful of the fact that I was born, than I used to be in the deadly serious nineteen-year-old days—which are the oldest days any human passes through though he outlive the traditional Methuselah. The only people I hate are night hotel-clerks, reformers, and people who say: "Here's a new one—and this actually happened." Best book to date, "Sunshine and Awkwardness."

[Tom! Is this any good? I'm blushing all over the place over it, but—you wanted me to be rather intimate, I take it. If I have left unstressed any point you'd like to have stressed, or if you find any lead in the above that might have been followed further to your benefit, say it, Tom, and I'm on the job.—STRICKLAND GILLILAN.]

CHAPTER XIII

MONTAGUE GLASS

ALTHOUGH he does not mention it in the letter he writes to me, which follows later in this article, I have a strong recollection of reading Montague Glass in the *New York Sun*, in the old days when the *New York Sun* was not only publishing news but literature. Certainly those inimitable Jewish sketches of his began there. Mr. Glass came after "Chimmie Fadden," by Ned Townsend. In those days everything good came out of the *Sun*, and was afterwards grabbed by the magazines and publishers. But the question we now have to ask ourselves is, "What place does Montague Glass occupy in American humor?" Is he not more essentially a dramatist than a humorist? I should say not, without, however, attempting to pose as an authority on these matters. Indeed, to pose as an authority on anything is much too shameless. The fact is that Mr. Glass has made as many, if not more, people laugh genuinely than any other man I know. I should not consider him so much a dramatist as an interpreter. It is quite difficult to define what I mean: nevertheless I shall try.

Mr. Glass has sympathy, insight, creative ability and a most intense sense of humanity. He *feels* people.

He is also intensely impersonal, in the sense of not caring, except only as one who cares as an interpreter. He is quite free from rancor of any kind: I could not imagine his harboring anything. He is not at all like anybody you have ever met, because he is so like everybody. I should think that if you were cast away on a desert island and could exchange, well, say the "Encyclopædia Britannica" that came along with you, for a human being, you would call for Glass. I mean no reflection upon Mr. Glass in stating this. Nobody ever has, or ever will, read the "Encyclopædia Britannica," and yet it is the kind of a book that you are always thinking of looking into and do not care to part with. Mr. Glass has all of the information contained in the "Encyclopædia" and besides this, he has a highly developed sense of humor and likes to talk about Max Beerbohm. In thinking of him in this way, it is almost impossible not to wish to be cast on a desert island with him. Besides, in this condition, I am convinced that he would be highly useful. I do not know what his mechanical abilities are, but let us hope that he hasn't any: nobody who is cast away on a desert island should have mechanical ability. That was the flaw in Robinson Crusoe: he is so much better when he isn't doing anything.

Now as to Mr. Glass, he has brought out the Hebrew temperament better, much better, than it has ever been brought out before. Before Potash and Perlmutter how many of us really understood the Jew? Even Mr. Henry Ford doesn't now, but that is because he has never read Mr. Glass.

But it is something much more than this. Mr. Glass

has gone quite beyond the Jew, and revealed to us all that those qualities which appear inherent in him are inherent in all of us. What astonishes me most about the Jew is that he never can explain himself. Undoubtedly the most introspective and imaginative human being in the world, he has always failed to tell us what he is. Mr. Glass interprets him to us accurately by humor; not by satire, but by atmosphere. In short, Mr. Glass is a reporter. He has reported the Jews, and we no longer laugh at them, but with them.

That is no mean achievement. My quarrel with most people I meet who think they know something (and especially that they know something about America), is that they don't take the trouble to read the people who do know and who interpret. I have said elsewhere that if one would know the American of the past two decades, he must have read "Mr. Dooley": it is equally true that, in what some one has been pleased to call this "melting-pot" of ours, there is an atmosphere, largely of cities, that can only be understood when one understands the Jewish mind. The Jewish mind is often unpleasant. The Jewish manners are often worse— they are frequently as bad as the manners of anybody else. There is a strain of something in a large proportion of Jews that nobody likes. It has been Mr. Glass's work to show the Jew like the rest of us—as a creature of God. For a great many generations, I should say even as far back as Moses, the Jew has been arguing and pleading and protesting that God made him, and he could get nobody to believe it. If Henry Ford thinks at all (I would not accuse him of it) he undoubtedly thinks that God, or somebody, made everybody else but the Jews: perhaps he thinks they were duly created and assembled by some previous rival merely for the purpose of being made to suffer by riding in his cars. I used to dislike the Jews cordially. But humor is a singular resolvent. When it is really right humor it softens down one's prejudices, gives one a sort of community spirit with the rest of the world. That is why really good humorists should never be allowed to die. Most of them are too clever when they are young. Age is a great mellower. By the time a real humorist is a hundred or so, he is then, or should be, about perfection. As for Mr. Glass, he didn't wait to be a hundred. Read what he has written about the Jews, and you will realize that he has given to us a new sense of proportion about them. Is he a humorist? I should say he is.

I was born in a house called Fern Bank, Cheetham Hill Road, Manchester, on July 23, 1877. I am, therefore, 45 years old, unless I have made a mistake in arithmetic, which I am quite likely to do, for the only reason that I am not in business to-day, is that I never could add up a column of figures with any degree of accuracy. To this fortunate circumstance, therefore, I owe my escape from the linen and cotton converting trade, in which my father was engaged. His business is now being carried on in part by my brothers, and as far as I am concerned, they are entirely welcome to it. My father moved his family to Lawton House, Baguley, Cheshire, when I was little more than an infant. Later we returned to Fern Bank, and in August, 1890, we came to New York. My father had places of business in Belfast, New York and Manchester, but as the

major part of his time was spent in New York, he
moved his family there so as to be with them for a
longer period than only a few months out of the year.
His name was James D. Glass. My mother's name was
Amelia Marsden Glass. She was the granddaughter of
the founder of E. Moses & Son of the Minories, E.
You will remember that in *Joseph Vance,* Old Joe tells
Mrs. Vance that young Joe is growing to be a heathen
and ought to be taught Bible history.

"Blest if 'ee don't think Moses is Moses's," old Joe
says, and then goes on to explain to Joey that Moses is
a character in the Bible and consequently in heaven, but
that Moses's are Jews and will most certainly go to
hell. Instead of going to hell, however, Elias Moses
went to live in Kensington Palace Gardens, W., and
changed his name to Marsden. His descendants are
now so merged with the Anglo-Saxon and Norman
blood, or shall we say bloods, of the British Isles that
most of them fondly believe they came over with the
Conqueror. As a matter of fact my ancestors came to
England from Holland during the Commonwealth and
settled in Ipswich. I have some old books of prayer
dated about 1708 in which somebody has scrawled on
the fly-leaf: "This book belongs to Moses Alexander,
his book." Underneath it, this statement is contra-
dicted. "And I say that this book belongs to Alexander
Alexander, his book."

These two young men were my remote great uncles.
Their descendants are living in Kingston, Jamaica.
In fact, like most Jews, my family is pretty well scat-
tered over the face of the globe. I have relations in
Italy, In New Zealand, Australia, and of course in
England. I had ten brothers and sisters of whom eight
survive. I married Mary Caroline Patterson, of Port
Jervis, New York, and I am a *Mayflower* descendant in

my wife's name, her remote ancestor Edward Doty having been ship's carpenter of that overcrowded vessel. We have one daughter, Elizabeth Mary, nearly five years old. We have been married fifteen years.

My education was received at the hands, at times literally, of a succession of Fräuleins of whom I remember three, Fräulein Arensburg, Fräulein Wallach and Fräulein Pierkowska. Later I went to Miss Pearson's select academy for young ladies and children, St. Luke's School, all these in England, the College of the City of New York, and the Law School of New York University. I studied music, off and on, with sundry foreigners; had a flyer at German with an old gentleman called Ross, and how he got that good Caledonian name, I never found out. I also had French lessons of a M. Delacourt, and under compulsion I studied Hebrew with an Australian gentleman called Samuel Green. I remember him with the utmost affection. He was a delightful character, full of good stories, patient to a degree, and whenever my mother asked him if he had seen me in synagogue the previous Saturday, he always said: "Yes." As a matter of fact, I spent my Saturday mornings in the Cheetham Free Library, principally reading bound back numbers of *Punch,* the *Graphic* and the *Illustrated London News.* It is due to Mr. Green that I possess a smattering of Hebrew and a large fund of Jewish humorous stories.

I wrote my first story for a school competition in England. I didn't win it. The headmaster thought it too flippant. I continued to write humorous matter and verse for the *University Item* of New York University. At about that time, 1895, I began to contribute to magazines and grew accustomed to receiving money for it. My first employment was with a lawyer called Augustus C. Fransioli, an Italian Swiss. He strongly objected to my writing stories during office hours, and I was obliged, therefore, to go up to the New York County Register's office ostensibly to examine a title, but in fact to work away diligently at a short story or an article, in a quiet corner of the old Hall of Records in City Hall Park. There, under the influence of Mr. Fransioli's clientage, I wrote some Italian short stories, notably one called "Papagallo" which *Current Literature* reprinted from *Short Stories* where it originally appeared. The compliment turned my head completely. After that I lost all interest in the law. Although I stuck to it for a number of years, I was a great deal more concerned with the material for fiction it provided than in the substantive law itself. It was in the Jewish law office with which I was associated that I gathered the ingredients for *Potash & Perlmutter,* and for all the characters in the plays and stories in which that firm appears. I had recently married,—a highly speculative venture, since I had taken a young lady of much attractiveness and charm from a perfectly good job as a teacher in the New York Public School System, where she earned more money than I did. It was, therefore, up to me to quit writing and set myself seriously to work at the law. This I did by ceasing to write during business hours. Instead I wrote at night and in the early morning, with the result that my income from my writing soon left my income from the law so far behind, that I threw up my job and have been writing ever since. This occurred in 1909. It was in the early part of 1909 that I published my first *Potash & Perlmutter* story in the *Saturday Evening Post.* Prior to that, in 1907 and 1908, I had written *Potash & Perlmutter* stories, which I was obliged to sell to magazines who carried so little advertising that the editors were willing to take a chance about offending the Jewish advertisers they didn't have. The first story was called simply *Potash & Perlmutter*. The first thing I did with it was to take it down to the *Evening Mail* office and read it to Frank Adams. Frank is a cousin of my brother's wife, and we have been close friends ever since he came to New York. Frank enjoyed it hugely. So did I, but nobody else did. I took it first to "Pop" Taylor of the *Associated Sunday Magazines*. He thought that perhaps it was funny but that there was no perhaps about Kuppenheimer, Hart Schaffner & Marx and a few other good advertisers canceling their advertising if he printed it. All the magazines to which I was by that time a fairly regular contributor, turned it down. I sold it after some months to the *Business Men's Magazine* of Detroit, Michigan. It promptly went into bankruptcy and I collected about fifty cents on the dollar for it. The same magazine had also taken another *Potash & Perlmutter* story called "Coralie and Celestine." That too netted me only fifty per cent of its purchase price. The first *Potash & Perlmutter* story that I sold to the *Saturday Evening Post* was called "Taking It Easy." The second, with which I landed Mr. Lorimer a week later, was called "The Arverne Sacque." That one made an impression on the *Post's* readers, and thereafter I became a regular contributor to its columns.

Up to 1909, I had been a writer of anything and everything that could be sold for a half a cent a word up. I wrote musical articles and legal articles. Christmas, Thanksgiving, New Year's Day, and in fact every public holiday, found me ready with an article on the significance of the celebration. I wrote verse, music and fiction. I worked on legal textbooks. I even did a bit of drawing. But after 1909, I wrote fiction almost exclusively.

My association with the theater began with a collaboration upon the first play *Potash & Perlmutter*. My collaborator was the late Charles Klein, who went down with the *Lusitania*. We started to do it for a company called the Authors' Producing Company of which the Selwyns and John Cort were the principal stockholders. After we had decided on the plot and began to write the scenes, Mr. Klein was approached by some of his Jewish friends, who told him that the play would be offensive to them and induced him to abandon it. I was only too glad to let him off. Subsequently A. H. Woods secured the dramatic rights to *Potash & Perlmutter,* a collection of short stories which had been published by Howard Altemus of Philadelphia. Mr. Klein and I then worked on the play which proved to be so successful. Mr. Klein insisted that his name should not appear as part author, so that when it was produced, no name appeared on the program. This was in 1913. It has been running constantly since. At present it is enjoying a long and prosperous run in Berlin, but, in the status of an enemy alien, I have received no royalties. Mr. Klein's name now appears on all programs as co-author. Had he lived, we would have collaborated on the later plays. I went to see him off when he sailed on the *Lusitania*. Not ten minutes before the boat left, we bought some afternoon papers which contained an account of the mysterious bombarding of Dunquerque. It was thought that the German fleet had broken through and was in the channel *en route* for the North Atlantic. I asked him if he didn't feel a bit uneasy about it. He said that he would sail if the entire fleet was stripped for action outside of New York harbor. He wanted to see his wife and his young son John whom he had left in London only a few weeks before, and he told me he would just as lief drown as die of homesickness. He was a gentle, charming little man, with every imaginable good quality of heart and mind.

I next collaborated with Roy Cooper Megrue on the play "Abe & Mawruss" and, in 1916, I began the series of collaborations with Jules Eckert Goodman, resulting in "Business Before Pleasure," "Object Matrimony," "Why Worry," "His Honor Sam Davis," which after a number of performances out of town, was changed into "His Honor Abe Potash."

There are various methods of collaboration. The one I pursued with Mr. Klein I do not recommend. We had decided on the plot and some of the scenes when Mr. Klein decided not to continue. I therefore obtained Mr. Klein's permission to work up the incidents and plot already decided upon into a story, which was published in the *Saturday Evening Post*. It was called "Brothers All." Later Mr. Klein wrote the first draft of the play in London. It was sent on to New York. There I rewrote it, preserving a great deal of Mr. Klein's work. The last act is entirely mine. I wrote in many new characters and scenes and did a whole lot of hard work which would have been avoided had Mr. Klein and I collaborated in the fashion that Jules Goodman and I now work. We start in at nine and knock off at lunchtime. We then resume for a couple of hours at about three o'clock or so and call it a day. Sometimes he sits at the typewriter and I lie on the sofa. At other times our positions are reversed. The result is a sure-enough collaboration. The collaboration with Mr. Megrue was one in which Mr. Megrue matched his experience against my labor. Perhaps this arrangement is quite fair. At any rate it does not make for cordiality in the subsequent relations of the collaborators.

Collaborating with Jules has been continually a pleasure, which I am sure is not going to end for many years. We have had two successes, one artistic success and one play that the *Herald* said was a success. I have enjoyed writing them all.

My books are principally collections of short stories. There have been two volumes of comments upon the war and the Peace Conference put into the mouths of *Potash & Perlmutter*. The whole list is as follows: "Potash & Perlmutter," Howard Altemus, Philadelphia, 1910, later published by Doubleday, Page & Co.; "Abe & Mawruss," Doubleday, Page & Co., 1911; "Object Matrimony," Doubleday, Page & Co., 1911; "The Competitive Nephew," Doubleday, Page & Co., 1913; "Elkan Lubliner, American," Doubleday, Page & Co., 1912; "Abe & Mawruss, Philosophers," Doubleday, Page & Co., 1911; "Worrying Won't Win," Harpers, 1917; "Potash & Perlmutter Settle Things," Harpers, 1919.

How many magazines and newspaper articles I have written I cannot now remember,—probably many hundreds, including short stories. I have been a journeyman author since about 1895, and the mere lapse of time, in spite of a congenital laziness, accounts for them. I have also written some one-act plays and I wrote a new English version of "La Tierra Allegra," or "The Land of Joy," which ran for several months in New York and on tour.

I spend the winters in Pasadena, because of my little daughter's delicate health. I have a cottage in Lake Placid, where we go for the summer. My city address is 47 Fifth Avenue, the Salmagundi Club. I am a member of this Club, and the Lambs in New York,

the National Press Club of Washington, the Authors'
Club of London, and I belong to the usual number of
professional societies, viz: The Society of Authors
of London, The Authors League of America, and
La Société des Auteurs et Compositeurs Dramatiques
of Paris. I do not play golf and belong to no
fraternities or fraternal organizations. I am insured in
the Equitable Life, and play bridge, poker, auction
pinochle, pool, billiards and the piano.

CHAPTER XIV

MISS HERFORD AND THE MONOLOGUE

THE monologue is a distinct type of humorous character delineation which actually, in its dramatic qualities, belongs to the stage, but which the genius of Miss Beatrice Herford has transfused into a type of humor all its own. Miss Herford has a number of imitators, some of whom are extraordinarily good, but no one, I think, approaches her in her qualities.

What is it that she does?

She reproduces out of our common life a common character with such fidelity to nature, that it is all we can do to keep from holding ourselves back from that kind of laughter which might—although it never does —express our real emotions. Therefore we shiver with the delight of coming into contact with truth—a rare experience, revealing that, after all, the best satire is only truth in a thin disguise. Miss Herford not only writes her own monologues, but acts them; and she does this much better than any one I know. Her monologues, thus conceived by her and written with painstaking care, have appeared in our leading magazines and in an occasional book. As a part of our humorous literature their subtlety is recognized by all

lovers of the best.   Perhaps the best description of
Miss Herford is that written by another highly talented
Woman, Dorothy Parker, who not long since in
Everybody's Magazine, wrote of her as follows:

Certainly, the last place you would ever expect to
find her is in the midst of a vaudeville show.

Up to the time of her entrance, things have gone
along just about as usual.   The two young men in
the conventional jet-buttoned and velvet-collared black,
with the extra-size silk hats pressing the tops of their
ears outward, have danced individually and simultaneously, saving for the climax their inebriation specialty
in which, with hats tilted to one side by way of
atmosphere, they stagger rhythmically about the stage
to the overaccented strains of "We Won't Go Home
Until Morning."

The playlet about the young lady thief who robs
the house of the prominent judge who turns out to be
her father has reached its happy conclusion.   The
gentleman in the lavender dinner-coat and the basket-
weave hat has indulged in a successful flirtation with
the self-made blonde who trips on from the opposite
side of the stage, the romance blossoming into several
songs and dances, and a series of ever-shorter costumes
for the lady.   The individual who so sincerely flatters
Al Jolson has told a series of loud stories, and has
rushed back and forth, shaking the house with a song
about the purely speculative diversions of Mrs. Julius
Cæsar while her husband was away at war.   The well-
dressed black-face comedian has beguiled his hearers
by addressing elaborately worded insults to the shabbily
dressed black-faced comedian.

And the audience has drunk all this in, enraptured.
As the nature of the entertainment demands, they have

laughed, or thrilled, or brushed away a tear, or gurglingly repeated the jokes to one another. They have applauded at each finale as if they could not bear to let the acts out of sight.

Then comes the time when, according to the program, Beatrice Herford is scheduled to appear. Nothing particular is done about it on the stage. There are no custom-made velvet curtains, no special orchestra, no trick-lighting effects, not even a strip of red carpet unrolled for the occasion. The setting is just whatever drop-curtain the management may happen to have around the house; possibly a gentleman assisting a lady into a swan-encircled gondola is painted upon it, or it shows a vast flight of strikingly realistic marble stairs, mounting out of sight in admirable perspective. Before it stands one small gilt chair, looking pitiably alone. The orchestra plays something in which neither it nor the audience takes much interest.

And then Beatrice Herford enters, not dramatically, or laughingly, or even whimsically. She just enters. She looks as if the thought of appearing in vaudeville were the last thing that would ever come into her head. With her softly arranged wavy hair and her conservative frock, it seems as though she had just been going down to the drawing-room to welcome her dinner guests, and had somehow got up upon the stage by mistake. She walks casually over, and stands behind the little gilt chair, just as anybody might. When she announces the subject of her first monologue, "The Hotel Child," perhaps, or "In the Five-and-Ten-Cent Store," or "At the Box-Office," her voice is distinct, but outside of that it is not so different from other people's voices. There is no trace of the booming of the professional elocutionist; pronouncing her words seems to be an entirely painless operation to her.

For one bad moment you think that they are not going to like her. You look nervously around at that audience, and your heart sinks. You recall how, not five minutes before, they were shrieking with laughter, when the well-dressed black-face comedian told his ragged partner that he was going to "knock him so far that it will cost ten dollars to send him a post-card." You recollect how they writhed in agonies of mirth when the ragged comedian retorted that he would make the first one "run so fast that people would see so much of the soles of his shoes they would think he was lying down." Things look pretty black for that audience; you feel that they will never make the grade.

But once Beatrice Herford is started on her mono-logue, you cease to worry about the audience. You are too much occupied with your own affairs. You have all that you can do to restrain your whoops of laughter, not so much because they might annoy your neighbors as because they might prevent your hearing some of Miss Herford's succeeding remarks. You want to rise and beg her to stop for a minute so that you can get all through appreciating one line before she goes on to the next. You want to implore her, when she reaches the end, to go back and do it all over again, in case you might possibly have overlooked something. You have plenty to hold your attention to your own concerns, and keep your mind off your neighbors.

When you suddenly do remember, with a guilty start, and give a thought to the audience, you find that they have been shifting for themselves very nicely indeed. They are laughing just as helplessly as you are, sitting forward just as eagerly so as not to miss anything, applauding for more just as beseechingly. Just as you have been doing, they recognize the characters in the monologues, calling breathlessly to one another, "Isn't that just like Aunt Annie?" or "Haven't you heard Cousin Bertha go on that way a hundred times?"

The only one who is not surprised at Beatrice Herford's success with vaudeville audiences is Beatrice Herford. When she first considered going into vaudeville, people who had nothing but her interest at heart begged her with tears in their eyes to see the light. It was for her own good, they sobbed on her shoulder, that they felt that they must tell her that, as a vaudeville performer, she would be the sensational failure of the age. She might be a great hit in a parlor, they conceded, reciting some of those clever little things of hers while the chicken salad was being served; but on the variety stage, filling in the space between a troupe of trained Bedouins and a dog and monkey circus— they all but broke down at the picture. Patiently they pointed out that her monologue would glide smoothly over the heads of vaudeville patrons. Subtleties slipped through the generous gaps in the two-a-day mind. The appreciation of the efforts of a seemingly intoxicated comedian to lean against the lamp-post painted on the back drop was about as far as vaudeville hounds went in the line of humor. For her own sake, she ought to realize that her place was in the home.

Buoyed up by their words, Miss Herford signed her contract and went on at one of Keith's Theaters. And vaudeville audiences ever since have been repaying, in applause and laughter, the compliment she paid them by her confidence in them.

It happened all over again when she thought of appearing in revue. By that time, people had become accustomed to her success in vaudeville; indeed, several were letting it be rumored abroad that it was by their advice she had gone on the variety stage. But revue was markedly something else again, and her mono- logues—it wasn't easy for them to say it, but they were not ones to let themselves shirk a duty—would never go over with revue audiences.

So, after listening attentively to them, Miss Herford entered a revue, and history obliged by repeating itself. She was the only thing that one can bear to remember of "Let's Go," William Rock's production, which, shortly after its opening, lived up to its name. Re- cently she provided a welcome bit of humor in "What's In a Name?" for a season or thereabouts.

In between times she slips comfortably into vaude- ville again. And whenever she can do it, she eludes the theater altogether, and she and her husband go up to their home way off in Massachusetts, where she can be as virulently domestic as she yearns to be, cooking and darning and dusting, and taking part in all the other sports for which that part of the country is famous.

Beatrice Herford's career never had any definite starting-point. There never was any one great day when she suddenly felt the urge to go out in the world and do monologues. She was just born that way; that's all. Just as her clever brother Oliver was born the way that he is.

It began in England, in Manchester, in so many words—where she was born, the daughter of a clergy- man. As far back as her memory begins to function, she was always pretending that she was somebody else. She was not, it is gratifying to report, one of those quaint little things that go pallidly about making believe that they are Queen of the Snowflakes, or the Spirit of the Rosebush, or a little lost Sunbeam, or something of that delicate and whimsical nature. The

fancies of young Miss Herford were of a more sub-
stantial nature; she looked on life with the material
eye of Daisy Ashford. The parts that she allotted
to herself, in her games of pretending, were nice, fat
ones.

She was usually a rich and sought-after woman of
the world, who had generously dropped in for a visit
to the simple Herford family. A most unenthusiastic
sister was coerced into playing the game with her, act-
ing as a sort of feeder. It was no simple little pastime
which could be indulged in at a moment's notice whenever nothing more attractive offered; it involved much
preparation and many properties, for Beatrice Herford,
with the thoroughness of a true artist, insisted upon
a lavish amount of convincing local color. She carefully dressed in her conception of a traveling costume,
commandeered a bag and umbrella, and arrived impres-
sively at the front door. With sophisticated politeness she inquired of the apathetic small sister as to
the health of her family, and, that over with, got on
to the really interesting part of the game, an exhaustive
recital of her doings, concerns and opinions as a woman of the world.

It was the birth of her monologues. At that time she
had not quite caught the idea of sketching, in a few
words, the characters she was impersonating. The
game would go on for days at a stretch. From morning until night, not exclusive of the necessary time
spent at the table, young Miss Herford played the part
of the wealthy visitor; her abundant words were the
words that would have been spoken by the distinguished
guest. She lived the part, as the critics would say.

Then she would suddenly grow tired of being that
particular rich lady, and would conceive a rôle for
herself of an even wealthier and more important per-

sonage. After a time, she grew bored with playing only society rôles, and she began pretending to be certain of the people she saw about. Several of these impersonations she tried out on the family, meeting with instantaneous success. She had always liked reciting, and almost from the time she could speak at all, her father had encouraged her in it, listening attentively while she declaimed across the spaces of his study to him. He did it for her amusement, first, and for his own after a while.

It was just a step from giving her monologues in her own drawing-room to giving them in other people's. Then, after a while, she came over and tried them in American drawing-rooms. From there, any one can go on with the story.

Miss Herford writes every monologue that she uses. She sees potential characters for them everywhere— shops, railway stations, employment agencies, street-cars, and listens hungrily for them to say something that she can use. Unfortunately, they seldom do; people aren't like that. The things they say either aren't funny at all, or else they are incredible. Once she selects her type she must prayerfully work out the logical things for that character to say. Lines that are merely funny in themselves are of no use at all; they must be the exact lines that the character would say under the circumstances in which Miss Herford places him or her—it's always her, of course. It means that she can't dash off her monologue while humming a sprightly tune; they are the result of good, honest toil. But it also means that each one is perfect as a character study. Which is the difference between Beatrice Herford and other monologists.

Usually the word monologist brings to mind the picture of a nervous girl in a white dress, with the

golden chain of her eye-glasses coiled behind one ear
and a home-made silk rose tucked behind the other,
reciting "Miss Hepzibah Sunnybrook's Thoughts on
the First Robin," and receiving at its conclusion a
bouquet of wired asters addressed in her mother's hand-
writing. You know you never think of Beatrice Herford as a monologist in that sense of the word. She
manages it, somehow, so that you don't think of her
at all. She hides behind each of the characters that
she represents. There isn't any Miss Herford for the
time being—there is a bored five-and-ten-cent store
shopgirl, a weary servant-seeker, a friendly shopper
for theater tickets, an harassed mother taking her
offspring for a trolley ride, any one of dozens of
familiar people.

You meet an old friend in each of her creations.
Every one in the company she presents may be promptly
identified as Mrs. Chaney, or Cousin Abbie, or that
woman in the apartment up-stairs. Sometimes she
comes even nearer home, and does a portrait of you,
yourself, and a startling likeness, too.

The curious thing is that you never recognize yourself. You go blissfully on saying, "Well, if that isn't
just like that Mrs. What's-her-name, that moved to
Utica last October—the one that had the two little
boys and the husband in the hardware business!"

CHAPTER XV

OLIVER HERFORD

If this little world to-night
Suddenly should fall through space
In a hissing, headlong flight
Shriveling from off it's face,
As it falls into the sun,
In an instant every trace
Of the little crawling things—
Ants, philosophers and lice,
Cattle, cockroaches and kings,
Beggars, millionaires and mice,
Men and maggots all as one,
As it falls into the sun—
Who can say but at the same
Instant from some planet far
A child may watch us and exclaim:
"See the pretty shooting star!"

Years ago Oliver Herford wrote and rewrote this
verse (as he always does) and it was published in
Life. Afterwards he used it for the Epilogue of his
little book, "This Giddy Globe," published a year or
so ago, and the dedication to which reads:

TO PRESIDENT WILSON

(With all his faults he quotes me still)

Probably, indeed, over a considerable period of
time, Oliver Herford has been, and still is, the most
quoted man in America. Presidents have come and
gone, but the things that Herford has said linger
on. It would be quite impossible to get together
in any sort of complete array all of these good
things. Much of what some witty people say
lies either in the saying of it or in the immediate
occasion. This must be true of course of him; but
doubtless it is less true of him than of the others. A
unique combination of philosopher, wit, poet, and
artist, he remains practically indefinable. To describe
him is to commit a kind of sacrilege. Not that he is
above description; on the contrary, he is perfectly offhand and agreeably dull and silent when the occasion
warrants or necessity confronts him. He has a
Shakespearean sense of words, with which he loves to
play, as a kitten does with a ball of yarn, raveling it
and unraveling it. This sensitiveness to sound which,
in a low mind, would lead to the most violent puns, is,
in Herford's hands, a medium for the most delicate
construction and unerring insight. Truly a person of
most nimble wit and delicate fancy, one who loves
fairies and bears a kind of innocent and withal wonderful contempt for material things; who possesses
an unerring faculty for selecting the threads of gold
running through all things, and winding it about so
that it is seen by those who have eyes. Shy to the last
degree, shrinking from any kind of that sort of personal exploitation so dear to the hearts (and pocket-
books) of the rest of us, Oliver Herford is the only
one of his kind in America. It is really with a sense

of genuine guilt that one writes about him at all. His remarkable influence over those with whom he comes into contact is due to the very qualities that he is supposed to lack. It has been said of him, and repeated so often that he has come to believe it himself, that he never keeps engagements. Once at a dinner party, the hostess remarked a vacant seat near him. "Yes," replied Herford, "if I weren't here I should know that seat was mine."

Yet as a matter of fact, no one is more punctilious. The great difficulty with him is that he is never satisfied with what he does. He will do over a drawing fourteen or fifteen times to get it right. This sort of thing is of course maddening to practical people, and especially to printers and editors. After having written a piece of verse, he will reluctantly hand it in. He will say: "Now, what do you think of this line? Perhaps another word would be better here." He is assured that this is the very word. "Do you think so?" he will repeat. "I have my doubts."

Finally the copy is released to the editor. It is sent to the printer. The telephone rings. It is Herford.

"Could you manage to change that last line?"

He repeats the last line.

"And this is so much better. You *must* change it you know." Money is no object. Perfection is the only goal. The agonies that Oliver Herford has suffered from misprints, and from faulty reproductions of his drawings, it would be wrong to dwell upon. And his spirit of resignation, in the light of his wise maturity!

Herford draws better than he writes, and writes better than he draws. The broad farcical effect is not his. He has no sense of the crowd. The thing that most men strive so earnestly for—applause—he doesn't even know about. But he is so sympathetic that I think he would envy any man almost anything that he would not take as a gift for himself.

Here are three of his epigrams, taken at random from my memory.

"Many are called but few get up."

"Actresses will happen in the best regulated families."

"In the midst of life we are in Brooklyn."

The son of an English clergyman and born in England, he received his education partly in England and partly in this country; afterwards he studied in Paris. He has written plays, verses (and such verses!) and has drawn such inimitable things as send shivers of delight over one to look at. Here is a piece of his prose, taken from "This Giddy Globe." In fact, it is a whole chapter. The book itself can easily be read through in half an hour, yet it contains practically all that is known about this world.

The Giddy Globe

Men of science, who delight in applying harsh terms to things that cannot talk back, have called this Giddy Globe an Oblate Spheroid.

Francis Bacon called it a Bubble; Shakespeare an oyster; Rosetti, a Midge; and W. S. Gilbert refers to it familiarly as a Ball——

Roll on thou ball, roll on!
Through pathless realms of space,
    Roll on!
What though I'm in sorry case?
What though I cannot meet my bills?
What though I suffer toothache's ills?
What though I swallow countless pills?
    Never *you* mind
    Roll on!

But these people belong to a privileged class that is encouraged (even paid) to distort the language, and they must not be taken too literally.

The Giddy Globe is really quite large, not to say obese.

Her waist measurement is no less than twenty-five thousand miles. In the hope of reducing it, the earth takes unceasing and violent exercise, but though she spins around on one toe at the rate of a thousand miles an hour every day, and round the sun once a year, she does not succeed in taking off a single mile or keeping even comfortably warm all over.

No wonder the globe is giddy!

Questions

Explain the Nebular Hypothesis.

State briefly the electromagnetical constituents of the Aurora Borealis, and explain their relation to the Hertzian Waves.

Define the difference between the Hertzian Wave and the Marcel Wave.

The story of Herford's that ex-President Wilson quoted so often—indeed, I believe it was the only story that he quoted in his speeches—runs something to the effect that one man met another and said to him:

"Do you remember me?"

The other man replied: "I can't remember your name or face, but your manner is very familiar."

Another story told by Herford relates to a lady who persisted in asking him to her house. She asked him first to come on Monday.

"Impossible," said Herford.

"Then make it Tuesday," said the lady.

"No," replied Herford, "I really cannot come on Tuesday."

"How about Wednesday?"

"I am sorry but I have something important on hand Wednesday."

"Then come Thursday."

"Oh, well, make it Monday."

There are several stories of Herford's that I am aching to tell in this chapter, but he will not let me do so. They are perfectly proper, of course, but he does not like to hurt people's feelings, and he thought the retelling of these stories might. As a matter of fact, there is absolutely nothing in them that ought not to be told, and I am convinced that if they were told they would do much good; yet he is obdurate. That is what embarrasses me, because, as Herford remarked to me recently, one may remain silent all the evening in company if one has something that one wishes to say and doesn't feel that it ought to be said. There are so many things of a delicious nature about him that

I recall, it does seem a shame that I cannot now put everything in. I remember just here his story about meeting in Boston—just as he was about to sail for Europe—John Ames Mitchell, the one-time editor of *Life*.

"What are you doing in Boston?" asked Mitchell.

"I am about to sail for Europe," replied Herford.

"But why do it from Boston?"

"Because it is so much easier to sail away from Boston than anywhere else in America," said Herford. Mitchell was so much amused with this reply that he asked Herford to write it out, and I believe it was afterwards published in *Life*.

It should be understood that the kind of repartee that is peculiar to Oliver Herford is impossible to translate into words. Merely to repeat a saying of his and see it later in cold type is to destroy almost the whole effect.

Once, trying to persuade him to play golf or croquet, of which he had his choice, he said: "I take all my exercise in a rocking-chair." And upon my asking him, after he had stopped smoking, if he had really kept his resolve, he said, "I am obliged to smoke occasionally so that I will not fall into the habit of not smoking."

I have tried to analyze the difference between Whistler and Oliver Herford, and think it lies largely in the fact that Whistler delighted to hurt people, and Herford is gentleness itself. Apparently he has only one dread—that of being bored, and all of his prejudices and emotions that might otherwise be personal have gone into that channel. Nothing could induce him to go to a public banquet, which I should say he regards as a kind of saturnalia of vulgarity. To him publicity of any sort, other than the publicity of his ideas is, in a sense, a shocking affair. I once showed him a publisher's circular where it was proposed to have an entire "week" devoted to a popular author. It appealed to me as being a grand idea, and the audacity and blatant vulgarity of the affair delighted me, as an example of the methods resorted to by the American advertiser. Herford snorted with rage. Words utterly failed him to express his emotions.

I can remember him as far back as I can remember anything that is good and wholesome and witty. He did chance things for *Life* in the nineties, and some years later on, when George Harvey was running *Harper's Weekly*—and afterwards, when Norman Hapgood was its editor—he was attached to that journal as its chief cartoonist. It is very seldom that a man has talents in both directions—that of art and literature; or perhaps I should say that where he has it in both, both are like to suffer. In Herford's case the union of the two seems essential in order to complete his idea. His drawing of Queen Victoria would hardly have been complete without the verses underneath it. Herford, without doubt, is the greatest wit and the most vicarious editor in America.

CHAPTER XVI

KIN HUBBARD

I WAS born at Bellefontaine, Ohio, and attended local schools; learned the art preservative in my father's newspaper office. In 1891 I took a place on the *Indianapolis News* as a caricaturist, developing a little natural ability along that line after accepting the place. With the exception of a brief tryout on the old *Cincinnati Tribune* I have been a member of the *Indianapolis News* staff all of these years. Almost seventeen years ago I created the character, Abe Martin, who is supposed to be a small town philosopher in Brown County, a wild, hilly county without telegraph or railroad, in the southern part of this state. Every day, except Sundays, for seventeen years I have written a single paragraph dealing with two unrelated subjects to set beneath a picture of Abe Martin, and each day the picture has shown the same old character in a new pose and a different background. This little feature has been syndicated for about eleven years. To-day it appears in about 195 American and Canadian newspapers. For eight or nine years I have contributed a weekly essay to the *News*. This feature appears under the caption of "Short Furrows." The essays have been syndicated for seven years. "Abe Martin's

Sayings" have been published in book form each November for sixteen years. To my notion the best thing I ever wrote was the biography of a fellow who took up the cornet so many different times during his life, hoping to master it and devote himself to it, and who finally died in th' radiator repair business. Of all the thousands of paragraphs I have written the two that seem to have had the greatest appeal to vaudeville performers are these:

"Th' first thing t' turn green in th' spring is Christmus jewelry."

"Women are jest like elephants t' me. I like t' look at 'em, but I wouldn' want one."

CHAPTER XVII

WALLACE IRWIN

I HAD started to write something in this book about Wallace Irwin, and in trying to get together the facts I was in despair because there were none; at least there was nothing but a series of adventures and interviews I had had with him, and out of this there was only an impression; a very strong impression it is true, but nothing to write down in a sober book about humorists. The only concrete thing I could recall at the time was what Mark Twain once wrote about Irwin's "Togo," and even the text of this had slipped me. But I knew it was very favorable and I recalled that Mr. Clemens had declared that the Togo letters were quite the best thing he had seen in American humorous literature. And while I was thinking of all this and wondering what to do, lo and behold; Irwin suddenly appeared, and I got him to write what follows about himself.

There was some difficulty in persuading him of the importance of doing this; not that his modesty is of that false kind that makes a pretense of not wanting to be talking about oneself when it is essential that one should, but only that he could not come to see himself in quite the right perspective, or at least that, having become immersed in family cares, he was reluctant to break loose from the thoughts of others to himself. At any rate, we debated for some time as to the thing that he should write, and thereupon a few days later he sent me what follows.

But before I come to it I want myself to say a few words about Wallace Irwin, and after he has had his say about himself, I shall go back briefly to what he has written, merely to wind up this chapter.

I recall now quite vividly Lincoln Steffens coming into my office one day, and the talk we got into about getting on in literature. It was quite a practical talk, just as one might talk about one's method of playing parcheesi, or any game that requires a moderate degree of attainments. Steffens said that the trouble with most young writers was that they were afraid; that is, they became attached to one thing and didn't dare quit, whereas the very life of a writer depended upon his continually cutting loose. And then he told me about Wallace Irwin. Wallace, some time after his birth and his being got out of college (in the manner he mentions in his story), came on to New York. He says also (as you will read a little later) that he sold his first verse to *Life*. I dimly remember reading it and liking it, but I can recall nothing more than this. But, at any rate, he secured a job on a New York evening paper. His daily stint was to write a poem a day, and for this effort he received the magnificent stipend of $25 a week. His verses were good and attracted wide attention—among others that of Steffens. Now anybody who knows Lincoln Steffens knows that he is always helping other people, and so, as he told me, he dropped in one day on Irwin and asked him why he did that sort of thing; why he didn't write for other papers.

"I wouldn't dare give this up," replied Irwin. "It's a steady thing; my God, what would I do without it?"

Thereupon Steffens saw the proprietor of the paper and got him to fire Irwin.

"He'll never get anywhere unless you fire him," he declared. So Irwin, having to sink or swim, was forced into prominence and affluence by the Man that Knew.

Here follows his story:

Mainly About Myself

In my infancy there was always some one to inform me that Opportunity—quite unlike the prevalent income tax—arrives but once to any man. Opportunity, according to my sage advisers, consisted in meeting great men, and in improving one's mind by their company and example.

In those days we were living in Leadville, Colorado, a mining camp that pinned its faith on free silver and lived up to its reputation of being the highest incorporated town in America—or was it the world? We dwelt in an atmosphere of rarefied ideals, but suffered from a chronic shortage of fresh fruit, drinking water, and famous men. All of these commodities had to be hauled over a rocky spur of the D. & R. G.; hence, came seldom and expensive. Celebrities especially were rare; hence, at a premium.

I went to public school when I was six, and my earliest memory of that environment was of a large, greenish gentleman—I think he was somebody on the board of education—who used to stand on the platform

Friday afternoons and chant in a Welsh accent under his black horseshoe mustache:

"I live to tell their story
    Who labored for my sake,
To em-u-late their glory
    And follow in their wake.
Bards, geniuses and sages,
The noble of all ages
Whose deeds fill Hist'ry's pages
    And Time's great volume make."

Therefore it was pretty generally agreed that I should get busy, pick out a genius to emulate, and emulate to the best of my ability.

As though to further my ambitious scheme, General Grant came to Leadville, Colorado, bent on one of those tag-and-follow-me excursions known as ex-Presidential Tours. The sojourn of the much-wandering Ulysses in Leadville was of such brief duration that a local paragrapher was quite justified in his quip, "General Grand has come and gone—principally gone." But, while he was in town, my father saw in the great soldier a chance for my advancement in the study of emulation.

My memory of the occasion is, necessarily, vague. The mountain streets were dim with early twilight; the I. O. O. F. band was playing; a carriage came lurching around a slushy corner, and everybody set up a cheer.

"There's General Grant!" exclaimed my father, holding me high in his arms.

Entranced, I beheld the majesty of a silk hat and the perfect poise of one who sat his kingly, elevated seat just behind two spanking grays. If I were a general, thought I, just such a prominence would I occupy, only the seat and the hat would be at least two inches taller than those the hero of Appomattox affected.

The carriage stopped. Many hands were reached out to clasp the hand that had clasped the sword of Lee.

"And what a nice little boy!" I heard a kindly voice exclaim.

"He's pretty fine," agreed my father, "but you ought to see Bill. Shake hands with the General, Wallie."

I reached up and tried to shake hands with the General, upon whom my eyes had been fixed, but when I had twined my fingers with those of the high-throned gentleman in the silk hat I received, I thought, rather a poor response. The crowd uttered a deep-throated mountain yell. The carriage moved on.

It was only next day that I learned the truth. I had shaken hands with the coachman.

It was during the same year and in the same town that I made my first stage appearance in the company of William Gillette. Mr. Gillette, should he happen to read this article, will be surprised, but the statement is too literally true. He was touring in "The Private Secretary"—I am sure of this play, because the other one I saw in Leadville was the "Black Crook."

I don't remember much about the plot, further than an impression, which I still cherish, to the effect that "The Private Secretary" was the funniest play ever written. The art of Gillette was then, as now, satisfying; but it was the work of that brilliant child actor, Wallace Irwin, that most deeply interested me. Vaguely I recall that Mr. Gillette, in his farce, was a very comic English curate whose wife and eleven children had an embarrassing habit of showing up at romantic crises in his life.

Well, the Irwins, as a family, went to the show. The second act was delayed and, had I been a few years older, I should have realized that something had gone wrong with the properties. I well recall the stage manager coming down the aisle and whispering to my father in the cool, impersonal manner peculiar to slave dealers of all time, "Dave, the infant prodigy's down with measles. We've got to have a baby in the third act or the show's cold. Will you loan me yours?" Meaning me.

Possibly I was consulted in the matter; but what I said was of small consequence in the ensuing movement during which I was smuggled down a dark alley and into a giant's cave where tier on tier of painted canvas partitions loomed from a cobwebby zenith to a grimy nadir and made me feel like the smallest boy that ever walked into a nightmare.

In a patch of brilliant light beyond I could see people with beautifully decorated faces walking about and saying witty things in loud, unnatural voices. It dawned upon me that I was seeing the play wrong end to. I asked my mother about it, but she said, "Hush!" Then a very tall, very thin gentleman in the raiment proper to a minister of the gospel came up to our family group, pinched my cheeks and whispered, "Yes, he'll do very nicely, just as he is. Thank you, Mrs. Irwin."

A moment later, when I saw the clerical gentleman, coat tails flying, capering across the stage, I was sure he was the funniest man in the world. My screams of delight were properly hushed, with the caution that I was disturbing Mr. Gillette. An artistic ecstasy filled my veins, made me wild to dash behind the gassy footlights and share the honors. I was told that it would not be my turn until next act. Such are the disappointments that wait upon genius.

In the chaos between acts ten larger children were lined up and I, the smallest, stood at the end of the row. They ranged in size like the pipes of an organ, from big double-bass to little vox humana. We were told to await the signal, then to file on the stage and stand, pipe-organ fashion, just as we stood in that brief rehearsal.

So at last the procession of stage children filed on as per cue amidst the appreciative guffaws of a Leadville audience. A nice lady passed down the line and wiped our noses, which graduated in size from the big boy's at the other end down to mine. The lady pinched my nose slightly and whispered, "Don't stand so far out, dear." Then Mr. Gillette came in and had a distressing scene with the nice lady, who turned out to be his wife—in the play—and proved ever so stubborn when he begged her to take us away and not disgrace him before his friends. A great confusion ensued. There was much running back and forth and, from the heartless audience, much ribald laughter.

In the general stage panic I turned around, and was stiff with fright to see that the other ten children were being led off the stage. I, also, sought to flee, but kind, firm hands restrained me. I looked up and saw that it was Mr. Gillette, who had taken me on his knee. It was rather a thin knee and I began to struggle, filled with the hysterical conviction that the act had gone far enough. As I look back adown the years I think of that moment and sympathize with the distinguished actor whose duty it was to hold a struggling little fat boy under one arm and with the other to deliver gestures appropriate to his truly comic lines.

"I say, little man," he managed to whisper at last, "what's wrong?"

"I wanna get down!"

"You'll be down in a moment. Try to sit still. What's your name, my boy?"

"Wallace Irwin. And I wanna get down!"

This last speech in a clear, loud voice, audible to the very back seats of Leadville's leading playhouse.

At that instant one of the actors addressed to Mr. Gillette a speech which called for immediate reply. It was necessary for the author-star to raise both his hands in an expressive gesture. I saw my chance and slipped eel-like off his knee. I caught a glimpse of my mother's frightened face somewhere in the wings. There safety lay. Brisk as a squirrel off the stage, tripping up the soubrette in my headlong flight. I managed to get myself tangled in the scenery and was finally removed by a stage hand.

Fifteen minutes after this exit my family went into conference and decided to retire me to private life.

One quick and rosy path to prominence, they tell me, is the way of public speechmaking. There are two reasons why I never make a public speech: I hate to, and I am never asked.

But, stay! I *was* asked once. And since the episode illustrates several points in this wandering confession, let me tell it to the end.

It was several years ago, and the publishers of America were planning a great dinner to entertain the authors of America at the New Willard Hotel, Washington. A doomful letter came to me one morning requesting me to appear at the speakers' table and deliver a few choice remarks. For a month after that I lived under a drizzle of cold perspiration. Libraries were searched for appropriate thoughts, reams were written, committed to my poor memory, forgotten, destroyed. At last I decided on something slightly jocular, not too personal, nimbly evasive. Those were before the days when I rose, or fell, to a fiction-writer's estate; I bore the brand "Humorist" seared upon my forehead and never managed to grow my hair so as to conceal the damned spot.

So I wrote a speech which I thought would do. This I had typewritten on a series of small cards, my idea being that I could hide it in the palm of my hand.

The day came and I went down to Washington supported by two as able comforters as ever padded Job in his day of soreness. James Montgomery Flagg, the famous illustrator, guarded my right hand and sought to divert me by means of horrifying sketches, representing somebody who looked like me dying of fright at a long banquet table. Julian Street—who, judged alone by the mileage consumed in compiling data for his eminent volumes on the quaint inhabitants of North America, might be called the "Longest Street" and certainly one of the most amusing in the world—bounded me on the left.

I was surrounded. Flagg and Street held upon me the wary eyes of secret service guards.

I was not permitted to approach an open window. By the time the train had reached Washington my keepers had read over my speech and succeeded in agreeing on only one point: it was all wrong. Street held that it was too broad, Flagg that it was too narrow. Street declared the thought imperfect, Flagg contested that the thought was all right, but stuck to it that it was entirely lacking in local cracks. As soon as I reached the New Willard I hunted up a stenographer and sat until dressing time dictating a new speech. I had it typed on larger sheets, because the kind-hearted typist assured me that I could hide it inside my menu card. She had seen President Taft do the same thing.

A reception was being held outside the banquet hall. The dinner was late. In the very center of the carpet stood Hon. Joseph G. Cannon, shaking hands at a furious rate and saying the very things that Uncle Joseph would say to a magazine writer when dinner is late and his feet were beginning to hurt him. Presently a distinguished novelist approached me and said in the most matter-of-fact tone:

"Old man, how would you like to meet Joseph G. Cannon?"

I had never thought the matter over, but since he mentioned it I could find no objections. Therefore I was incorporated into the line, forming from left to right, and after a patient interval I found myself within easy radius of the twinkling eyes and witty chin-beard which have furnished pepper for a generation of congressmen.

"Mr. Cannon," said my friend in the easy voice of one familiar with the habits of the great, "I want you to meet Mr. Wallace Irwin, harbor commissioner of Honolulu."

"Pleased to meet you, Mr. Irwin," declared the National Uncle. "Fine place, the Islands. Fine, fine."

Whereupon he relinquished my hand for the next glad clasp. But my friend the novelist had been a humorist in his struggling days; therefore he persuaded me to take my place again in the line.

"This time we'll meet him right," he said. Therefore, when we had advanced to within shaking distance, he again introduced me:

"Mr. Cannon, permit me to present to you Mr. Wallace Irwin, president of the Cheeseborough National Bank."

"Glad to know you, Mr.——" He hesitated for the name, and when it was supplied he added, "Great work the bankers can do these days."

And I went my way.

The dinner was unusually late. During my famished wandering from door to door, again the novelist got me by the arm and swung me around the circle toward the great Speaker's busy hand.

"Mr. Cannon," he said this time, "I want you to meet Mr. Wallace Irwin, collector of the port of Guam."

The crowd was thinning by now, and Mr. Cannon had more time to consider my case.

"Glad to know you," he began; then, retaining my fingers in an unescapable clasp: "Say, young man, I don't know who and what you are. But I'll say this, you've got enough alibis to be a regular politician."

This should have been the end of my adventure, but it wasn't. I still had that awful speech folded in my inside pocket. The fatal dining-room doors opened at last. As I was going in I asked Julian Street, in passing, "Am I pale?" "All but your lips," he whispered consolingly. "They're bright blue."

It was the longest banquet table in the history of conversation. I sat at one end and Sam Blythe—who has made most of the public speeches I want to make—sat beside me.

"What are you doing with that essay?" he asked as soon as I strove to conceal my speech inside my menu.

"My speech," I gasped, moistening my cerulean lips with a little ice water.

"Oh," said Sam, who, being a kind soul, never willfully hurt a fellow man.

Later in the evening he turned and inquired, "What's that machine under the table?"

"My knees," I explained.

"I thought the table was over a dynamo or something," he said.

"What's the best way to begin a speech?" I at last found voice to inquire.

"I usually wait till I'm called on," he advised, "then I get up and talk."

I tried to keep his advice in mind.

F. Hopkinson Smith was, of course, toastmaster. The song birds of the Publishers' Association were warned that their time would come as soon as the official guests had finished. The official guests included President Taft, Hon. Joseph G. Cannon, several senators and the Mexican Ambassador. After a period of expensive malnutrition the speechmaking began. A great deal was said, I suppose; but I sat listening to the voice of my inner self. I would have torn up the typewritten pile, but the tremor of my fingers prevented me. Dimly in the audience I could see the great sad eyes of Julian Street. They were trying to convey some sort of helpful intelligence. Either they were advising me to go while the going was good or to brace up and take it standing. The President of the United States had a great deal to say, as was his right. The Speaker of the House had more. I sat in a horrid torpor, the electric chair yawning for its prey.

During the course of the evening I managed to steal over to F. Hopkinson Smith's chair and tremblingly

to plead that my speech come first among the publishers'
speakers.

"After the Mexican Ambassador finishes I'll call
on you," he conceded. "He'll only say three words
and sit down."

I resumed my seat, which had got hard and cold
in my absence. Life with its short pleasures and long
pains swam before me. Something told me it was
getting late. Sam Blythe informed me that the last
senator had taken an hour and thirteen minutes.
Finally out of the blur I heard the voice of F. Hopkinson Smith announcing the Mexican Ambassador.
Words of doom for me. I tried to pick up my
manuscript. Several pages of it, I found, had spilled
under the table and skidded beneath the feet of nation-
wide celebrities. Even as the Mexican Ambassador
arose, I was down on my hands and knees trying to
collect my scattered thoughts.

Then occurred the unexpected reprieve. The Man
from Mexico, it seemed, was not going to be content
with the three promised words. Something in the
international relations incensed or delighted him—
nobody knew which, because the gentleman spoke in a
Latin-American English which was a mystery to all
but himself. He went on and on. He quoted from
the little known Spanish poet, Ambroso del Todos los
Toros. He complimented the American magazines
and had a good word to say for each and every one of
them. Which was remarkable in itself. At last his
throat showed signs of giving out. He paused. Mr.
Smith glanced my way. I was icy cold from the waist
down. I saw the manuscript lying before me at page
11. The rest had vanished. My lips had grown dry
and hard as a cow's horn. The Mexican Ambassador
sat down amidst a torrent of congratulations.

"Mr. Wallace Irwin comes next on our program," proclaimed the toastmaster in ringing tones, "but, due to the lateness of the hour—it is now seven minutes past one—we must forgo the pleasure of listening to any more speeches."

After the banquet broke up I shook myself back into life and sought out the Mexican Ambassador and took him warmly by the hand. Tears were in my eyes as, almost hysterically, I thanked him again and again. He didn't know who I was nor what I was blessing him for—but by every nerve within my shattered system, I knew, I knew!

And the moral of my tale is this: If you are an author, remember that success lies hidden in the pad of paper on the blotter on the shelf of your writing desk. Your battle lies at that desk, struggling with all your might to put your heart and soul on the surface of white paper. Outside of that you may be an international tennis champion or an expert safe-breaker. That will not make you any better writer, but it may make you a more famous one.

For my part I was born to blush unseen in the small but not unknown town of Oneida, New York. It was on the morning of March 15, 1876, that I first saw the light, and my advent was a great encouragement to my father, no doubt, because it was less than four years later that he decided that the perils of the Wild West were preferable to slow starvation in Upper New York State. Therefore the Irwins, accompanied by their infant sons, William and Wallace, struck boldly out for Leadville, Colorado, a silver-camp situated several miles in the air among the Rocky Mountains.

Only a sunny disposition and maternal care saved me from becoming a Wild West writer, for the Irwins

subsisted on local color for several years. Between
my ninth and fourteenth years I lived on a broncho
and learned to read Elizabethan poetry from the
saddle. In my sixteenth year, when our establishment
was moved to Denver, I could quote pages of Shakespearean verse, which I spelled with more originality
than even the Bard of Avon could achieve. I graduated from the West Denver High School in 1895 and
went to college after a post-graduate year among
assayers and deputy sheriffs in Cripple Creek.

I graduated from Leland Stanford a year ahead of
my class—by special request of the faculty. From
this to newspaper poetry was an easy step, and I
earned a sparse livelihood writing rhymed headlines
for the *San Francisco Examiner*. Contributory to my
training as a humorist, I was morgue reporter for a
time, then Chinatown reporter—and in the latter
capacity I saw and learned more of Asiatic life than
ever went into the daily print.

A famous magazine editor came to San Francisco—
that was in the early days of the century—and I was
stunned by an invitation to meet him at luncheon.
Shortly before that I had written "The Love Sonnets
of a Hoodlum," which gained for me the passing
notoriety which, no doubt, inspired the invitation.
Half blind with glamour I basked in the presence of
the great man through six laborious courses, and upon
the arrival of coffee I gained his attention.

"What are the chances for a man like me in the
East?" I managed to ask.

"Immense!" cried the great man, who was an
enthusiast. "You're the type we're looking for, Irwin.
Don't waste your talents out here. And when you
come to New York see me at once."

I followed him two weeks later. I had nothing to

show, save a broken typewriter and a great eagerness.
I engaged rooms in the least expensive of the slums,
and upon the very day of my arrival, attacked my
typewriter with a frenzied determination to keep ahead
of the rent. Love, politics, domestic problems, holiday
humor—I choked the mails with rhymed manuscripts
which came back with such regularity that the branch
post office knew my address by heart before the month
was over.

Then, one drizzly morning, I bethought me of the
celebrated editor who, under the influence of San
Francisco fog, had stamped me as the type he was
looking for. Then and there I determined to sell
myself into bondage to his famous magazine.

I called at his office. He was in.

"How are you, Irwin!" he cried rapturously. "Have
a seat. Try one of these cigars. Been in town long?
Why didn't you let me know? Not trying to raise
your children in town, I hope."

"I haven't any children," said I meekly.

"Well," he snapped, "take 'em out into the country.
Town's no place for children."

I waited.

"Look here, Irwin," he demanded, coming suddenly
out of the silence, "how would you like to go to
Russia for us?"

"How would I like——" I could have kissed the
royal hand.

"Well, come round next Wednesday at 11:30 and
we'll talk it over."

I glided through air out of the office and into the
elevator. To think of it! In New York less than
a month and already a successful foreign correspondent,
practically.

On Wednesday I was in his office at 11:29. He

was there to receive me. He was obviously nervous about something.

"Oh. Hello, Irwin!" he cried, seeing me at last. "Been in town long? A month? Well, why didn't you look us up? Bring your children? Don't try to raise your children in New York . . ."

It was still forenoon when I returned to my inexpensive slum, uncovered my typewriter and went back to my thankless task of providing verse for a world which will always prefer prose.

I sold my first verse to *Life*. It was a rhyme about Abdul Hamid and the illustrator, as often happens, lost the manuscript. That was no trouble for me, as I knew it by heart. I became a daily rhymester for the *Globe* and from there went on the staff of *Collier's Weekly* where I began with a series of metrical satires, usually abusive, directed at the heads of public characters.

There I invented "The Letters of a Japanese Schoolboy," the dialect being founded on actual letters written to me by Japanese while I was a college student. The first of the Togo articles was written as an experiment, its inspiration being an attack upon Japanese coolies in British Columbia. They became a weekly feature after that, and for six months or so the public was allowed to believe that Hashimura Togo was a real Japanese.

I attempted fiction rather late, although I carried around with me an invertebrate short story—something about a comic Mexican bull fight—and only managed to dispose of it after it had undergone many deaths and as many rebirths. My first short stories appeared in *McClure's* about 1913. My first novel was "Venus in the East" and was published in the *Saturday Evening Post*.

The rest of my life, as we might say, is fiction. Or, in so far as I am a fact, I am a mild-mannered bourgeois of forty-six, undustrious, sedentary, of medium height, a hater of rice and Sir Walter Scott. I love my wife and should be taking up golf, but I have a Complex to the effect that, should I be discovered swinging a mashie, somebody will be saying, "It's good for a man of his age. We knew he'd come to it sooner or later."

P. S. BY T. L. M.

It chanced that I was present at the dinner to which Irwin refers, and I can vouch for the truth of his account in every particular. He has written nothing more humorous—or so it appears to me.

His advice about oratory should not be taken too literally however. It is possible to be a good writer and also a good speaker. Mr. Irvin Cobb is both, and so is Mr. Simeon Ford. And then Irwin is much better on his feet than he would like to admit. Most humorists are.

CHAPTER XVIII

BURGES JOHNSON

BURGES JOHNSON voices the popular discontent among successful humorists when he writes me that he should feel "most uncomfortable," if he found himself appearing in twice as many pages as given to a writer of three times his ability. Well, as a matter of fact, the amount of space given in this book to anybody or everybody is no gauge. If a man were absolutely nothing else but a humorist he would be entitled to no space at all. When he is a humanist and a humorist also he begins to grow. The truth is that Burges Johnson is altogether too modest in his estimate of himself—as a humorist, in the sketch that follows. Also he has given absolutely no indication of what he is, as a man. The truth is also, that, as a man, he is a "corker." When I die, it is possible that I shall invite some humorists to sit with me at certain times of every day. I haven't quite made up my mind about that. But, if I do, Burges Johnson will head the list. And he probably will not accept my invitation. He knows me.

This is what he writes about himself:

Mr. Burges Johnson says that he was born in Vermont in 1877. He followed his father (who was

182

a clergyman) to several successive parishes, where he
may or may not have assisted in the parochial labors.
In Chicago, he prepared for college, and graduated later
from Amherst. He states that the ambition to be a
writer led him, after many fruitless attacks upon
editors, to solve the problem of publication in the only
really effective way. He, himself, became an editor
and bought his own stuff. This accounts for the fact
that his writings first appeared in the pages of *Harper's*
and *Everybody's* magazines. For one eventful year
he was editor-in-chief of *Judge*.

The academic life always had allurement and, after
some experimenting with educational publishing, he
accepted an invitation to teach at Vassar College, where
he is at this present time, directing the official publications of the college and conducting a course which he
calls "journalistic writing." During the six years that
he has been there, thirty-five per cent of his graduates
have begun earning their living in journalistic pursuits.
Mr. Johnson admits that his underlying purpose in this
teaching work is to place so many of his students in
editorial positions that, in his old age, he can sell his
own manuscript to them without inconvenience. He
has published various books, including verse and
essays. Just why he appears in this compendium he
does not know. Reports that he is a humorist are
greatly exaggerated.

CHAPTER XIX

PHILANDER CHASE JOHNSON, who for more than thirty years past has contributed verse, dialogue, editorial paragraphs, and dramatic criticism to the *Washington* (D. C.) *Star,* was born in Wheeling, W. Va. His father, S. E. Johnson, was a well-known writer in Cincinnati and editorial correspondent in Washington, D. C. After newspaper service in various capacities in Cincinnati, Chicago and Washington, D. C., Philander Johnson established a connection with the *Washington Star,* and developed the characters "Senator Sorghum," "Farmer Corntossel," "Uncle Eben," "Mr. and Mrs. Torkins" and a number of others that have long been prominently identified with current newspaper humor. He has been remarkably prolific in versification, his uninterrupted daily production including at least two examples of this form. His most popular verses, "Somewhere in France Is the Lily," was set to music and became one of the conspicuous ballads of the World War period. He is a character number of King Solomon Lodge, the daylight Masonic Lodge of Washington, and has contributed prominently to the unique entertainments of the Gridiron, of whose music committee he was, for many

years, the chairman.   His home is in Cleveland Park,
D. C., much of his working and leisure time, however,
being passed on the shores of the Manasquan River, in
New Jersey.

CHAPTER XX

THE *Saturday Evening Post* literature has come to be known, to use the language which is assumed to be familiar to those that use its columns, as "in a class by itself."

Whether the *Saturday Evening Post* has stifled what literature may have been about to spring up among us, or whether it has stimulated its growth and been the medium through which it has been expressed—all this is the subject for a passionate debate. My own opinion is, that it is one of our greatest and cleanest educational influences.

It may be said that those that decry the *Saturday Evening Post* literature are the ones that have not succeeded—again descending into the vernacular—in "breaking into" it.

The actual fact is that the *Saturday Evening Post* has published more readable stories, many of them in the very first class, than any other magazine in America. It has introduced more new writers to the public during the past decade, than any other magazine. And, among these, not the least is Ring Lardner.

Mr. Lardner once told me that his success as a writer could be summed up in two words: he "listened hard."

Undoubtedly he sprang from the soil. And he caught
the language of those that, like him, had also sprung
It is always a debatable matter of course, how far a
writer can go in his delineation of character by using
the vocabulary of the common people. Every great
writer has done it, but has done it with unerring insight.
The dialect of some of Shakespeare's characters strikes
us now as barbaric, particularly his Irish characters.
His grave-digger's scene in "Hamlet" is immortal, as
is his Justice Shallow's patter. But, it is in the contrast
between the language of the slums and the heights of
thought, as expresesd through the finest shades of
meaning, that Shakespeare is supreme.

Ring Lardner is naturally not quite like this. He
would be willing to admit that Shakespeare had him up
against the ropes when it comes to "hitting off" a
human being. Ring Lardner is more modest than
Bernard Shaw. He is so modest, indeed, that I don't
think he has ever thought of modesty as applied to any
writer. He appears to me to be a perfectly normal type
of American, with a fine talent for expression, who
has used the only medium that he is familiar with,
namely, the language of the people. It is not fine
language—on the contrary, it may give to some of us
a hopeless feeling that, if these things are the best things
the average American is talking about, we would better
revise our school system. But it is human language—
the kind you hear, and Ring Lardner reproduces it with
fatal familiarity. He attempts nothing more. He has
no need of doing so. Within his scope, he has produced true humor—a kind of humor that carries along
with it a gentle glow of freshness and gayety—an

atmosphere in which we can actually smell the soil itself. It is often horrible, but it is true.

That is to say, it is true in so far as Ring Lardner is a true reporter of it, and this is all that any writer can be, for every good writer is only a reporter. He carries to us the news about human beings. And books are interesting only as they are able to convey this news. For example, Shakespeare reported the news about human qualities. He was able, through his genius, to show them off in contrast with the vast background of humanity. He told us things about human beings that we might have known before, but he recast them, gave them vividness of color and setting, and thus brought out their contrasts. Unless the writer can give us something of news about his people, he will invariably fall flat. So, when we read Ring Lardner, we recognize that he is reporting for us a certain kind of atmosphere. He has listened, and this is the result.

But, in addition, he has a dramatic talent of high order. He would not be a humorist if he did not have sentiment. He is, therefore, able to produce a story that (once more to descend) "gets" us. It is low-brow stuff. But it is the best of low-brow stuff.

I have heard so many high-brows dismiss Ring Lardner as not being a part of the scheme of literary things—as they understand literary things—that I feel some obligation to report Ring Lardner himself. I have interviewed him. And he has written things about himself, not only for others, but for me. It was with the greatest reluctance that he did this. But he did it.

First, however, let me give a small extract from his writings. It is not the best. But it is characteristic. It is not a story. It is just a so-called humorous sketch.

A Small Vocabulary May Have a Big Kick

To the Editor:

The other night I was to a party where they had a argument in regards to how many wds. is in the average man or lady's vocabulary which they meant how many wds. does a person use in their regular every day conversation and one lady said 4 or 5 thousand and one of the men give her the laugh and said 700 was nearer the mark, and of course I didn't take no part in the argument as they was all my elders but that didn't keep me from thinking over the question and maybe some of my readers would be interested in doing the same.

Well, in the first place you would naturally suppose that a woman's vocabulary was a lot bigger than a man's on acct. of them talking so much more, but on second thoughts that don't prove nothing as you will notice that the most women say the same thing over and over and a woman might say 10,000 wds. per day but only 10 different wds. like for inst.:

"I wished we had a fire. The house is cold," which she is libel to say a 1000 times makeing a total of 10,000 wds. that don't mean nothing.

As a matter of fact, a man though he don't talk nowheres near as much, don't repeat himself nowheres near as often, a specially since they fixed it so he had to quit saying, "Give us another," so wile a man may talk 100 wds. a day to a woman's 10,000, still they's libel to be 50 different wds. amongst his 100 and sometimes even more than that, though if a man does say

100 wds. the chances are that at lease 50 of them is "Well."

Some men of course has more to say than others and they's been evenings in my career when I only said 2 wds. the whole evening namely "stay" and "pass" and a few afternoons spent outdoors when my conversation was just the numeral wds. "seven" and "eight."

When all is said and done I suppose the number of wds. a person talks depends on what line of business they are in, like for example a doctor talks practically all the time where as a engineer on a R. R. or a fisherman don't hardly say nothing, and even some people talks more than others in the same business like for inst. a elevator man in a 22 story bldg. has twice as much to say as a elevator man in a 11 story bldg. and a train man on a subway local has to name maybe 30 or 35 stations while a train man on a express only names 4 or 5, but as far as that is conserned for all the good they do, the both of them might as well keep their mouth shut.

A box office man in a N. Y. theatre only has to say 2 wds. all day, namely, "Seventeenth row."

A man that runs a garage can get along on even less, as all he has to do is say, "No," when people call up to ask is their car ready yet.

In the old days, barbers use to do a lot of talking. They had a vocabulary of about 1000 wds. which they would repeat them the same number of times per day as they had clients in their chairs, but the funny papers and etc. begin to kid barbers about talking so as now a barber is almost scared to even say your hair is falling out, but it's agony for them to keep their mouth shut and their wifes must get he-ll when they get home.

A traffic policeman's conversation varies according

to what time of day it is. In the morning he only has
to say "What do you think you are trying to do?"
which is 9 wds. all together and only 7 of them different, but along in the afternoon when he ain't feeling
so genial he adds 2 wds. makeing it:

"What the hell do you think you are trying to do?"

As for the motor man on a st. car they's generally
always a sign that says don't talk to the motorman and
I use to think that meant you mustn't talk to him on
acct. of it bothering him and takeing his mind off his
work, but wile rideing on the front platform of st. cars
in N. Y. and Chicago I come to the conclusion that he
don't want to be interrupted.

The facts of the matter is that nobody likes nobody
for their vocabulary and no man ever married a gal
because she could say 5000 wds. besides yes or because
she couldn't, and on the contrary one of my best
friends is a man that don't hardly ever open his mouth
only to take a fresh chew, but they say its nice for a
person to know a whole lot of wds. even if they don't
use them so when they are in church or rideing on a
train or something they can amuse themselfs counting
up the wds. they know.

As for a big vocabulary getting a person anywheres
or doing them any good, they's a party liveing in our
house that is 2 yrs. old and I don't suppose he has got
a vocabulary of more than 200 wds. and even some of
them sounds foreign, but this bird gets whatever he
wants and I don't know of nobody who I would rather
trade jobs with.

Which is about all the wds. I can write about wds.,
only to recommend to the reader a kind of a game
I tried out the other day which was a couple of days
after the party and the game was to try and think
every time before I spoke and count the number of

wds. I used and count how many of them was necessary
and how many could be left out and of course I forgot
a couple times and said things without thinking or
counting them, but you would be surprised at the few
number of wds. it is necessary for a person to say
in the course of a day and personally I come to the
conclusion that a dumb mute ain't so much to be pitied
after all and the people around him less.

RING W. LARDNER.

This piece is undoubtedly strained in spots; it is
reminiscent; it shows the defects of its qualities. In
miniature, it is representative of the weakness and
strength of the greater part of our writing. Ring
Lardner, at his best, is much better than this. But, in
"sizing up" such an important figure in our contemporary letters, (and do not believe for a moment that
Mr. Lardner is not important) one must be accurate.
He is an American humorist of no mean proportions.
His "stuff" is read by millions. He is popular, and deservedly so. We should not be fooled by what appears
to be his commonness. In fact, he is not common at
all, or common only when he brings in such allusions to
poker as he has done in this sketch: that is to say,
drawing on the old stock jokes. We are all guilty of
doing that. There is a sense in which the reader would
not understand us if we didn't. It has been my own
experience that a man, give him rope enough, can talk
much faster than a woman, and often much less to the
point; yet, for generations, a woman's tongue has been
a subject for jest; therefore, in any humorous article,
it may be proper to allude to this matter, as Lardner

does in his sketch. I remember quite well the visit of a widely known reciter to my own home town. The chairman of the committee that engaged him was fearful that he would "spring" too many old jokes, and so took him aside before the entertainment and requested him to be as original as possible, bearing in mind that the audience (as usual) was a very "cultured" one.

The reciter was quite game. He declared his sympathy and appreciation of the whole situation. And, during the first part of the evening, regaled his hearers with lofty humor—humor that was quite "literary," but produced nothing but intense silence. The chairman was greatly alarmed. During the recess, he remarked, with sobs in his voice, that the "evening wasn't going at all."

"You would have it so," replied the reciter with a bland smile. "It is not, however, too late; if you will allow me, I will save your reputation and mine."

He thereupon proceeded, during the latter half of the evening, to tell them about mothers-in-law, about poker, and about ladies that talk, until it is no exaggeration to say that the entire audience was convulsed, and voted him the funniest speaker they had ever listened to.

This is what every humorist knows. He must play to the gallery. At the same time, it is extremely unjust to judge a humorist altogether by the old jokes he may spring. To be a real humorist, he must have that other thing—real originality, real insight. Ring Lardner undoubtedly has these. The people know, quite largely. You cannot fool them all the time. Personally, I have been able to get out of Ring Lardner some of the most pleasurable glows I have ever had. He is a real Amer-

ican, a delightful story-teller, a quite unique repro-
ducer, or reporter, of the feelings that we all have.

And this is what he says about writing:

Inside Facts of the Writing Game

In the first place the average party has got a magazine editor all wrong witch they usually are. They
think he is a man that will give everybody a square
deal where as the most of them lets their personal feelings and tempermunt get the best of them. For inst.
a new beginner is libel to be discouraged because their
manuscript comes back on them and they think to
themself that the story couldn't of been no good or
the editor would of eat it up and they may as well
give up writeing and try something else.

Well the U. S. is probably dirty with these kind of
people that would of made grand authors if they hadn't
of became discouraged on acct. of their ignorants of
editors and how to handle them. The best rule for a
new beginner to follow is to 1st. get a idear for a story
and then forget the idear and go ahead and write the
story out or dictate it to somebody that has got a good
hand writeing or better yet one of these new fangle
machines called a typewriter that makes it look all most
like print.

Then put a good suggestive title on the story like for
inst. "Clara's Calves" and then give it to your family
to read and if they say it reads good why it must be
good and the next question is how to get it before a
magazine editor and get a square deal. The most
magazine editors don't want good stories as it crowds
out the ads and in the 2d. place the most editors won't
read manuscripts themself because it keeps them away
from hockey so they give them to the wife and kiddies

and leave them pass judgment or if they do read them themself, why the chances are they have got a secret grudge vs. you for something that maybe 1 of your relatives done to them, or you got the same name as somebody they don't like and that is enough to knock your chances for a gool from field.

But 1 of the biggest mistakes a new beginner makes is to send return stamps along with their manuscript as most of the editors is air tight and the minute they see stamps that somebody else has boughten why they can't wait a minute till they use them, and whist, back comes your manuscript. I remember once, before I became a wise cracker, that I sent a stamped self address envelope along with a good story I wrote and the old skin flint shot it back to me pro tem all because he couldn't do nothing else with a addressed envelope with the stamps stuck to it and couldn't bear to see it wasted. Both my sisters read the story I speak of and said it was a pip, and I wished the old Shylock could of heard what they said about him for sending it back.

Well, then the only way to get a square deal from a editor is to scrap up a acquaintance with somebody that is all ready in the writeing game, and the editor knows who he is and got respects for him, and then have this bird write a letter for you to send along with the manuscript, and have him say in the letter that your story is O. K. and the editor is a sap if he don't accept because you have got a lot of friends that will stop their subscription if that story comes back. These kind of letters makes a editor think twice, and they tell me that even a author like Irvin Cobb don't never think of sending in a mss. without getting somebody down in Washington to write and tell the editor where he will head in at if they's any monkey business.

So much for how to get a square deal after your
story is wrote. As for the writeing itself, a good many
new beginners falls down because they try and write
their story without the right atmosphere to work in.
I can't give no advice on this subject, as different
authors demands different working conditions.   For
inst. they say Rupert M. Hughes can't write a line unlest the water is running in the bath tub, and Fannie
Hurst won't attempt to work without the room is full
of sardine cans, where as when the editor wants a story
out of Mrs. Rhinehart they get somebody to stand
and snap a rubber band at her neck.   Personally I
never feel comfortable at my desk unlest they's a dozen
large rats parked on my ft.   These inst. will give you
a idear of how different tempermunts effects different
writers but, as I say, each writer has to chose for themself what tempermunt to have, and I might advise you
to try writeing in a public garage, whereas you might
do your best work setting in a eel trap.

Ring Lardner, in my opinion, has not yet written
his best work.   In fact, he is only just beginning.
There is a sense in which he is much too popular to be
as good as he might be.   That is really the difficulty
with America.   We have as much raw talent—indeed
positive genius—as any other country, if not more.
But our popular writers get carried away by their own
success.   Form is what counts in literature, as in everything else.   Many of our best writers start out with
the best intentions and the best form, but they become
swamped later by their own success.   It is not their
fault.   We are too material, that is to say, we are too
wasteful, and wastefulness leads to large materialism,
because one can afford to throw away a thing that is

only half done and take up something new. We do
this with our resources, and our writers naturally come
to think they can do this with theirs. No American
writer has a chance to develop himself to the utmost.
When he gets about halfway, he is successful, and to
be successful is always fatal.

The real trouble with our literature is that it has
never produced any failures.

The real trouble with Mr. Lardner, as with so many
others, is that he has been able (again!) to "get away
with it." The question now remains whether he will
grow better. He *must* grow better. He has got to
get better. We need him. This is what he writes
about getting to be thirty-five, for his friend, John
Siddall, of the *American Magazine:*

In regards to this article: When the Editor asked
me to write it up I said I didn't see how more than
only a few people would be interested because they
was only a few that is this old. So he told me that, as
a matter of fact, pretty near everybody in the world
that can read is either 35 or a few mos. one way or
the other and if I didn't think that was so to go and
look it up in a book. So I looked up in the encyclopedia
and they was nothing in there like he said, but I found
out a whole lot of other things that was news to me
and maybe the reader don't know them neither so I
will write them down.

In the 1st. place, it says that most people dies when
they are 1 yr. old and the 1st. 10 yrs. is the most
fatalist. But if they's a 100 thousand people that can
manage to get to be 10 yrs. old why then 749 of them
is pretty libel to die the yext yr. After that, the older

you get the longer you live up to when you are 59, and then you can just about count on liveing 14 and 7-10 yrs. more. In other wds. if you ain't one of the 749 that crokes between 10 and 11, why you are safe till about June of the yr. when you are 73. So a person is a sucker to try and take care of themself at my age, and from now on I am going to be a loose fish and run wild.

Out in Benton Harbor, Mich., however, near where I use to live, they have got a sex that calls themselfs the Holy Terrors or something that claims you live as long as you are good and as soon as you do wrong you die. But I notice that they all wear a beard so as the encyclopedia can't tell if they are 73 or 21.

Another thing it says in the book is that figures compiled in Norway and Sweden shows that the death rate amongst bachelors is a lot more than amongst married men even includeing murder. So anybody that is between 11 and 73 yrs. old and got a wife is prac-tally. death proof especially if you are a Swede.

But all that is either here or there. The idear is to tell how it feels to be my age and I may as well get to it. Well, in the 1st. place, I am speaking for myself only. I don't know how how the other 35 yr. olders feels about it and don't care. Probably the most of them don't feel near as old as the writer. Laughter is supposed to keep a man young but if its forced laughter it works the opp. When a guy is named Ring W. and is expected to split their sides when ever somebody asks if your middle name is Worm which is an average of 365 times per annum over a period of 35 annums, why it can't help from telling on you. Or it don't lighten the wgt. of the yrs. none to half to snicker every time they say Ring give me a ring, or Ring why ain't you a ring master in Ringling Bros.

And yet a number of birds has asked me if that was
my real name or did I assume it. They would probably
ask the kaiser if he moved to Holland to be near the
tulips.

I suppose that, on the morning of their 21st. birthday, the right kind of a American citizen wakes up
full of excitement and says to themself "Now I am
of age and can vote and everything." And when they
come to what I often call the 35th. mile stone they are
even more smoked up with the thought that now they
are eligible to be President, and go around all day
stoop shouldered with the new responsability.

Well, I don't recall how I woke up the day I was
21 if at all but my last birthday is still green and sour
in my memory. I spent the most of it in Mineola
signing mortgages, and if I thought of the White
House, it was just to wonder if it would do any good
to write and tell President Wilson about the Long
Island R. R.

At the present writeing I have got so use to being
35 that I don't know if it feels any different from
34 or 33. But I can at least state that being 35 don't
feel nothing like being under 30. For inst. when the
telephone rings now days I am scared to death that its
somebody asking us to go somewheres for dinner or
somewheres. Six yrs. ago I was afraid it wasn't. At
29, home was like they say on the vaudeville stage, a
place to go when all the other joints was closed up.
At 35 its a place you never leave without a loud
squawk.

A man don't appreciate their home till you are up
around par for 9 holes. Under 30, you think of it as
a dump where you can't pick out what you want to
eat, like roast Vt. turkey or a filet mignon or some
of that prune fed muskrat a la Biltmore. If Kathleen

decides in the A. M. that you are going to crave spare ribs at night, why you can either crave spare ribs at night or put on a hunger strike that won't get you no more sympathy than the hiccups.

In them ribald days home is just a kind of a pest where you half to choke down breakfast or they will think something ails you and talk about sending for a Dr. And 1 or 2 evenings per wk. when you can't think of no reason to go out, its where you half to set around and wait for 9 o'clock so as you begin to talk about going to bed, and sometimes things gets so desperate that you half to read a book or something.

But at 35 you spell it with a big H. Its where you can take off your shoes. Its where you can have more soup. Its where you don't half to say nothing when they's nothing to say. Its where they don't wait till the meal is all over and then give you a eye dropper full of coffee raw. Its where you don't half to listen. Its where they don't smear everything with cheese dressing. Its where you can pan everybody without it going no further. Its where they know you like doughnuts and what you think about a banana.

When you was 29 you didn't care for the band to play "Home sweet Home." It was old stuff and a rotten tune any way. Now you hope they won't play it neither. Its a pretty tune but it makes you bust out crying.

Bud Kelland that lives over to Port Washington wrote a piece for this magazine a wile ago where he said in it that it kind of shocked him to find out that young people didn't act like he was one of them no more. Well he ain't, but it took the old gaffer a long time to find it out. Here he is pretty near 39 and I guess the old Methuselum wants folks to hide I Mary Mac Lane when he comes in the rm.

Well it was 5 or 6 yrs. ago when I realized that I was past my nonages as they say. It come to me all of a sudden that the only compliments I had for a long wile was what a pretty tie you got or something. Nothing about my natural charms no more. It was an egg's age since anybody had called me to 1 side and whispered "I got a T. L. for you. Gertie thinks your ears is immense."

I seen then that I wasn't no longer a larva and I guess maybe it hurt at first. But its like falling hair or the telephone service or anything else. When you have lived with it a wile you don't mind. Which is just as well because they ain't a wk. passes when you wouldn't get touched on the raw if they was any raw left.

Like for inst. a few wks. back I was up in Boston where I got a young and beautiful sister-in-law. When it come time to part from she and her husband she kissed me 6 times, which was supposed to be once for me and once apiece for the Mrs. and 4 kiddies. Well I thought it was pretty nice and got kind of excited about it till I looked at her husband to see how he took it. He took it without batting an eye. To him it was like as if she was kissing an old cab horse on a bet for the benefit of the Red Cross. And when I had left and they was alone together, instead of lepping at her throat with a terrible curse he probably says "Janey, you're a good game gal," and she give him a kiss that meant something.

Now an incident like this would of spoilt my whole trip if I didn't look at it in a sensible way, which is to say to yourself, "Well if I wasn't in the Sears and yellow I wouldn't of got them 6 kisses. And 6 kisses is ½ a dozen kisses in any language."

Or for inst. out on the golf course. Suppose I and

Grant Rice is playing with some young whipper snapper like say Jack Wheeler and they's only 1 caddy for the 3 of us. "Take them two" says Jack pointing to my and Grant's bags but the caddy has all ready took them any way as soon as he found out which ones belonged to which. Or when one of my young brother in laws is around the house and I come in the rm. and they are setting in the easy chair, why they jump up like food shot from guns and say "Here take this chair."

All and all when you get hardened to it they's many advantages in reaching your dottage. When they's 7 passengers for a 7 passenger car its never you that has to take one of them little torture seats. When your brother in law is here on a visit and the Mrs. thinks it would be nice to have a fire in the fire place, you ain't the one that has got to ruin his clothes. Yes, friends the benefits is many fold but if them ½ a dozen kisses and a few stray others pretty near as good was all, why you could still think to yourself Youth may get good service, but 35 ain't makeing no complaints to the management neither.

As for the gen. symptoms of 35 and vicinity as I have found them, and not speaking for nobody, only myself you understand, the following points may interest science:

1. The patient sometimes finds himself and one lady the only people left at the table and all the others is danceing. They seems to be nothing for it but to get up and dance. You start and the music stops and the young buddies on the flr. claps their hands for a encore. The patient claps his hands too but not very loud and he hopes to high heaven the leader will take it in a jokeing way.

2. For some reason another its necessary to find

some old papers and, in going through the trunk, the
patient runs acrost a bunch of souvenirs and keep
sakes like a note a gal wrote him in high school, a
picture of himself in a dirty football suit, a program
of the 1907 May festival in South Bend and etc.
"Why keep this junk" he says and dumps them all in
the waste basket.

3.   The case develops nausea in the presents of all
story tellers except maybe Irvin Cobb and Riley Wilson
and Bert Williams.   Any others has to work pretty
fast to get him cornered.   Violent chills attends the
sound of those saddest wds. of tongue or pen "I don't
know if you heard this one or not but it struck me
funny.   It seems they was a woman went in a dry-
goods store in Detroit to buy some towels.   Stop me
if you heard it before."   You couldn't stop them with
big Bertha.   The best funny storys is Balzac's because
they are in a book and you don't half to buy it.   But
when you get up vs. one of these here voluntary stag
entertainers you either got to listen and laugh or they
put you down as a dumb bell.

4.   The invalid goes to a ball game and along comes
the last ½ of the 14th. innings and the score is 1 and
1 and the 1st. guy up makes a base hit.   The patient
happens to look at his watch and it says 11 minutes to
6 and if he leaves the park right away he can make
the 6:27 home where as if he waits a few min. he
will half to take the 6:54.   Without no hesitation he
leaves the park right away and makes the 6:27.

5.   The subject is woke up at 3 A. M. by the
fire whistle.   He sniffles but can't smell no smoke.
He thinks well it ain't our house and goes back to
sleep.

6.   He sets down after breakfast to read the paper.
The mail man comes and brings him 3 letters.   One

of them looks like it was a gal's writeing. He reads the
paper.

7. He buys a magazine in April and reads the first
instalment of a misery serial. The instalment winds
up with the servants finding their master's body in bed
and his head in the ash tray. Everything pts. to the
young wife. Our patient forgets to buy the May
number.

8. Somebody calls up and says they are giveing a
party Thursday night for Mabel Normand and can you
come. Our hero says he is sorry but he will be in
Washington on business. He hasn't no more business
in Washington than Gov. Cox.

9. They's a show in town that you got to see like
Frank Craven or "Mecca." "It's a dandy night" says
the Mrs. "Shall we drive in or take the train?"
"We will take the train" says our hero.

These is a few of the symptoms as I have observed
them and as I say I am speaking for just myself and
maybe I am a peculiar case. They may not be another
35 yr. older in the world that is affected the same
way and in fact I know several suffers about that age
which I am as different than as day and night. Take
Jess Willard for inst. He was somewheres around
35 in July 1919 and Dempsey knocked him down 7
times in one rd. He wouldn't do that to me, not 7
times he wouldn't. Or look at Ty Cobb. Do you
think they would get me to play center field and manage
a ball club for $30,000? Or would Jim Thorpe's
brother-in-law look on him as too frail to hobble down
in the basement and get a few sticks of wood?

On the other hand they might be 2 or 3 brother
eagles in the mediocer 30s that is even more mildewed
than me, but I am afraid they's a whole lot more of
them feels like a colt. They take care of themselfs.

When they get up in the A. M. they take a cold plunge
and then hang by their eye teeth on a hook in the
closet while they count 50 in Squinch.   And noons,
when they come back from their lunch of hot milk and
ferns, they roll over on the office rug 10 times without
bending their shin.

I can't compete with these babies.   I slice a few
golf balls in season but bet. Nov. and May the only
exercise I get or want to get is twice a wk. when
I take the buttons out of shirt A and stick them in
shirt B.

They's still another crowd yet that renews their
youth by going back every yr. to commencement or a
class reunion or something.   Well, I don't know if I
want to renew my youth or not.   Leave bad enough
alone is my slogum.   And in the 2d. place I don't half
to go nowheres to a class reunion.   I could hold it in
the bath tub.   I was the only one that graduated when
I did, as it was in March of my freshman yr. and they
didn't seem to be haveing no commencement exercises
for nobody else.   I guess I must have been one of these
here infantile proteges like that 11 mos. old junior they
got up to Columbia.

No article of this kind would be complete without
shooting a few wds. of unwanted advice at my youngers
and betters.   For inst. John D. tells the boys how to
build up a fortune and John Jones tells them how to
rise from a white wings to a steeple jack.   So it looks
like it was up to me to tell them how to get to be what
I am, 35 yrs. old.

Well, my lads, they's 4 rules that I made and have
stuck to them and I think you will find they'll bring
you the same results.   The 1st. rule is don't die the
1st. yr.   The 2d. rule is don't be one of the 749 that
dies when they are 11.   The 3d rule is don't pick a

quarrel with a man like Dempsey.   And the 4th. and
last rule is marry a girl like Sue.

In explanations of that last rule I will say that the
one I married ain't Sue but the name don't make no
differents if she is the right kind of a gal.   And the
reason I say that is because its customary in these
intimate capital I talks to throw in a paragraph of
blurb about the little woman.   What ever success a
man has had he has got to pretend he owes it to Her.
So if they's any glory to be gleaned out of my success
in reaching 35 and looking even older, why she can
have it.

What fooling that is!   One may read on and on,
knowing that one is not going to get anywhere so far
as Ring Lardner himself is concerned, and not caring
whether one does or not.

I wanted to put it in this book, and got his permission to do so, and after it had been placed, it then occurred to me that it was too interesting.   And besides,
it had none of that dull and useful information about
Lardner himself that one is bound to expect in a book
like this.   It was impossible for me to tell just what
had happened to Ring Lardner that had made him as
good as he is, without calling upon him once more.
And so I got him—with much preliminary pain—to
write what follows about himself:

I was born at Niles, Michigan, on the 6th of March,
1885, and soon entered the high school.   I kept right
up with the rest of the class, and we all graduated
together.   In those days the graduate with the best
scholastic record was awarded a scholarship at Olivet

College. It wasn't offered to me, possibly because it was a Methodist college and I was an Episcopalian.

I wanted to go to the University of Michigan and take football and dentistry, so I was sent to Armour Institute, Chicago, to study mechanical engineering. At the end of the first semester, I passed in rhetoric and out of Armour.

That was in the early spring of 1902. During the next year and a half I took part in two minstrel shows, and then came an opening as bookkeeper at the gas-office. I felt exhausted and didn't want to take it, but my father coaxed me into it in a few well-chosen words. I learned one thing on this job—That there's a lot of cheating done in the gas business, and it's all done by the consumers. The company doesn't have to cheat.

When I had been there two years, the editor of the *South Bend* (Ind.) *Times* came to town to see my brother. He was a (the, to be exact) reporter on the *Niles Sun* and the *Times'* Niles correspondent. The *Times* wanted him to join its reportorial staff. He was out of town, so the editor came to the gas-office and hired me. I had no newspaper experience, but a two years' course in a gas-office teaches you practically all there is to know about human nature. Besides, I had been class poet at the high school, and knew I could write.

My position on the *Times* was sporting editor and staff, dramatic critic, society and court-house reporter, and banquet hound. My hours were from 8 A. M. on.

In the fall of 1907, I attended the world's series games at Chicago, met Hughey Fullerton, and, through him, landed as a sport reporter on the *Inter-Ocean.* Thereafter, reading from left to right, I was baseball and football writer on the *Chicago Examiner* and *Chicago Tribune,* editor of *Sporting News,* a St. Louis baseball publication, baseball reporter on the *Boston American,* copy reader on the *Chicago American,* once more baseball writer on the *Examiner,* and column conductor on the *Chicago Tribune.*

In January, 1914, I wrote a baseball story and sent it to the *Saturday Evening Post.* It was accepted and published. I wrote some more and they were accepted and published. Mr. Lorimer is a good man and a great editor. The same may be said of a great many editors of big magazines.

But now I am trying to horn into the play-writing game and may deal less with editors and more with theatrical men. And may God have mercy on my soul!

CHAPTER XXI

STEPHEN LEACOCK

WITHOUT this dishonorable explanation issued as a mean method of circumventing critics, I should probably receive a number of letters asking me why I write about Stephen Leacock in a book presumed to be exclusively about American humorists.

I know in advance all the reasons why I shouldn't do it—that Stephen Leacock was evolved in Canada, dating from the year 1876, that he is a political economist, that he is too funny to be an American humorist, and so forth and so forth.

And what difference does all this make to me? I am determined to write about Stephen Leacock. If he had been born in Patagonia I should write about him. There are others that I've got to write about: but I haven't got to write about Leacock, and that is why I am writing about him.

Besides, he is worth writing about, and he is just as much an American for my purpose as if he had been born in Ohio. There are no fences between Canada and this country, and Leacock has more readers here than anywhere else. He writes for us, and about us, and the first recognition he got as a humorist came through us. I recall even now one of his earliest sketches (if not his first), that was published in *Life*, "My Financial Career." It was not only copied broadcast and is now a classic, but still remains one of the best bits of humor in the anthologies.

Mr. Leacock had his handicaps. He became a political economist. Think of the courage of any man who is a political economist daring to become a humorist! He was once asked how the university dignitaries regarded him, especially the humor written at their expense. "At first," he said, "they were rather upset, but now they don't mind a jot. Of course if I had failed I would have been called a jackass; as it is I am a pet product."

Perhaps it was because he started his career on soda biscuits that he came to be so eminent. Of this he writes:

When I was a student at the University of Toronto thirty years ago, I lived—from start to finish—in seventeen different boarding houses. As far as I am aware these houses have not, or not yet, been marked with tablets. But they are still to be found in the vicinity of McCaul and Darcy, and St. Patrick streets. Any one who doubts the truth of what I have to say may go and look at them.

I was not alone in the nomadic life that I led. There were hundreds of us drifting about in this fashion from one melancholy habitation to another. We lived as a rule two or three in a house, sometimes alone. We dined in the basement. We always had beef, done up in some way after it was dead, and there were always soda biscuits on the table. They used to have a brand of soda biscuits in those days in the Toronto boarding houses that I have not seen since. They were better than dog biscuits but with not so much snap. My contemporaries will all remember them. A great many of the leading barristers and professional men of Toronto were fed on them.

This chapter about "Steve" Leacock, as the reader is doubtless already aware, cannot be an orderly proceeding. I tried to make it so, mapping it out as if I were a first-class understudy to an efficiency expert: but when one thinks of Leacock, all order must be abandoned: in the end, if you don't mind literary disorder, you will know as much about him as I have learned, and you may then rearrange it to suit yourself.

I recall the first time I saw him, after having read him for many years. To be frank, it was disappointing. It generally is. A friend said to me recently: "I never want to meet a genius personally," and so our first impressions of eminent persons, and oftentimes our later ones, are apt to be disappointing.

He talked about "whiskers"—when they began and where they left off, their relationship to literature, their moral effect and so on. It was excruciatingly funny, but appeared to me to be too superficial, too purely materialistic. It didn't mean anything: it wasn't worth while. Afterwards I saw that I was wrong. The fact is, that nobody else but Leacock could have talked about whiskers in the way he did, and recover from it without injury. I visualized other humorists I knew trying to do it, and saw plainly what would have happened. It wasn't, certainly not!—the best that Leacock could have done, but the fact that he could do it at all was enough to stamp him as Leacock and nobody else.

Then again—sometime later—one of my daughters suddenly caught me one day just before I was about to submerge myself in toil and said: "We have been reading the funniest book—'Winsome Winnie.' We screamed with laughter. You simply must read it."

Thereupon I got the book and started to read it aloud. It was subtitled "New Nonsense Novels," being the last volume of Mr. Leacock's works. I read "Broken Barriers." Certainly nothing, read aloud, could be more laughable. I have mentioned elsewhere that George Ade's "Fables" are not so easy to read aloud, except to a highly sophisticated audience. Leacock has an astonishing gift in the use of words and images that compel laughter. Not all of his nonsense novels come up to this test: some of them we found dull reading, but there is none better than the best of them. Of this kind of writing Leacock, writing of his first volume of "Nonsense Novels" says:

The stories in this book I wrote for a newspaper syndicate in 1910. They are not meant as parodies of the work of any particular author. They are types done in burlesque.

Of the many forms of humorous writing pure burlesque is, to my thinking, one of the hardest—I could almost feel like saying, is *the* hardest—to do properly. It has to face the cruel test of whether the reader does or does not laugh. Other forms of humor avoid this. Grave friends of mine tell me that they get an exquisite humor, for instance, from the works of John Milton. But I never see them laugh at them. They say that "Paradise Lost" is saturated with humor. To me, l regret to say, it seems scarcely damp.

Burlesque, of course, beside the beautiful broad canvas of a Dickens or a Scott shrinks to a poor, mean rag. It is, in fact, so limited in its scope that it is scarcely worth while. I do not wish for a moment to exalt it. But it appears to me, I repeat, a singularly difficult thing to do properly. It is to be remembered, of course, that the work of the really great humorists, let us say Dickens and Mark Twain, contain pages and pages that are in their essence burlesque.

Mr. Leacock has another handicap besides being a political economist. He has come out of Montreal. By some this is considered apparently a severe test. Mr. J. P. Collins (the *Reader*) writes of him thus:

Can anything good come out of Montreal? The late Samuel Butler, who is vaunted as a kind of modern Buddha, appeared to think not. He wrote a lampoon, one remembers, intended to wither the devoted city up, and all because he had found in its museum a classic statue stuck away in a lumber room, and a busy taxidermist much to the fore, engaged in the harmless occupation of stuffing an owl. Hence the "Psalm of Montreal," and all that apostrophic pother about Mr. Spurgeon's haberdasher and his precious brother-in-law. Montreal strikes one as rather a long way to go in search of incongruities, when the worthy Samuel could have found specimens flourishing triumphantly at South Kensington or his beloved Bloomsbury; but satirists must have their little fling, so let Butlerians boast that he converted the Canadians from the error of their ways. Other men have not been so successful. Mr. Kipling, for instance, paid Canada years ago a compliment worth having when he christened her by the title of an old church in Quebec "Our Lady of the Snows": and he must have been quite unprepared for the snort of disgust this accolade aroused in her official circles—regions disturbed by the thought that poetic liberties of this kind might interfere with immigration business. But there are inklings of a better frame of mind in Canada to-day, and even Montreal is ahead of the rest of the world in one important respect. She can appreciate a man who unites in himself to an exceptional degree the double capacities of scholar and wit, philosopher and humorist.

Most halls of learning have harped too heavily on the dividing line, and ruled off the wholesome spirit of mirth with a kind of bar sinister. McGill University does better, for it can boast a man whose titles to our admiration are evenly balanced as between levity and gravity, and, in Professor Stephen Leacock, it possesses a savant in politics and economics who is also a brilliant jester, and recognized in both rôles in both the hemispheres. As such, and not merely as the author of several volumes of philosophy and *belles-lettres,* he enjoys a place of his own in modern English-speaking literature. The only difficulty is which of his aspects to take first—the grave or the gay, the lively or severe. Stevenson stood out for the happy paradox that a man's recreations were the main affair in life, and work was only the negligible day-drudge, so there is authority and warrant for treating the Professor's lighter volumes first. But usage and tradition are all in favor of taking the solid courses before the sweets, quite apart from the question of chronology.

Of the quality of Mr. Leacock's humor Mr. Collins speaks with sympathy:

Having never met the Professor at the breakfast table, I can handsomely acquit him on all those disparaging points that make up an appearance of intimacy and are supposed to supply the "personal" touch to a composite portrait like this. But a talk he gave me years ago went far to explain by its pace and tone as well as its substance how he turns his leisure to such blithe results. He denies, by the way, that his lighter work is the product of idle moments; but this, I suspect, is because the plague of idleness hardly ever disturbs so keen a temperament. To a mind well stored with the best reading of the older hemisphere he adds the audacity and energy of the other. In answer to a remark of mine, he said that, while in Europe here, we did our reading carelessly, and were content to absorb the best literature in fragments or flying allusions, a keener generation in the Colonies did its reading for itself, and devoured all the right reprints instead of arranging them along a decorative but dusty shelf. He might have gone further and said that, in the Old Country here, we are so bemused with passing talent and polemic garrulity, that we lose sight of the greater and more abiding forces except as names to garnish paragraphs and tattle. But as far as he went, I found it refreshing to hear Dr. Leacock lay about him in his quick, outspoken way, and to find my suspicions verified that his wit is the outcome of deep sincerity and hard sense. Beyond the cynical autobiography he prints in front of "Sunshine Sketches," I know nothing of his career, but I should say that the gist of it has gone into that bitter indictment, "The Lot of the Schoolmaster," reprinted in his essays. To take up the challenge he there throws down on behalf of the humbler walks of an ill-paid profession would be daring and difficult; to endorse it is unnecessary. One can only quote and quote again, or refer the reader to the paper itself; and if that is the case with his criticism, it is certainly the same with his other writings, facetious or otherwise. One of the best of his critical papers he devotes to a generous laudation of the late "O. Henry," and Mr. St. John Adcock quoted this in his admirable monograph in miniature in these pages. A classical training preserves the Professor from that looseness in terms which could allow O. Henry to call a bow a 'genuflection'; but, happily, years of concentrated study and drudgery have not lessened his rapid and prolific originality, while it has only deepened that sense of justice which he vents at times with such towering indignation.

Too much emphasis has been laid on his faculty for parody, which is only one weapon after all in his well-filled armory. It seems only the other day that "Nonsense Novels" arrived to prove that a vogue in which Thackeray and Bret Harte excelled is still a living force in criticism, and that a Canadian professor is equal to either of those master-satirists in the power of turning the eccentricities of modern fiction against itself. If he turns on its practitioners as well, he is not content with mimicry of their accent and locutions, but tries to reconstitute their view-point, and always with an imperturbable good humor. You perceive very soon that, with him, the mimetic stage has never been more than a kind of reserve trench in the "big push" against humbug and literary pretension, and that the parodist in this case is also a creative humorist of the first water. Certain critics rose, I remember, at his "Literary Lapses," and strained their arguments needlessly without diminishing anything or anybody but themselves. Some of them complained that a western humorist without dialect or Bowery slang was an

exotic, an importation from the East, and a geographical contradiction, which is all pure nonsense. The
Old World, as we have long discovered, enjoys no
monopoly of wit. You cannot bring sense and nonsense into collision without striking a tell-tale spark,
and whether the clash occurs on this side of the Atlantic or the other, the chances are that you will get the
same kind of a spark from the same shape of head.
If the longitude of Greenwich can produce university
brilliance like that of a Hilton, a Godley, an Anstey
or a "Q," there is no reason why the same perception
of values and contradictions should not produce their
equal in a Stephen Leacock, even in the longitude of
McGill and the latitude of a political professorship.
One of our author's fiercest assailants revealed himself, I remember, in the book column of a lofty London
daily, and showered out all the ineffable contempt this
organ reserves for everything American except peeresses and advertisements, and the American Ambassador; but presently, observing that the *Times* (which
it hates like poison) had given up a segment of its
Supplement to a consideration of Dr. Leacock's merits,
this enlightened organ lay in ambush for his next book
and then swamped it with green gush. But I hesitate
to touch on the vagaries of reviewers when the Professor has turned them to such diverting account in
his books; they constitute a grand assault on all sorts
of pests from the club bore and the platform quack to
the cheap millionaire and the expensive lap-dog. That
truly modern martyr's rack, the boarding house, has
made a text for all the American masters of humor,
from Holmes and Stockton to Wallace Irwin and
George Ade, but none of them has touched off the
horrors of the "hash bazaar" as deftly as our Professor
has done. Years ago he wrote a series of Euclidean

axioms which appeared in *Truth* and then had a come-
tary orbit of republication, from *Punch* downwards.
Even now one hears the jest attributed to all sorts of
brilliant mathematicians, dead and gone, and those who
have ever met it in those cold shades of anonymity will
recognize it from one example:

"If there be two boarders on the same flat, and the
amount of side of the one be equal to the amount of
side of the other, each to each, and the wrangle between
one boarder and the landlady be equal to the wrangle
between the landlady and the other, then shall the
weekly bills of the two boarders be equal also, each
to each. For, if not, let one bill be the greater. Then
the other bill is less than it might have been, which is
absurd."

* * *

It is usual to greet a new writer with discourage-
ment, just as the astronomer tackles a new sun-spot
through a smoked glass. One cannot find that, on the
whole, Professor Leacock has ever met with want of
recognition, certainly since he first appeared in print;
and, indeed, he is not the sort of person to have suffered from it if he had. But I have no doubt that, like
the pearl in Æsop's fable, he has been pecked with the
query as to why he wasn't something else? Carlyle
chilled William Black after his twentieth successful
novel or so, with the brutal inquiry as to when he was
going to do some "worrk," and there are doubtless
people who ask our author when he is going to write
a sequential book, instead of a series of fugitive chapters. Well, there is "Sunshine Sketches" on the one
hand, a racy presentation of a typical western town and
its inhabitants, and on the other there is the
"Elements," already dealt with; and if it were not for
the matter of date, one might even suppose that treatise

had been written in reply to this very taunt. The Professor's humor is certainly equal to this *riposte* or any other. He believes, with Erasmus, in saying even serious things lightly; and he has loudly proclaimed he would rather have written "Alice in Wonderland" than the whole of the "Encyclopædia Britannica." That is also why, like Garrick in the picture, he may be torn between comedy and tragedy, but at least he smiles under the ordeal. Such is the effect of a true conception of the office of humor in a miscellaneous firmament of bounty. In an unpublished essayette he once remarked that it is "better to take your place humbly and resignedly in the lowest ranks of the republic of letters than to try to go circling around on your own poor wings in the vast spaces of Milton's 'Paradise,' or the great circles of Dante's 'Inferno.'" The individual modesty of this is balanced by the fact that he stands up handsomely for the craft of humor and his brethren who follow it. A member, as he says himself, of the Royal Colonial Institute and the Church of England, he does not hesitate to remind us in another fragment somewhere else that it is "much harder to write one of Owen Seaman's 'funny' poems in *Punch* than to write one of the Archbishop of Canterbury's sermons"; and that whereas, in his immortal hymn, Newman only cried out for light in the gloom of a sad world, Dickens gave it. Which is profoundly true, as far as it goes. One might pursue indefinitely this contrast in the man which is characteristic of so many true artists—a passion for the vindication of his calling, whatever the niche that is allotted to himself.

On an occasion lately which should have been enough to tempt the humblest of men to glorify himself for once, Dr. Leacock showed some anxiety to stay in the background with his books, and to set in front of them a masterpiece of his special predilection—his son and namesake of a year old, and his second self. Of this prodigy he remarks that he is "guaranteed to eat more, sleep deeper, shout longer, and cry harder than any boy of his age in the British dominions outside of Zululand." I beg to leave that challenge as it stands with all its unnecessary reservations on its head, and to leave its author at the mercy of a myriad progenitors prepared to take it up; but at least the episode illustrates the idiosyncrasy of authors that their pride invariably lies far outside the circle of your conjecture. Let me conclude with another fragment from the Professor's pen, which strikes me as truer and deeper than anything ever written by Professor Bergson or Professor Pogson on laughter or free will or anything else:

"The world's humor in its best and greatest sense is perhaps the highest product of our civilization. One thinks here not of the mere spasmodic efforts of the comic artist or the black-face expert of the vaudeville show, but of the really great humor which once or twice in a generation at best, illuminates and elevates our literature. And here, in its larger aspect, humor is blended with pathos till the two are one, and represent as they have in every age the mingled heritage of tears and laughter that is our lot on earth."

Personally, it remains only to indicate a fund of unutterable thanks for the pure and healthy enjoyment that Dr. Leacock's books have given me for years. If I were called in to prescribe for the restoration of Europe after this present convalescence, I should prescribe the free circulation of an unlimited number of his books at Germany's expense, in all languages and dominions outside the circle of the Central Powers, with a strict embargo on their entering the land of the Huns. They deserve it.

Mr. Collins writes of Dr. Leacock's rapid and prolific originality as having survived his classical training, and infers that he was also immune to that "looseness in terms" which his native American brothers (O. Henry for example) reveal. True. Yet Dr. Leacock's training does not save him from being a careless writer, and often a dull one. That, of course, is not to disparage his best work, which is all that Mr. Collins writes of it, but it is only to sympathize with him in the enforced production of his worst—a blight of which most of us are conscious.

As to what Stephen Leacock thinks of himself, and the somewhat orderly and chronological procession of his life, let me give it in his own words:

I know no way in which a writer may more fittingly introduce his work to the public than by giving a brief account of who and what he is. By this means some of the blame for what he has done is very properly shifted to the extenuating circumstances of his life.

I was born at Swamoor, Hants, England, on December 30, 1869. I am not aware that there was any particular conjunction of the planets at that time, but should think it extremely likely. My parents migrated to Canada in 1876, and I decided to go with them. My father took up a farm near Lake Simcoe, in Ontario. This was during the hard times of Canadian farming, and my father was just able, by great diligence, to pay the hired men and, in years of plenty, to raise enough grain to have seed enough for the next year's crop without buying any. By this process my brothers and I were inevitably driven off the land, and have become professors, business men, and engineers, instead of being able to grow up as farm laborers. Yet I saw enough of farming to speak exuberantly in political addresses of the joy of early rising and the deep sleep, both of body and intellect, that is induced by honest manual toil.

I was educated at Upper Canada College, Toronto, of which I was head boy in 1887. From there I went to the University of Toronto, where I graduated in 1891. At the University I spent my entire time in the acquisition of languages, living, dead, and half-dead, and knew nothing of the outside world. In this diligent pursuit of words I spent about sixteen hours of each day. Very soon after graduation I had forgotten the languages, and found myself intellectually bankrupt. In other words, I was what is called a distinguished graduate, and as such, I took to school teaching as the only trade I could find that needed neither experience nor intellect. I spent my time from 1891 to 1899 on the staff of the Upper Canada College, an experience which has left me with a profound sympathy for the many gifted and brilliant men who are compelled to spend their lives in the most dreary, the most thankless, and the worst paid profession in the world. I have noted that, of my pupils, those who seem the laziest and the least enamored of books, are now rising to eminence at the bar, in business, and in public life; the really promising boys who took all the prizes are now able with difficulty to earn the wages of a clerk in a summer hotel or a deck hand on a canal boat.

In 1899, I gave up school teaching in disgust, borrowed enough money to live on for a few months, and went to the University of Chicago to study economics and political science. I was soon appointed to a Fellowship in political economy, and by means of this and some temporary employment at McGill University, I survived until I took the degree of Doctor of Philosophy in 1903. The meaning of this degree is that the recipient of instruction is examined for the last time in his life, and is pronounced completely full. After this, no new ideas can be imparted to him.

From this time, and since my marriage, which had occurred at this period, I have belonged to the staff of McGill University, first as lecturer in Political Science, and later as head of the department of Economics and Political Science. As this position is one of the prizes of my profession, I am able to regard myself as singularly fortunate. The emolument is so high as to place me distinctly above the policemen, postmen, street-car conductors, and other salaried officials of the neighborhood, while I am able to mix with the poorer of the business men of the city on terms of something like equality. In point of leisure, I enjoy more in the four corners of a single year than a business man knows in his whole life. I thus have what the business man can never enjoy, an ability to think, and, what is still better, to stop thinking for months at a time.

I have written a number of things in connection with my college life—a book on Political Science, and many essays, magazine articles, and so on. I belong to the Political Science Association of America, to the Royal Colonial Institute, and to the Church of England. These things, surely, are a proof of respectability. I have had some small connection with politics and public life. A few years ago I went all around the British Empire delivering addresses on Imperial organization. When I state that these lectures were followed almost immediately by the Union of South Africa, the Banana Riots in Trinidad, and the Turco-Anglican War, I think the reader can form some idea of their importance. In Canada, I belong to the Conservative party, but as yet I have failed entirely in Canadian politics, never having received a contract to build a bridge, or make a wharf, nor to construct even the smallest section of the Transcontinental Railway. This, however, is a form of national ingratitude to which one becomes accustomed in this Dominion.

Apart from my college work, I have written six books. All of these are published by John Lane (London and New York), and any of them can be obtained, absurd though it sounds, for the mere sum of one dollar or a dollar and twenty-five cents. Yet these works are of so humorous a character that, for many years, it was found impossible to print them. The compositors fell back from their task suffocated with laughter and gasping for air. Nothing but the invention of the linotype machine—or rather, of the kind of men who operate it—made it possible to print these books. Even now, people have to be very careful in circulating them, and the books never should be put into the hands of persons not in robust health.

Many of my friends are under the impression that I write these humorous nothings in idle moments, when the wearied brain is unable to perform the serious labors of the economist. My own experience is exactly the other way. The writing of solid, instructive stuff, fortified by facts and figures, is easy enough. There is no trouble in writing a scientific treatise on the folk-lore of Central China, or a statistical inquiry into the declining population of Prince Edward Island. But to write something out of one's own mind, worth reading for its own sake, is an arduous contrivance only to be achieved in fortunate moments, few and far between. Personally, I would sooner have written "Alice in Wonderland" than the whole "Encyclopædia Britannica."

So much for Professor Stephen Leacock of McGill University and Canadian-American, or American-Canadian humorist, as you will. But a much more intimate view of him is given by an anonymous writer who, under the pseudonym, "A Canadian Soldier" writes (in the *Bodleian*) "An Impudent Sketch of the Professor":

There are three persons of my acquaintance whose signatures absolutely defy interpretation; one of them is a professor of philosophy whom I shall not name; the second is an officer in the Canadian Army, whom I dare not name, and the third is—Stephen Leacock. We do not say Doctor Leacock or Professor Leacock, though, when I was a boy, that was how he was known. It would now seem as absurd as does speaking of the ex-President of the United States as Doctor Wilson.

He is now Stephen Leacock, or just Leacock, and will be so long as his books are printed, and read, and known. Already he is growing into a "phrase." An article appeared in the *Daily Chronicle* not long ago speaking of the "Peacock Cult" of a past generation. I doubt if many are familiar to-day with that eccentric author's books. For myself I can only remember them as an immaculately clean set of volumes, uniformly bound in spotless red art cloth, standing in inenviable peace, undisturbed year after year upon the Library shelves.

The Library.—I do not refer to any private library, but to the Library of McGill University at Montreal, where as a boy I was employed, and where I first met the author of "Literary Lapses." At the beginning of my time there he was known as the author (if one ever thought of him as an author at all) of "Elements of

Political Science" and of another book which treats of Canadian politics, published in the "Makers of Canada" Series. But now who thinks of him as other than in connection with the "Arcadian Adventures" or the "Larger Lunacy"?

He was, of course, and is, I imagine still, a daily figure in the Library, where his deep resonant voice and his gruff, peculiar manner sometimes caused confusion to the staff, which always afforded me intense satisfaction. His method of signing his name, when he left a receipt for a book which he wished to borrow, was considered very "liberal." For as I have already hinted, Stephen Leacock's signature is like a Hindoo mystery—it transcends explanation.

I was quite a youngster at the time, and was at much confusion of mind between these two questions: "Does one write badly because one is clever; or is one clever because one writes badly?" I had no known reason for my belief in Dr. Leacock's "cleverness," for political science leaves little of an overawing impression upon a lad of twelve, but somehow the Hindoo soul of that indecipherable signature, which conveyed to my physical being nothing whatever but the image of a long-legged spider squashed by a merciless thumb, haunted me, until I decided the matter finally for myself by asking the Professor to give me an autograph for my cherished collection. And it rests now, still undecipherable in its unshamed illegibility, among my favorite names. Every little while I take it out and look at it, and wonder, as Thomas Bailey Aldrich did over his friend's letter, if the day will come when I shall be able to make it out.

Dr. Leacock gave a number of the lectures of his course in one of the upper rooms of the Library, and when three o'clock came round it was no unusual thing to see him, a host of books and papers under his arm, make giant and hasty strides into the Library to the delivery counter. I was always there ready for him. With great excitement I made note of his quick instructions and, a few moments later, breathless and aglow, I would follow him to his lecture-room, loaded down with the reference books for which he had asked. It was to me the height of satisfaction to be able to give him the books that he wanted without obliging him first to hunt for them in the card catalogue, and it was probably my evident eagerness to please him that earned for me his friendly recognition. It became a byword in the Library that whenever Dr. Leacock wanted anything in a hurry (and he always wanted books in a hurry) he called for "the boy." So much so was it that it became his habit to trust me with tasks which were beyond my power to perform, such as looking up statistics, population returns, immigration figures, etc., etc. And, in spite of my zeal, it was with more than a sinking of the heart that I approached that formidable and seemingly endless collection of pumpkin-colored volumes which constitute the statutes of the Dominion of Canada. I spent many a weary hour thus in tearful confusion, and I imagine that in most cases the figures that I did eventually secure were not correct. But Professor Leacock was invariably most kind, and my remuneration measured in his estimation with the time I had spent upon my task, and not with the extent of its results. I blush still when I think of those liberal dollars that he gave me from time to time for my services, and that I so little earned.

But with the coming of "Literary Lapses" Dr. Leacock appeared before me in an altogether different light. His familiar figure assumed a new meaning. His fine, grave face, that boy's mop of hair that always looks as if it had just been washed the night before, and simply refused to be brushed, the deep vibrating tones of his voice, and his peculiar stride had always appealed strongly to me. But I realized now with a new glow that I actually *knew* him, that I numbered among my acquaintances one who belonged to that group, thrice blessed, in my imagination, of men who write!

Publishing a textbook on Political Science was not writing in my estimation, but it was indeed being an author if one could produce such a book as "Literary Lapses," and such screamingly funny sketches as "My Financial Career."

One evening I was left alone in the Library in charge of the reading-room. There were quite a number of students in that evening, but for me there was little work to do. A friendly student lent me a copy of "Literary Lapses," which had just been published. I read it, but didn't quite understand. Was this Leacock? Then what a new Leacock to me! I was amused, soon I was convulsed, and very shortly afterwards had to desert my post to laugh in shameless noisiness in the furnace-room downstairs. To this day I cannot begin reading, "Whenever I go into a bank I get rattled" without the memory of that night coming over me, and how I disgraced myself by breaking the awful stillness, over which I myself should have been the stern sentinel, with my uncontrollable mirth.

From that time onward I have read Leacock. Long before his articles were published in book form I knew them as they appeared in the magazines and periodical publications. I always knew where to find them. The University magazine, a *very* dignified and academic publication, became readable in my eyes only when it published, "The Apology for the Professor."

But it was with the "Arcadian Adventures with the

Idle Rich" that I began to see something deeper in Dr. Leacock's writings besides a mere sense of fun. And as Peacock laughed at Coleridge with a purpose, so I saw their affinity. And although I do not always agree with Dr. Leacock, I have to laugh with him, too.

For he is inimitable. He is Mark Twain and Artemus Ward; he is Josh Billings and Sam Slick (The Clockmaker), he is Dickens—but above all he is Leacock, and nobody else is quite like him. What valuable services he has rendered to Political Science must be recorded in the publications devoted to that laudable subject. But just as Charles Dodgson, the mathematician, is overshadowed by Lewis Carroll, the author of "Alice," so will Professor Leacock, the Political Scientist, be overshadowed by that *larger* personality, Stephen Leacock, the Humorist.

It is platitude to explain that in employing this term one is merely saying *Humanist* with a smile. For a Humorist is above all that also. A question of title, however, has but an insignificant interest when dealing with Stephen Leacock.

I remember being present at a large students' gathering at McGill University when an incident occurred which I think gives the keynote to what I have been trying to bring forth in this sketch. I forget what the meeting was about. I can remember only that, at a given moment, the entire audience rose and shouted with one voice: "We want Stevie!"

Stephen Leacock's public, I think, has the same desire. It does not worry much about his title. It reads his books as they appear, then cries out to "Stevie" that it must have more.

CHAPTER XXII

C. B. LEWIS

("M QUAD")

IN that wise and charming book entitled "The Opinions of Anatole France"—a book that I can heartily recommend to every struggling writer— M. France deliberately removes the props from many preconceived ideas about literature in general. "Now what is a scholar?" he asks and replies: "A deadly creature who studies and publishes, on principle, everything that is fundamentally uninteresting." He declares that all the great men were bad writers, and that their reputations for doing a particular thing changed from generation to generation. The real point is, of course, that there is no rule to writing, and instead of saying that the style is the man we might just as well say that the man is the style.

And what ought to cheer up every writer, so far as America is concerned, is that it is such a big country, and if you have really anything to say, you can always get some of the people to listen to you. Also, the people who are listening to you may be very much more important than those who are listening to some one else who thinks himself much more important than you are. Here is M. France, one of the first writers in the world, coming down to first principles, just as M. Renan remarked that, after reading and reflecting for thirty years or more, he found that the first street gamin he met knew as much as he did. "For my part," declares M. France, "I have no excessive confidence in reason. I know how weak and tottering it is."

Now the same thing is true of style, or literary talent. The great things of the world have been said, not by clever people but by great people. If in his youth Abraham Lincoln had taken lessons in style from Walter Pater, he never could have written the Gettysburg address. So it seems to me that, in our judgments of men who write, we must consider many more things than mere smartness. In this book, for example, there are gathered together an incongruous company of humorists. I have no doubt that many among the so-called intelligentsia have never heard of Mr. Lewis, or if they have, would scorn to read anything he has written. Also, there are probably, especially among the younger, a number of whom Mr. Lewis himself has never heard, or if he has—but I shall not pursue this painful subject further. I am already in too deep.

The fact is that Mr. Lewis, take him for all in all, is one of the most remarkable men of this period. Over a quarter of a century ago I was a cub editor and had the weekly pleasure of passing his copy through the typographical mill. I recall quite vividly his Bowser sketches, and his weekly story of adventure, and the astonishing clarity of his copy, written with scarcely an error, week after week. Suddenly there came the "Arizona Kicker," I think the first of its kind—that is to say, that kind of satire on the American western editor, recently become more common, filled with the most robust humor, side-splitting often in its primitive revelings. And here is Mr. Lewis, after all these years, still at it—truly an immortal! The oldest and cheerfulest humorist in the United States! Perhaps, indeed, the only cheerful one! The following sketch of him has kindly been supplied to me by his son.

The Anecdotal Side of M. Quad

At the Age of Eighty the Creator of "Bowser" is Still in the Journalistic Saddle and Going Strong

BY J. SEYMOUR WALLY

Probably the easiest man in the world to interview is Charles B. Lewis, better known as M. Quad, the famous humorist, who has made a million homes rock with laughter over his Bowser stories, his Lime Kiln Club philosophy, and the escapades of the "Arizona Kicker." All that is necessary to secure enough copy for the whole Sunday edition of a newspaper is to hand Quad a long cigar—the blacker and stronger it is the better. Mention the city of Detroit, and he will talk to you until a big collie comes around and noses the old man as a hint that it is time to stop such nonsense and think of the more important matter of dinner. That canine is the apple of Mr. Lewis's eye, and you may put away your pad and pencil and make your best exit bow when the dog shows signs of hunger.

At the very ripe old age of eighty the creator of "Mr. and Mrs. Bowser" is still at work supplying a New York syndicate with six columns of humor weekly. He is never at a loss for a funny idea, dictates his copy as rapidly as the typist can take it on the machine, and says he could furnish a whole page daily if there were any call for his articles by the wholesale. Since he began writing for the *Detroit Free Press,* some sixty years ago, he has never written less than a column a day, besides furnishing many special articles, and incidentally turning out a book or a play just to keep in working order. His career as a playwright, however, was short and not sweet. During the rehearsal of Mr. Lewis's first and only drama the villain in the play reported in an intoxicated condition and thrashed the entire cast, including the brave hero, and the humorist decided then and there to write exclusively for his newspaper. M. Quad has never forgotten his work and friends in the Michigan city. When he talks of Detroit one can see that he longs for the days when he filled the job of reporter, editor, humorist and advertising salesman all at the one time.

"We had to hustle back in those days," smiled the author, in telling of his early career in journalism. "I wrote my regular column of humor in the morning, edited copy and drummed up advertising in the afternoon, and worked as an all-around reporter in the evening up to midnight. When I received my eighteen per on Saturday it seemed a princely salary, but I felt that I had earned it. I well remember that when this sum was increased to $25, owing to a big scoop I had put over, I used to lie awake nights and wonder if the paper could possibly stand the terrific financial strain. One day William E. Quinby, the beloved boss and owner of the *Free Press,* turned me loose on humor alone, and boosted my wages to such a figure that I trembled every time a stranger entered the office, thinking he might have come from the Sheriff's to close us out; and it was only after I learned that I was working for one of the richest newspapers in the country that I could get the proper sleep."

Asked about his fads and favorite sports in his younger days, the eighty-year-old humorist smilingly continued:

"I think my greatest out-door sport in those days was in painting my house on Pitcher Street, for I dearly loved to see our frame domicile looking as bright as a new penny. It was great fun, too, to wield the brush and originate new shades to astonish the natives. The very smell of the 'turps' made me think of spring and robins and romance, and I always left the task and started for the office full of inspiration—and paint. I beautified that house with linseed and white lead every summer regularly, and while I had numerous escapes from falling off the roof and ruined many a good suit of clothes, I smeared away annually until the neighbors held an indignation meeting and planned to ride me out of town on a rail if I didn't stop it. You see, I had the whole neighborhood working overtime, for one newly painted house will make all the other homes around look shabby. Of course I took the hint, being a poor equestrian, but it was some time before I felt that it was safe to go out at night, for fear some one might throw a brickbat, and thereafter the outside appearance of my house was no concern of mine.

"When the dance craze hit Detroit I became so enthusiastic over that indoor sport that I hired an uncle of mine, who was a carpenter out of work, to build an upper addition on the house for use as a private dance-hall. I agreed to pay him $10 per week and board for his superior knowledge with the saw, but he hadn't lived with us long before we realized we had taken in the champion eater of Michigan. He also could out-snore any human being in the country, and between the midnight serenades and the awful wallops the grocery money was getting, I began to wonder if dancing wasn't as wicked as the ministers proclaimed it. While he was pounding and measuring, I also hired a colored youth to teach me clog-dancing at $1 per lesson, so that I could show our guests something novel when it came to 'balance your partner.' It took one solid year to build that addition, and it was one year to the minute before I could do the most simple clog, and I have always thought that the coon and the carpenter put their heads together and figured it out that I would stand the financial strain about that length of time.

"Every one for blocks around attended the first dance in the new hall, and I shall never forget the shrieks of laughter and yells of terror when I let out a war-whoop and began to clog. In my endeavors to show those folks a thing or two I ripped off evening gowns and trod on tender toes and finally landed on my back in a cloud of dust, but what hurt me most was the fact that most of the guests departed without saying 'good-night.'

"I ached for just one more chance to show my skill with the boot, but the prayers and pleadings of my family prevailed, and I promised to take only the part of a wall-flower at the dances thereafter. I cannot claim to have originated the short-skirt, but I will insist that my *cavort de nouvel,* as they would say in Paris, furnished the idea that finally led to them. Probably that dance-hall stands to-day, but it used to shake and wobble so when eight or ten couples waltzed over its floor that we all doubled our life insurance and opened the weekly dance with prayer."

M. Quad got his start as a humorist after he had

been blown up on a Mississippi steamboat, for while he was convalescing in a hospital after the accident he wrote a story entitled; " How It Feels to Be Blown Up," that was copied all over the world and made him famous as a funnyman. Here is his account of that aërial affair:

"The managing editor seemed to think I needed a little vacation, so he sent me South during one of the hottest summers Detroit had ever known to cover a mysterious murder in Louisville. Baked to a cinder, and feeling quite sure that I was now immune from any climate I might find in the hereafter, I was returning home on the bow of an old side-wheeler when she blew up with a bang, from an overheated boiler, and the fun began. The last I remember as we went skyward were the yells of terror and fervent prayers of an old darkey who took the flight alongside of me, and when I leaned over his bedside two weeks later in the hospital he was still rolling his eyeballs and praying.

" 'Cheer up, Uncle Tom,' I tried to assure him, 'you're all right now and will soon be well again.'

" 'Go 'way, boy,' he advised me in husky tones. 'Go 'way down in de Co'nfield an' hide yo'self. Ize a big long skyrocket bound fo' de moon, an' yo' bettah keep out o' my path fo' I sizzles yo'.'

"Shortly after the explosion my 'corpse' was duly laid out on the banks of the river alongside the other victims, my wife notified by wire to hunt for mourning bargains, and Bowser would never have had a publicity man had it not been for a morbid native, who came to the big show, discovered a twitching of my eyelids, and was thoughtful enough to report such a trivial matter to the doctors.

"My enemies have always claimed that not until a

full quart of rye was poured into my system would I
show signs of life, and that my first words were, 'more,
please,' but I want to state it as a fact that just one
bucket of black Mississippi river water thrown over me
had the desired effect, and that my first words cannot
be found in the hymn-books. My story, 'How It
Feels to Be Blown Up,' pleased the managing-editor
so much that he wired me to get kicked by a mule or
run over by a steam-roller and rush another good
story, but I refused to consider it. I had gone up, but
I had been lucky enough to remain whole and come
down again, and I proposed to stick around for a
while with two feet on the earth. In fact, for a year
or two afterwards, I would not even cross the river
on a ferryboat, job or no job."

Mr. Lewis keeps cheerful despite the fact that he is
a victim of rheumatism and has been somewhat of a
cripple for the past fifteen years. Seldom does he get
further than the front gate of his home on an outing
and then only by the aid of a long staff. Since the
death of his wife about fifteen years ago he has lived
with his son and daughter-in-law in Borough Park,
Brooklyn, and his granddaughter writes his copy from
dictation on the typewriter and carries it to the syndicate each week.

I had almost succeeded in starting the humorist on
another story when the collie began to bark and walk
about my chair in a suspicious manner, and I took the
hint. The last I saw of M. Quad he was smoothing
the beautiful coat of his chum and assuring the dog
that there was roast beef for dinner and they would
divide it "fifty-fifty," as usual.

CHAPTER XXIII

ROY L. McCARDELL

BY R. L. McCARDELL

ROY LARCOM McCARDELL believes, like all modern men and women, that he has a strong sense of humor, but isn't so sure he is a humorist.

He comes of a newspaper and writing family connection, and a livelihood in journalism has, in consequence, been gained by him along the lines of least resistance.

A great aunt and namesake was Lucy Larcom, the poetess; although all he remembers of her work is fugitive bits from "Hannah Binding Shoes," and just how shoes were bound or why, he has but the vaguest idea. Another great aunt of literary renown, although a lesser light than Lucy Larcom, was Maria Louisa Eve, of Augusta, Georgia, a Southern poetess of at least local repute and of the didactic, Mrs. Sigourney and *Southern Messenger* school.

Roy L. McCardell's father, Capt. Thomas F. McCardell, was a noted Maryland editor and Democratic-reform leader. The elder McCardell was sometime editorial writer on the *Baltimore American* and *Pittsburg Dispatch,* and later editor of the *Cumberland*

(Md.) *Daily News* and *Evening Times*. Of the latter newspaper, Capt. McCardell was the owner for some years, and it was, and most likely still is, the leading daily of Maryland, maugre such Baltimore papers as the *American* and *Sun*.

Besides all this, his father's brother, Willoughby McCardell, was for forty years the editor and owner of the *Williamsport* (Md.) *Leader,* and two of his maternal uncles, Charles and Dorsey Eve, were noted Southern editors and writers, long connected, respectively, with Asheville, North Carolina, and Richmond, Virginia, newspapers.

Roy L. McCardell was born in Hagerstown, Maryland, June 30, 1870, his father being the editor of the *Hagerstown Mail* at the time. Later, his father was made the editor of the *Evening Times,* Cumberland, Maryland, and the family moved to that city— the second in size in Maryland.

Roy McCardell attended the public schools of Cumberland until he was twelve. He had been an omnivorous reader as long as he could remember— devouring Dickens, Scott, Thackeray, Dumas, Bulwer Lytton, Lover, Lever, Shakespeare and all the poets, not to mention dime novels and nickel libraries.

At twelve he decided that, although he was weak in spelling, mathematics and grammar, he was so well informed in reading, history and geography, he might conclude his schooling and go his way in the world.

He also determined to go the way of all flesh in his family and become a newspaper man. In such a career he could not see where his weakness in spelling, grammar or mathematics would be any drawback. The copy desk would correct his spelling and faulty grammar, and, as for mathematics, what writer has to keep books?

At twelve McCardell had contributed some satires of scholastic significance to a school paper, and had narrowly escaped being expelled. During the summer vacation that followed he demanded at least one of the *Evening Times'* tickets to the circuses, the baseball games and Buffalo Bill's Wild West, and, in return, reported these amusement events for his father's paper in a satisfactory manner, after the grammar and spelling of his articles had been amended and corrected. He was in no sense hypercritical in his reviews, his critiques being unvaryingly favorable and commendatory.

At about this time, *Puck,* edited by the late Henry Cuyler Bunner, was the most popular paper of national circulation, holding a place in general esteem about parallel to that held nowadays by the *Saturday Evening Post.*

Young McCardell had a penchant for writing light verse and, at about this time, he had written some rhymes for his father's paper on baseball as Tennyson would have reported it, and the issue of *Puck* of the following week, the late R. K. Munkittrick had written parodies on the same theme and the same poet.

Well meaning but doubtless falsely flattering friends made comments on the coincidence, to the advantage of the younger versifier. But he knew better then, as now.

However, it encouraged him to send his next batch of verses to *Puck* and, to his great happiness, they were accepted. From that on, almost up to the time when *Puck* fell into the hands of Hearst, and then gave up the ghost, young McCardell was a constant contributor to *Puck,* both in prose and verse.

When he was seventeen he went to Birmingham, Alabama, and applied for and obtained a position on the reportorial staff of the *Age-Herald,* of that city, one of the leading journals of the South.

He reported hangings, lynchings, riots and other social affairs, for Birmingham was a lively city, in a bright and cheerful style, and also contributed sketches of local color—generally concerning the colored population—and verses on current events of local interest to the Sunday edition of the *Age-Herald* and as fillers for the editorial page.

Many of these ephemera were copied in *Current Literature, Leslie's Weekly* and other periodicals of clipping propensities, including the New York newspapers, especially the *Sun* and *Evening Sun.*

The *Evening Sun* was then edited by Arthur Brisbane and had on its staff such youths of promise of Richard Harding Davis, Mickey Finn, Mortimer McMichael 3rd, John Harrington, Acton Davies, W. S. Moody and Frederick Gregg.

Henry Gallup Paine, then assistant editor of *Puck,* and later, editor of *Harper's Weekly,* recommended to Arthur Brisbane that he might give young McCardell a try-out on his staff, and Brisbane wrote, offering $15 a week. Young McCardell was getting $25 a week on the *Birmingham Age-Herald,* but New York was worth the difference.

He came on at once to the *Evening Sun* and was

assigned to cover the Tombs Police Court's morning sessions. Judge Duffy, and other notable Tammany humorists of Hibernian extraction were on the police court bench in those days, and all a reporter needed to do was to "play straight," as they say in vaudeville.

McCardell supplemented his humorous and "human interest" police court reports of the morning by the merry-thoughts, so to speak, that he had of afternoons. His *Evening Sun* burlesque dime novels, such as "Ironbound Ed, the Elevator Boy; or, from the Bottom to the Top," and his parodies of Laura Jean Libbey's deathless works—and Laura Jean was then at the zenith of her vogue—gained him both esteem from the *Evening Sun's* readers and innumerable raises of salary from his appreciative editor, Arthur Brisbane.

From the *Evening Sun* McCardell went to the *New York World,* and from the *World* to the staff of *Puck* to work with and associate with such notables as Bunner, Harry Leon Wilson, H. G. Paine, F. Opper, C. J. Taylor, Louis Dalrymple, James L. Ford, John Kendrick Bangs, R. K. Munkittrick, W. C. Gibson and Harold McGrath, artists, editors and visiting contributors.

While on *Puck* he contributed to all the leading magazines and periodicals and kept in touch with Park Row journalism. In the summer of 1896 he learned that the *New York World* had built a color press and contemplated issuing a woman's fashion supplement in colors. Morrill Goddard, since editor of the *New York Sunday American,* was then editor of the *Sunday World.* McCardell suggested to him that the *Sunday*

World first experiment with a comic supplement in color. Goddard approved of the idea but ascertained that all the comic artists of reputation were under contract with *Life, Judge* or *Puck*. But McCardell knew of a young free-lance comic artist of much originality, in the person of Richard F. Outcault, and he brought Outcault to Goddard, and Goddard turned over the first issues of his novelty supplement to the two young men; although he closely supervised it.

The first Sunday paper to put out a comic supplement in color was the issue of the *Sunday World* of November 6th, 1896. At that time the circulation of the *Sunday World* was about 140,000 copies. The colored comic supplement—the famous "Yellow Kid" was an outgrowth of its first issues—was received with loud acclaim and high favor, and at once seemed to fill a longfelt want with a lot of people.

In six months the circulation of the *Sunday World* increased to 800,000. Then Hearst started a colored comic supplement with his *New York Sunday American,* taking over Outcault; and, within a year, had a circulation of 400,000, the *Sunday World's* circulation dropping to the same figure.

This was either evidence or proof that, in the area of Greater New York, just 800,000 people wanted colored comic supplements and no more.

As suggester and first getter-out of a colored comic supplement, now an affliction with almost every big Sunday newspaper, McCardell gained neither riches nor renown; but, on the other hand, the world at large has seemed to hold no animus against him regarding it.

Since then McCardell has been connected, off and

on, with almost every newspaper in New York, being one of the first editors of the *New York Morning Telegraph,* the *Metropolitan Magazine,* the *Herald,* the *Telegram* and others.

In 1900 he began writing moving pictures, and has since been identified with this new amusement art-industry as a writer of scenarios. He has written over a thousand in all, including the screen version of "A Fool There Was" that made the movie vampire an international institution.

But it is as a prize winner that McCardell has functioned most successfully. He has been connected with the *New York World* as a special-article contributor for almost the whole time of his journalistic activities. The *World* continuously offers cash prizes for ideas and suggestions from its staff, and McCardell has more than often figured in the money—first, second or third prize.

He has won short-story prizes in the *Herald* and *Collier's* competitions, and the *Puck* prize for the best humorous story printed in *Puck* in 1916.

In moving picture scenario prize contests he won the *Morning Telegraph-Flamingo Film Company* first prize of $1,000 for the best screen comedy manuscript, with a scenario entitled, "A Jay in Peacock Alley." He was one of the prize winners of the *Evening Sun-Vitagraph* contest with a five-reel scenario, "The Money Mill."

In 1915 he won the *American Film Company-Chicago Tribune-New York Globe* prize of $10,000 for the best scenario for a moving picture serial, from nearly 30,000 contestants.

His serial was entitled "The Diamond from the Sky," and was shown to great profit for its promoters in over 8000 theaters in the United States, and is still going strong, after playing all Europe, in Asia and Africa.

Mr. McCardell personally supervised the production of this picture, which was in sixty reels, the biggest moving picture ever taken. It was shown a la serial story, in two reel chapters.

Mr. McCardell also won the Leaders of the World advertising prize for the best short advertisement phrases or slogans for 32 leading American advertisers' products—such as the Ford Automobile, the Remington Typewriter, Walk Over Shoes, Waterman Fountain Pen, Washburn-Crosby Flour, etc. He also won a new model Cadillac automobile offered by the makers to the owner of a car of that make who could give the best account of his satisfactory experience with the same.

He is the author of "The Gay Life," a comedy produced at Daly's Theatre in 1914, a half-dozen vaudeville sketches, several popular songs, and contributes to the *Saturday Evening Post* and other leading magazines and periodicals.

His newspaper and syndicated articles such as "The Chorus Girl," "The Kind Kids Klub"—a burlesque "Children's Corner," "Mr. and Mrs. Nagg," "The Jarr Family," etc. Of all these, his daily "Jarr Family" stories have been the most durable, having run continuously in the *Evening World,* and in several hundred other papers, in syndication throughout the United

States, every day except Sunday, for the past twelve years.

Mr. McCardell wishes to state that he for one is tired of it, but if others are they do not complain as he does. He would have stopped writing it long ago, but the Jarr Family is the McCardell family's most reliable meal ticket, and he needs the money.

He has taken the Jarr Family all around the world and to Central and South America with him, but could never shake them off.

In his earlier years he aspired to be a poet, but in the year 1905 he had verses in the fifteen leading American periodicals of the time, in one current month's or week's issue—*Life, Puck, Judge, Truth, Leslie's Weekly, Harper's Weekly,* all the leading monthly magazines and, he thinks, the *War Cry* and *Police Gazette.*

No other versifier, with the possible exceptions of Arthur Guiterman or Walt Mason, ever equaled that record.

But the fifteen checks altogether only totaled $121.50, and McCardell decided that poetry didn't pay, or verse either. He collected his best lyrical efforts in a little volume entitled "Olde Love and Lavender," and reformed from rhyme, except where ideas fail him, or he is writing lyrics for musical shows.

He resides in New Rochelle with such as is left of a once large family, and, as a humorist, prefers to write moving picture scenarios.

They pay best, and he says they are always funny when they reach the screen, whether he intended them to be that way or not.

CHAPTER XXIV

DON MARQUIS

SOME of those friends of America who look at us from the outside have expressed the opinion that Don Marquis is the best writer of humor among us. That is always a difficult matter to decide. Don is uneven. I think, at his best, he is the best. But this is highly unimportant; it is sufficient to know him and to read him and to get pleasure out of what he does. He is almost the only one who can write about himself without offense; he is interested in everything, like Arnold Bennett—only more so. He is undoubtedly an artist in words, if not in ideas. He has all the faults of his environment, the unerring ability to express what we all feel, and to do it in such a manner that we are continually being brought up with a round turn. It would be unfair to some of the others to say that he is our leading columnist, because it is unfair to judge any columnist in that manner, although I have had the audacity elsewhere to make this claim for F. P. A. The column of type presented by a columnist is only an accident, although there is of course an atmosphere about the column all its own. Don Marquis is always slopping over his column and reaching out into unheard of spaces. Perhaps he indulges in fewer parlor fireworks than some of the others, depending not always so much on the trick of words as on ideas, or on expressions that are the result of impulses running towards deep convictions, and then suddenly being halted by the inevitable interrogation of "What are we all here for anyway?" He voices better than any one I know the struggle of the soul (or the thing that we term soul) but he does this more by byplay than anything else. And he has the trick of being readable no matter what he writes about, until both he and the reader suddenly look up and blush at each other for liking it. For example, take this piece, out of his daily column:

One of our favorite dissipations . . . we use the word advisedly, because it draws upon and diffuses our slender reserve of nervous energy . . . is worrying over the Terrible Condition of Things in General. We try to keep it out of the Sun Dial as much as possible, but our anxiety and pain and bitterness and sense of pathos when we think of the condition of the earth-bound multitudes of men often get into print in spite of us.

In the course of every twenty-four hours we find ourself going through a complete cycle of beliefs, from passionate conservative to impassioned radical. At times we are certain that the world is ready for the communal idea, and should we pick up an article or talk with a man disagreeing with us we damn the writer or speaker as a mud-headed Tory. Three hours later we have grown disgusted with liberalism and the conviction suddenly seizes us that popular government is the mistake of the ages . . . that the only reason this country has done as well as it has is because its professed republicanism, its democracy, has seldom really been genuine: there has been the form of a popular government, but the masses, the majorities, have usually been tricked: the control of affairs has been juggled away from them.

Under the influence of any of our moods we are apt to say things . . . not merely say things, but write them and send them to the printers . . . which we will not believe at all by the time the type is set. But we do not stop their publication: we know that, whatever they are, whatever complexion of political belief they represent, there will come a time when we believe in them once more.

Such tolerance as we have . . . and we pride ourself upon our tolerance . . . really arises from the conflict of a dozen jarring intolerancies.

There are only two things constant and stable in us: the wish to see the grosser injustices of human existence wiped out at once, and the conviction that it will be thousands of years before the human race will have developed sufficiently mentally and spiritually to wipe them out.

We have not the faintest idea why we are writing this totally unnecessary, this distressingly candid exposition of our own mental unreliability. But now that it is written, we shall print it . . . first, because a person who writes for a daily paper is obliged to keep up with the printers, and therefore cannot afford the luxury of writing anything he does not publish; secondly, because of a belief that the Sun Dial readers know us well enough by this time to forgive us such a tactless aberration from the usual. Of course when we see the stuff in print we shall repent having published it. We had intended writing an entire column of epigrams and witticisms concerning government

under the title of THE ALMOST PERFECT STATE,
when it suddenly occurred to us that in spite of
our knack of throwing our notions into epigram the
result was unimportant because of our own instability
. . . that is to say, no matter how clever the epigrams
might be, in themselves they would be entirely unrelated to ourself as a person, fatally divorced from
any course of action we might pursue as a human
being. So why cumber the earth with the fore-damned
things? We don't know how to run the world any-
how . . . at least we feel this afternoon that we don't
. . . although we know more about it than most of
the people who are actually doing it. Don't you?

There is nothing like writing to get a thing off your
chest. We feel better already. To-morrow you shall
have a column that is actually readable. It may be
about THE ALMOST PERFECT STATE after all.

DON MARQUIS.

One reads on and on, knowing that it is all nonsense, and perhaps not the best nonsense. After one
is through, nothing has happened, and yet here we have
a great piece•of literary business; it is actually, though
quite subtly, a satire—a satire on *any* form of expression. He seems to be serious; you know of course
that he is not. Yet when you get through you have
learned more, or at least realized more, than if you
had been reading some erudite dissertation on science
or theology. And the reason is, of course, that here is
personality, and Art after all is nothing but personality. The principles that lie under personality lie under
all literary work, even the dullest. And if you should
try to express yourself in the way that Don Marquis

does, you would see that it was impossible unless you had the secret of doing it. Among so many prolific American writers, I should say he has the most invention, and the most grotesque sense of invention; yet he never fails to come back to first principles. Here is one of his characters, archy the Cockroach. The whole thing is too utterly impossible, and yet what archy says is more important to a whole lot of people than what the President says or what a solemn college dean says—than what almost anybody says:

Maybe the Ku Klux Klams get the information on which they act from the Ouija Board.

archy Sings Another Song

boss i can
throw some light
on the two paragraphs
above perhaps
as follows
said the scrammel to the weasel
as the kleagle wiggled by
theres the passion of a measle
in his sad and strangling cry
said the weasel to the scrammel
as the kleagle sang his note
theres the gurgle of a camel
in the gargle of his throat
said the werble to the wobble
as his larynx looped the loop
he burbles like a bobble
that is scalded eating soup
and they went and asked the ouija

the secret of his song
and it said his brain was squeegy
and his mind wasn't strong
yours for the higher
ministries of poesy

archy

Don once told me an amusing thing about one of
his characters, Hermione, the girl who is always talking about the almost perfect state, that type of girl
who poses as being intellectual. He lectured once
before a large audience of girls and said he had quite
a hard time of it until he got talking about Hermione
and suddenly everybody realized that they were all
Hermiones more or less, including himself, and after
that it was a very merry party. That, of course, is
always the quality of true humor—no matter how hard
it hits, it hits the humorist as well. The grave-diggers
in "Hamlet" were only grave-diggers in the great soul
of Shakespeare.

Don Marquis has great passions, terrible finalities.
Nothing exceeds his wrath over shams, which is the
mark of true humor. Prohibition caused him to invent
The Old Soak, who sprang full born, a radiant being
who has come to delight us more and more. Here is
only just a small part of him:

The Old Soak Laments

"I ain't gonna turn Prohibitionist or nothin'," says
the Old Soak, "but I'll say this—these days I don't
relish my liquor none. I dunno w'ether I'm too old or
the hooch is too young. I always did like my liquor
to meet me half way, but these days you ain't more'n

made a home fer a drink before it begins to henpeck
you. It moves in an' starts to yank the furniture
around like a red-headed widow that's aimin' to show
her third husband who's boss five minutes after the
weddin' cerements has been uttered. I like to get
acquainted with my drinks more gradual. But nowadays one minute you're so sober you hate yourself,
an' the next minute you're so drunk you hate the world.
One of the greatest pleasures I useter have was hangin'
onto a bar and wonderin' if I was drunk yet. But
these times the' ain't no opportunity to speculate;
you don't wonder if you're drunk, you wonder if you're
gonna live. Booze uster be a king, but now he's turned
into one of these here redical anarchists. I ain't gonna
quit, nor nothin', but I'd like once more to ride on top
of a souse instead of bein' drug for miles under the
wheels. I don't know what kind o' grief berries they
make it out of these days, but I know I can't find but
two kinds of liquor—one kind ain't right an' the other
kind ain't liquor."

Should this, or his other fulminations, shock anybody? Certainly not. Prohibition is one thing. The
Old Soak is quite another. It was almost worth having Prohibition to incite Don Marquis to create The
Old Soak and to put him into a play. One can be
deeply committed to the Thirty-nine Articles and enjoy
him just the same. And among all the reformers, is
there one who cannot enjoy what follows?

Reform the Lower Animals!

Before we go on our vacation—or while we are in
the act of going on it—we give one backward thought

to the world from which we are retiring, and in-
augurate a new reform.

* * *

*Mankind is being reformed, but conditions among
the lower animals are frightful!*

* * *

We have received the following letter from Mr.
John Frew, which shows the *shocking conditions
among pigeons in and about New York City.*

"Knowing your interest in reform I have ventured
to send you the following observations:

"Yesterday, while musing over your brilliant theory
that the one-piece bathing suit is responsible for over-
work on the part of reformers, spots on the sun and
the present heat wave, and reflecting on what small
causes produce far-reaching results, my attention was
attracted by the actions of some pigeons on the roof
just outside my window. A male pigeon was going
through the absurd genuflections of his kind before
an unwilling female. This, I may here interject, is
a scene of frequent occurrence in this neighborhood—
hardly a moment passes that some pigeon is not making
an exhibition of himself. They strut and swell their
necks, they bow and swagger, tripping over their trail-
ing wings, until one's heart bleeds for the harassed
females. For it is plainly evident to a close observer
that these attentions are unwelcome to the female . . .
Unwelcome, did I say?—Nay, repugnant! Let me not
err on the side of understatement. The female pigeon
is a hardworking bird, untiring in her efforts to pick
up a living for her family, and the misdirected energy
of the males interferes sadly with her true mission in
life. Indeed, one might almost say that it would be
better for the pigeon race if all the males were

destroyed! Then the females could carry on the work of incubation and the feeding of the young undisturbed, and something might be done in a scientific way toward artificial fertilization of the egg.

"The destruction of the male, however, brings up a problem that requires careful thought. Questions arise. Is it better to destroy than to ameliorate? Would it not be better to punish these birds? To break down their pride by confinement, to purge their haughty flesh by pain? Pain, the purifier! Pain, the perfecting agent; dreaded and shunned by all animated nature, but yet so necessary as a preparation for a higher and nobler state! Following this thought I evolved a plan which I believe would be efficacious in purging away the grosser elements in the nature of the male pigeon.

"A great number of cages might be made, single cells, each accommodating one pigeon. They could be attached to the cornices of public buildings and the male pigeons placed in them. So imprisoned they could see the females going about their daily avocations, but would be denied access to them. Instinctively they would go through their absurd evolutions, prancing and bowing and strutting. A mechanical method of utilizing this waste energy would have to be devised —something in the nature of a miniature treadmill, in each cage. The power thus generated would operate a small chain of buckets passing through a reservoir of ice water. At stated intervals (far enough apart so as not to permanently discourage the prisoner from all effort) one of these would arise, a clutch would be released and the frigid contents discharged on the prisoner's head. There is nothing like a good healthy douche of ice water to cool off these affectionate birds!

"I am sure that good results could be obtained in this manner. To say nothing of the chastening effect on the pigeons themselves it would serve as an object lesson to all observers in proving that punishment inevitably overtakes the carnal minded. Regarded in this light it would be educational, and as such, would commend itself to the American public.

"The necessary expenses for installation of cages, machinery, ice, services of iceman, &c., could easily be taken care of by a slight increase in the tax rate. Indeed, the whole installation could be financed by an additional tax on tobacco alone, thus forcing the addicts to this noxious drug to make some slight return for the annoyance caused to non-addicts by their selfish indulgence. This last consideration should cause the scheme to endear itself to all right-thinking people."

* * *

It is not only pigeons, but *all birds and beasts!*

Who will join us in a crusade to reform the lower animals?

* * *

All the Lower Animals!

* * *

We must, if necessary, *Amend the Constitution once more!*

DON MARQUIS.

I have ventured, in this chapter on Don Marquis, to quote direct from my subject much more than usual because, only in this way, can he be revealed. He appears to me to be a special dispensation of Providence, set here to keep us all straight. God knows we are wicked enough in our moralities. What would America do without people like Don? I wanted him, also, to give some literal account of himself if he could, and so I caught him on the fly one day and got him to write down as follows:

Don Marquis, whose full name is Donald Robert Perry Marquis, was born at Walnut, Bureau County, Illinois, on July 29, 1878, at three o'clock in the afternoon, during a total eclipse of the sun, and a few minutes later his father had him enrolled in the Republican party. Mr. Marquis has left the Republican party and returned to it again a great many times since.

Walnut, Illinois, is one of those towns that prop two cornfields apart. Nothing ever happens there, except the sort of things chronicled in the "Spoon River Anthology"—which happen so slowly that one never catches them happening, just as one never sees the hour hand of the clock moving.

Mr. Marquis was graduated from the village high school at the age of fifteen, and explains that it would have taken him longer if the high school had been higher. He went to work in the local drug store— accepted a position, rather—the same year. He might have been there yet except for a fortunate accident which grew out of a series of chemical experiments which he was making. The drug store was blown up and the hearing of the experimenter's right ear was permanently impaired.

During the next four or five years Mr. Marquis worked at almost all the trades and professions that flourished in Walnut and vicinity. He clerked for a Semitic gentleman in a clothing store, he sold sewing machines, he was employed in a chicken abattoir, he taught school, he was an assistant in the village post office, he plowed corn, he worked on a hay press, and he hired out as a printer's devil for one of the local papers.

This was his first false step. Never since then has he succeeded in getting any distance away from printer's ink and white paper. Before he had been setting type six weeks he discovered that a sonnet—the regulation fourteen-line sonnet of commerce—just exactly fits and fills a printer's stick. After this discovery it was almost impossible to get Mr. Marquis to do anything but compose sonnets and set them into type as he composed them. He never bothered to write his copy first—right into the stick it went.

In 1896 Mr. Marquis deserted the Republican party for the first time, and put into type a series of sonnets in praise of William Jennings Bryan. It is hard for him to believe to this day that Mr. Bryan was not really elected President in 1896. Unfortunately, these sonnets have perished.

In 1898 Mr. Marquis went to Knox College, at Galesburg, Illinois, with the intention of getting an education. But he did not seem to be much good at it, and left, after working at it only a few months, and went back to teaching country schools and working for country newspapers—occupations in which a college education is only a handicap.

In 1900 Mr. Marquis returned to the Republican party and accepted a position as a clerk in the Census Office at Washington, D. C. After accepting this position he got a job on a daily newspaper, the *Washington Times,* as a reporter. In addition to this, he began to study art at the Corcoran Art School in Washington.

Mr. Marquis would go to work on the newspaper at 7:30 in the morning and work until 2 o'clock in the afternoon. From 2 in the afternoon until 5 in the evening he was in attendance at the art school. From 5 in the evening until midnight he worked at the

Census Office. The rest of his time he gave to dissipation, sleep, poetry, study of the workings of the National Government, attempts to write the great American drama, and other in- and out-door sports.

From Washington Mr. Marquis went to Philadelphia, where he was employed on the *Philadelphia North American,* and from Philadelphia to Atlanta, Georgia, where he wrote editorials, first for the *Atlanta News,* and later for the *Atlanta Journal.*

When the late Joel Chandler Harris started *Uncle Remus's Magazine* in Atlanta in 1906, he asked Mr. Marquis to be his assistant, and Mr. Marquis remained as associated editor of that magazine until 1909, when he came to New York. In June, 1909, he married Miss Reina Melcher, of Atlanta, Georgia, who is also a writer.

Since coming to New York Mr. Marquis has been employed on the *New York Sunday Tribune,* the *United Press,* the *New York American,* the *Brooklyn Eagle* and the *New York Sun,* formerly the *New York Evening Sun.* Since 1912 he has conducted on the *Sun* the column known as "The Sun Dial," contributing verses, short stories, serial novels and articles of various sorts to magazines at the same time and in September, 1922, he moved over to the *Tribune.* He has published two novels, "Danny's Own Story," in 1912, and "The Cruise of the Jasper B.," in 1916; "Prefaces," a book of whimsical essays; "Hermione," a volume of sketches delineating the vagaries of the Modern Young Woman who thinks she thinks; "Dreams and Dust," a book of serious verse; "The Old Soak" and "Hail and Farewell," a collection of prose articles and verses that deal with all aspects of the liquor-prohibition movement; and three other books of his have been announced for publication during the year—"Carter and Other People," a collection of short stories, "Poems and Portraits," a second volume of serious verse, "Noah and Jonah and Cap'n John Smith," a collection of humorous verses and "Sonnets to a Red-Haired Lady."

CHAPTER XXV

I T is impossible to write about any one with such an intimate personality as the one controlled and owned (presumably) by Christopher Morley without being intimate oneself. And yet the startling fact about him, which I discovered when I attempted to write, was that he had actually disclosed so little of himself, or at least, of the sort of self that I believed him possessed of, that I couldn't write about him at all.

I then—in the most brutal manner, a manner that only the editor of a humorous paper comes to acquire after long years of pain in the making—wrote and demanded of him that he write an autobiography of himself.

He did it. And then put me under oath not to publish it. That was quite like him. At first the subtlety of his humor didn't penetrate (I am Scotch). And then it gradually dawned on me that the article he wrote about himself was intended as a rebuke. This was also made more plain to my diminishing intellect by the last sentence in the letter with which he accompanied his manuscript in which he said: "But here's an amazing idea: why not write the book yourself?"

Morley is always doing things like that—trying to

incite people to superfluous things from a sense of duty. He was evidently secretly jealous and thought that if he could get me to do the book myself, instead of having it properly (or improperly) done by others, the sale would naturally fall flat. And yet I immediately absolve him from such a notion, for actually he is not that kind.

On the contrary, he is quite different.

After I was compelled by the horrid circumstances, actually to write about him, I was naturally compelled to think about him, and it then dawned upon me that what I had thought of all along as an intimate personality, was in reality intimate only as it concerned other people. That is to say, Morley is not so intimate with himself as he is with everybody else. Indeed, I doubt if he is intimate with himself at all. That is quite remarkable in one who, if he really cared to be intimate with himself, might easily extract considerable amusement from the contact.

The fact is that Morley is always amusing, not however in the sense of being common—for he never could be that—but because he has the superb faculty of being so interested in every one and everything else. I think it was Metchnikoff in one of his books about long life, who disclosed the consoling fact that, as one grows older, one should grow happier because of what he termed one's "sense of life." What Metchnikoff meant was that, as we come to study life itself, and become more intimate with it, the detail of its beauty and coloring is more evident to us, so that we enjoy things much more intensely in old age—that is, the right things—than we possibly can in youth; in youth, which is so detached and fleeting in its hurry-scurry.

And that is true. A picture that twenty years ago would have aroused only my passing interest, may now easily become a subject for complete absorption. Also, I find that people interest me more and more all the time. I seem to be on closer terms with everybody. The hues and tints of human beings, and the heretofore invisible beauties and qualities of their temperaments and characters, now affect me often very deeply, whereas before they passed me unnoticed.

Now Christopher Morley, it appears to me, was born with this "sense of life," and what a delightful and wonderful gift it was that the fairies presented to him! Of course that is the kind of thing that, when old men have it, keeps them young, but Morley, having had it when he was young, has been doubly blest in having been able, before he was thirty, to enjoy life just as if he was over fifty. No wonder his writing makes one feel very good indeed.

To classify such a seemingly joyous person is quite difficult. Is he a humorist?—that is, is he more of a humorist than anything else? I do not know. Lawrence Abbott, writing of Morley in 1920, said:

We should think Mr. Phelps, of Yale University, would like "Parnassus on Wheels" and "The Haunted Bookshop" very much indeed. Perhaps he does. If he has not read them, we advise him to. They certainly prove one thing—namely, that a "damn literary feller" need not necessarily be a highbrow, and that an American humorist of the most genuine sort can really like the best of literature.

How interesting that is as a comment!

But I have another one about Morley that I always delight in when I read it, not necessarily because I think it correct, but for certain reasons purely personal. It is by Mr. Vincent O'Sullivan, who visited America in 1919, and was the recipient of Morley's kindly intentions and hospitalities. And this is what Mr. O'Sullivan wrote:

Some years ago I was asked to lunch in New York at a restaurant in the neighborhood of Wall Street— one of those places where eating becomes feeding; where, as in a pew, men closely packed in a small room groan and sweat as they devour probable dishes while flying scuds of soup and gravy are blown in the face from plates carried at perilous angles by irritable and distracted waiters. . . . My host was a large florid young man rather ample in movement for the place, who looked as if he might have seized the restaurant in his arms and swung it across the river to the Brooklyn side. So far as looks go, he was the kind of a man you may meet on any misty morning in Essex or Suffolk riding about his farm on a stocky well-groomed cob or trampling through the worzels in thick boots and buskins, with a gun under his arm and a dog at his heels. This was Mr. Christopher Morley, sometime one of the editors of the *Ladies Home Journal,* and now an imposing pillar of the *Philadelphia Evening Ledger.* Amid the uproar, he gained my sympathy by calling "The Woman in White" one of the best English novels. He spoke warmly too of Anthony Trollope. I cannot read Trollope much, but I like people who like him. I suppose we all feel that way about some writer or other.

At the time of our lunch Mr. Morley had published in magazines some parts of his book of poems, "Songs for a Little House," whereof the inspiration takes its rise in the English intimists, Herrick, George Herbert, Cowper, Crabbe. He has since written a few books of essays (or as one would say in America "near-essays") whereof the inspiration is the prose counterpart of those worthies Izaak Walton, Addison (of Sir Roger de Coverley), Charles Lamb, Leigh Hunt, with something of Hazlitt and George Borrow thrown in. As you see, nothing could be more English. And as one reads these books, "Shandygaff" and "Parnassus on Wheels," it is easy to pick out his preferences among modern English authors. Stevenson, Kipling, Conrad, Chesterton, J. M. Barrie—there they are! It may be in deference to his surroundings that he professes an inordinate admiration for that didactic and boring writer, Samuel Butler—him of "Erewhon" and "The Way of all Flesh" I mean; heaven forbid that any one should think I mean the great author of Hudibras. . . . Such a list of preferences describes a man. You notice that if there was no Hall Caine there is no Galsworthy; if there is no Florence Barclay there is no Bernard Shaw; if there is no Arnold Bennett or Algernon Blackwood neither is there Mrs. Humphry Ward or William Locke. No non-English writers whatever, none of the great French, have said anything important for him. I have a notion that he regards Ibsen and Strindberg with dislike as not the kind of stuff that young America can profitably be nourished upon. His admiration of his own countrymen is also tempered by many exclusions. Among those he admires he takes a long slide from Walt Whitman to Mr. Don Marquis, who distributes parodies and proverbs. According to Mr. Morley the facetious Mr.

Marquis is the greatest writer, except Walt Whitman, that ever lived in the Brooklyn district of New York. This is perhaps not much of a claim; but however that may be, it falls to be said that Howard Pyle, admirable writer of fairy stories, of pirate romances, admirable black-and-white artist, too, lived in Brooklyn, and if he were still treading its streets, neither Mr. Marquis nor many other Americans would be worthy to walk in his shadow.

It has seemed worth while to dwell on Mr. Christopher Morley's literary formation because of his expression of the English literary tradition, which is indeed so singular in America to-day that one is not much surprised to learn that he is not very far off the original English stock—only a single generation I think. He has also been a Rhodes scholar at Oxford, and although in his latest book he calls a college cap a "mortar board," no doubt he came into sufficiently close contact with the real life of the place. He waxes enthusiastic about tea and muffins and open coal fires. Tea arouses no delight in the American breast, muffins mean something else than they do in England, and open fires are a privilege to the rich. He is, in his books, a great eater, his board is spread with a Victorian prodigality. To his mind, when the English Victorian era ended, something very good went out of the world. There is nothing in him that Victorianism would have frustrated: he does not want to do or express anything which would have shocked the Victorian sense of fitness. I do not know whether he would want to put drawers on the legs of a piano, but he would not want to discuss the subject of legs, or anything that may be implied in that. . . . Mr. Morley is by no means a realist, if realism means facing unflinchingly the sad and ugly among the other elements of life. He puts aside whatever is unpleasant, and, one can see in many another author, this is done by conviction, deliberately, like the effort of a Christian Scientist. He belongs to the domestic school; he is a homely writer. He tells you what they had for breakfast from sheer delight in telling it. People don't catch diseases in his book. They are very well. The doctor only comes to preside at the arrival of a new and healthy baby.

On the whole, if we want only the fair lights, Mr. Morley gives a true enough picture of the middle-class family in the United States—or more precisely, of the family of small means in New England and the Middle Atlantic States. . . . So much consideration it has seemed worth while to give to this American writer in an English paper, not upon any claim that what he has so far produced makes him a great and important writer, but because he is a pleasant writer, with whose books English readers might well make acquaintance, and particularly because he is one of the very few American writers who continue the English literary tradition in a country where that tradition is dying fast and where the spoken, and to a considerable extent the written, language is drawing farther and farther away from English as it is used in England.

Morley was doubtless consoled for O'Sullivan's article by the thought that there has devolved upon him the task of keeping the English language alive in America. And this is highly important, because if the English language is not kept alive in America, then no British celebrity can make even a decent living by coming over here to lecture—not to speak of getting his books read. And it was also kind of Mr. O'Sullivan to recommend Morley's books to the English public. I have ventured to quote quite largely from his lengthy article on Morley, because, as a piece of psychology, it is interesting to have had Morley entertain his visitor in such a horrible place as he describes and then to describe him in the way he did; and also because the description is not at all bad. One can see Morley fairly well through Mr. O'Sullivan's lenses— not as Mr. O'Sullivan thought of him but as we who live here can understand a man who also lives here by what somebody says about him who doesn't live here.

To understand and appreciate Christopher Morley it is of course necessary to read his books, because nobody who writes discloses so much of his personality as he does, and the reason for this, as I have already hinted, is that he discloses nothing! That may seem paradoxical, and I shall not attempt to explain it. If I were called upon to explain it I could not do so. There are plenty of things that never ought to be explained, and that is one of them. But I shall now make some attempt to give an idea of Christopher Morley, or at least, of his place in the present literary scheme of things. First then, here are the bare facts about him, what, in guide books, is termed the dull and useful information!

Christopher Morley was born at Haverford, Pennsylvania, May 5, 1890, the son of Professor Frank Morley, the mathematician. He went to school in Baltimore, graduated from Haverford College in 1910, spent three years at New College, Oxford, as a Rhodes scholar, and drew his first pay envelope from Doubleday, Page & Company, the publishers, in 1913. After four years with Doubleday, Page & Company and a year on the staff of the *Ladies' Home Journal* he entered newspaper work. For two years he conducted a column on the *Evening Public Ledger,* Philadelphia; and since 1920 he has had charge of "The Bowling Green," an editorial page column in the *New York Evening Post.* By the time he was thirty-one he had published thirteen books. When it is considered that this list of works comprises four collections of verses, three volumes of essays, two novelettes, one book of short stories, a fantastic skit on prohibition, a volume of city sketches ("Travels in Philadelphia,") and a book ("The Haunted Bookshop") which may perhaps be described as a novel, but is a novel of a very queer sort and an odd blend of seriousness, levity and satire, it will be seen that this writer possesses some of the true Elizabethan exuberance.

In a volume of literary portraits, "Pins for Wings," (written, if we remember, by Witter Bynner) Morley, was described as "an affectionate scorpion." The genial qualities of his domestic lyrics and more humorous essays and tales have somewhat obscured the fact that he is capable of implanting a satiric or ironic sting which carries a disinfecting acid. Consider, for instance, his burlesque, "Translations from the Chinese," or the portrait (in "Mince Pie") of the young English poet visiting this country. This must have cost Morley inward pangs to write, for Anglo-American friendship is the central doctrine of his creed. Anglo-American in origin and training and tastes, he is fitted to contemplate the quaintly stimulating contrasts and similarities of John Bull and Uncle Sam.

The chief literary influence of his boyhood was

Robert Louis Stevenson. Next after Stevenson, he fell under the empire of Keats, O. Henry, Kipling— a diverse assortment. But he has been writing ever since he was seven years old: conducted various family newspapers as a child, as so many writers have done, and served an editorial apprenticeship on school and college papers. It is curious to learn that in his college magazine—the *Haverfordian*—he wrote a series of stories, "The Adventures of an Irish Waitress," in which he treated the field of kitchen comedy which he has since developed in more than one story (e. g. "Kathleen"). The humors and moods of the household are a topic that he has found fruitful and congenial, both in prose and verse.

His first book was a slender collection of undergraduate verses, written and published in Oxford (1912), called "The Eighth Sin." This somewhat cryptic title, which might be thought to cover the Dowsonesque and absinthine moods of a young *fin de siècle* decadent, is however only a sprightly commentary on a remark of Keats, to the effect that "There is no greater Sin, after the Seven Deadly, than to flatter oneself into an idea of being a Great Poet." The author of this pleasant little collection of *juvenilia* is secretly proud (he confesses) of the fact that the entire edition of some 300 copies was, in the course of eight years, finally sold out by Mr. Blackwell, the persevering Oxford bookseller and publisher, and ultimately yielded an author's royalty of about eleven shillings.

His first regularly published book was "Parnassus On Wheels" (1917), a little romance of a wandering bookseller and a wagonload of second-hand books.

This rural comedy, with its bookish flavor, was kindly received, and has gone through more than a dozen printings in the four years since its appearance. It led to a sequel, "The Haunted Bookshop," which, in point of sales, has been Morley's most successful book. The booksellers have grown to look upon this author as a kind of informal laureate of their trade, and it is encouraging to see that stories of this distinctly bookish flavor have a larger public than might have been supposed.

In spite of the number (I was almost about to remark "high literary quality" of his books when it occurred to me that this would get me into no end of trouble) and bookish tone of his books, Morley is essentially a columnist. What a columnist is I have explained elsewhere. It is now sufficient to observe that this is Morley's trade. His column in the *New York Evening Post* is one of the three best known in the country, the other two being those of F. P. A. and Don Marquis. But Morley's column differs from the others markedly. He confines himself quite largely to books, to streets and to food. In all of these subjects he is on safe ground, but his geniality too often overcomes him, and he pays too much attention to other writers. Personally I don't think he knows anything about poetry, which shows at least that he is healthy, although the way he has played up some of our most terrible poets in his column is scandalous. I should say that, if he had a defect, it is that he writes too easily. He does not draw enough water, but dear me, the man is so graceful and slides you along so lovingly that it is simply no use to find fault with him. And he has done so much for those to whom so much should be done! There is William McFee; how much do we owe Morley for helping us to know McFee! And there is Edward Newton, who would have been known anyway but not so soon or so completely. I shall always remember that Morley made me get Newton's book when it first came out—before anybody else even suspected it. (It is called "The Amenities of Book Collecting.") I was so excited about that book, after Morley had recommended it and I had purchased a copy, that I kept buying it over again. I read it and then gave it to somebody else to read; then I bought another copy and forgot that I had it, and after that, the copies kept turning up unexpectedly. Once I thought I had given them all away, until in a happy moment, I discovered two of them on the same bookshelf. And then Morley made me read Barrie, and I blessed him for it—after that he went to Philadelphia, and I lost sight of him until he came back to the *Evening Post*. And this is the sort of thing that he writes for the *Post* and does so delightfully:

What authors would you give up your seat for in the subway? We didn't say *to,* we said *for.* The other evening, for instance, we saw a young woman standing, holding a copy of *Dodo Wonders,* by E. F. Benson. We did not hesitate a moment. E. F. Benson is a good enough writer to entitle any lady to a seat, and we gave her ours promptly. But ladies reading Ethel M. Dell, Ruby M. Ayres, Robert W. Service, Arthur Stringer, Eleanor H. Porter, and all that sort of thing, do not get our seat.

This particular young lady, we noticed, was using

as a bookmark a leaflet entitled *The Present Crisis of Simmons College.*

Morley (thank God!) is not a literary critic. He is not only too kind but in spite of the fact that he is so literary, he is intelligent. He is not only intelligent for a literary man but for a columnist. He supports his family, his opinions, and his motor car, and he once told me—but that is a secret.

As to whether he is more of a humorist than a writer on literature, I cannot tell; some will think one thing, some another. In a list that was made up by about fifty booksellers throughout the United States to determine the most popular writer of American fiction, he is number 17. This list was compiled by the *Publishers' Weekly,* and the writer goes on to say:

"It seems unfortunate that American humor did not have any outstanding figure that should be recognized for his contribution to our literature, as we have always complimented ourselves on our production in this field. Of those who fell below the line in votes, the four following deserve mention: George Ade, F. P. Dunne, Don Marquis, Ring Lardner."

And yet Morley is 17 in a list in which these writers do not appear—which in reality means very little because Morley's books that place him in this list, while undoubtedly charged with humor, are distinctive for other qualities, and the other writers mentioned are not to be classed with writers of fiction; their popularity is of another order.

Morley is undoubtedly a humorist. But it is hardly

possible to draw a distinction between him and, say, either Ade or Dunne or Lardner, and be fair to every one. I don't think he is as basic as these other fellows. He knows too much about books. He has read too much. Probably his experience at Oxford may have given him something that was less valuable than that which he had racially. I am frank to say that I do not feel competent to judge. I cannot give up one iota of what I have written elsewhere about Peter Dunne and George Ade and Ring Lardner, and at the same time, Morley delights me as much, but in another way. Is it because his passion for books has made him more indefinite, less unerring? He doesn't smell so much of the soil. I love to read what he says about books, but I don't want to believe it always because he reads too many of them. Perhaps all this is what makes him a humorist!

Bibliography

"The Eighth Sin": Blackwell, Oxford, 1912. [Out of print.]

"Parnassus on Wheels": Doubleday, Page & Co., 1917.

"Songs for a Little House": George H. Doran Co., 1917.

"Shandygaff": Doubleday, Page & Co., 1918.

"The Rocking Horse": George H. Doran Co., 1919.

"The Haunted Bookshop": Doubleday, Page & Co., 1919.

"In the Sweet Dry and Dry" [With BART HALEY]: Boni and Liveright, 1919.

"Mince Pie": George H. Doran Co., 1919.

"Travels in Philadelphia": David McKay, 1920.
"Kathleen": Doubleday, Page & Co., 1920.
"Hide and Seek": George H. Doran Co., 1920.
"Pipefuls": Doubleday, Page & Co., 1920.
"Tales from a Rolltop Desk": Doubleday, Page & Co., 1921.
"Plum Pudding": Doubleday, Page & Co., 1921.

CHAPTER XXVI

I FIRST met Dorothy Parker when she was writing dramatic things, and other things for *Vanity Fair* and *Ainslee's*. How she got started I do not know. All I know is that she is Dorothy Parker, that she lives in New York, that she is married to Mr. Parker, who happens to be the grandson of the man who married me, that she has a little cubby hole in the Metropolitan Opera House Building (or did have), and that she is the best humorous writer in America among the women. I fancy I hear some of her admirers exclaim, "Why drag in the women?" Well, I drag them in because I probably don't know any better. The fact is that you cannot make any comparison in humor between men and women. There are fewer humorists among the women than among the men. Many people declare that women have no sense of humor, but I have no doubt that there are people who will even deny them the talent for having children. I am not going to enter here into the difference between men and women. I am off that. It has been done too often already. Neither am I going to declare that Dorothy Parker is unique. She isn't unique. She is only Dorothy Parker, a delicate little thing of great beauty and charm, who writes and says the most cutting things with a lamb-like air that would melt the heart of an iron statue. She has the soul of an artist, hating to be ordered to do anything, and making all sorts of excuses not to do it, and usually surviving the not-doing of it. She refuses to have any alterations made in her copy. She toils over it like a slave, while it is underway, never thinks that it is any good but never (like Tolstoi and other great people) makes any attempt to revise it afterwards.

To get Dorothy Parker to write anything is one of the most hazardous sports in the world. At the start she completely fools you. She gazes upon you with her wonderful eyes, hypnotizes you completely with her wonderful smile, disarms you utterly with her sympathy, which she instinctively extends to you in advance. You don't, but she does, know fully what you are up against. Then you sit around and wait for her to finish what she has begun. That is, if she has begun. The probability is that she hasn't begun. In this respect, to reverse Professor Coué's formula, "Every day, in every way, I am getting better and better," of her it may be said, "Every day, in every way, I get worse and worse." Several days later, when you approach her again, she may confess that she has at last got an idea but that it "is perfectly rotten." However, she admits that she is working on it. She vows that she is working upon it. You run up through New England in your car and, there, sitting at the Red Lion Inn with Heywood Broun, and Mrs. Otto Kahn, and Marc Connelly, you will see Dorothy Parker sipping something through a straw. Does she

recognize you? Certainly. She has just recovered
from a long illness. Otherwise she would have had
that story ready. Months later, when you have quite
given the whole affair up, and have only memories of
a wonderful pair of eyes, of a dulcet voice, of a
shrinking charm, suddenly there lies before you something like this:

Hymn of Hate [1]

I Hate Books:
They tire my eyes

There is the Account of Happy Days in Far Tahiti;
The booklet of South Sea Island resorts.
After his four weeks in the South Seas,
The author's English gets pretty rusty
And he has to keep dropping into the native dialect.
He implies that his greatest hardship
Was fighting off the advances of the local girls,
But the rest of the book
Was probably founded on fact.
You can pick up a lot of handy information
On how to serve *poi,*
And where the legend of the breadfruit tree got its
    start,
And how to take *kava* or let it alone.
The author says it's the only life
And as good as promises
That sometime he is going to throw over his writing,
And go end his days with Laughing Sea-pig, the half-
    caste Knockout—
Why wait?

[1] Reprinted with permission from *Life.*

Then there is the Little Book of Whimsical Essays;
Not a headache in a libraryful.
The author comes right out and tells his favorite foods,
And how much he likes his pipe,
And what his walking-stick means to him,—
A thrill on every page.
The essays clean up all doubt
On what the author feels when riding in the subway,
Or strolling along the Palisades.
The writer seems to be going ahead on the idea
That it isn't such a bad old world, after all;
He drowses along
Under the influence of Pollyanesthetics.
No one is ever known to buy the book;
You find it on the guest room night-table,
Or win it at a Five Hundred Party,
Or some one gives it to you for Easter
And follows that up by asking you how you liked it,—
Say it with raspberries!

There is the novel of Primitive Emotions;
The Last Word in Unbridled Passions—
Last but not leashed.
The author writes about sex
As if he were the boy who got up the idea
The hero and heroine may be running wild in the
        Sahara,
Or camping informally on a desert island,
Or just knocking around the city,
But the plot is always the same—
They never quite make the grade.
The man turns out to be the son of a nobleman,
Or the woman the world's greatest heiress,
And they marry and go to live together—
That can't hold much novelty for them.

It is but a question of time till the book is made into
    a movie,
Which is no blow to its writer.
People laugh it off
By admitting that it may not be the highest form of art;
But then, they plead, the author must live,—
What's the big idea?

And then there is the Realistic Novel;
Five hundred pages without a snicker.
It is practically an open secret
That the book is two dollars' worth of the author's
    own experiences,
And that if he had not been through them,
It would never have been written,
Which would have been all right with me.
It presents a picture of quiet family life—
Of how little Rosemary yearns to knife Grandpa,
And Father wishes Mother were cold in her grave,
And Bobby wants to marry his big brother.
The author's idea of action
Is to make one of his characters spill the cereal.
The big scene of the book
Is the heroine's decision to make over her old taffeta.
All the characters are in a bad way;
They have a lot of trouble with their suppressions.
The author is constantly explaining that they are all
    being stifled,—
I wish to God he'd give them the air!

I Hate Books:
They tire my eyes.

Now if you should ask me, "What is the difference
between Dorothy Parker and other humorous writers?"

I will try to tell you but I shall be wrong. No matter
what anybody writes about Dorothy Parker, he will
be wrong. I am going to tell you what I think. It
is just as easy, and in many cases, easier to be wrong
in thinking as it is to be right, and also there is no
particular obligation to be right. Right-thinking is
only a kind of perversion. Practically all of the big
men and women who have amounted to anything have
thought wrong most of the time.

Dorothy Parker (I think) was suddenly, or at least
found herself suddenly (I mean that she woke up to
the fact) placed in a world that she didn't like. Most
of us of course are that way at times, and we employ
various means of self-defense. We start out to earn
a respectable living (I mean an outwardly respectable
living, for practically every method of earning a living
hitherto devised is more or less disgusting), and while
doing this we learn to conform. But Mrs. Parker
selected a method of self-defense that was unusual for
a woman. She determined, or at least it became necessary for her, to invent a method of quietly laughing
at the machinery that annoyed her. This machinery
annoys most of us, but we submit to it. When people
like Mrs. Parker come along and expose it, we laugh
with her. What has always amused me most about
those who have criticized her work (and some have
done this) is that they invariably accuse her of being
a cynic. "Oh, yes," they declare, "it is of course well
done, but so unbecoming in a woman." Well, anything
is always unbecoming in anybody when it is better done
than any one else can do it. That is the chief trouble
with Mrs. Parker. When she does a thing she does it

better than it can be done by any one else. Naturally this is very bad. She at once becomes a cynic. All the ordinary feelings that any woman has are immediately denied to her by everybody who wishes they could do what she has done. But the fact is, that Mrs. Parker, so far as I have been able to discover, is precisely like everybody else. For one thing, she loves dogs. And that is to her great credit.

And another fact about her is, and this also is a fact about most human beings, that she has an extraordinary talent, that she uses it for her own and other people's pleasure and profit, and that it doesn't interfere in any way with her other emotions and feelings. In short, Dorothy Parker is a born artist, a remarkable humorist in the best sense of that word, a quite unique person in this respect. (I expected to use that word "unique" once, but I warned everybody, or at least prepared them for it in advance.)

You will now ask me something that is going to inspire me to curses, and that is, What is Dorothy Parker's place in American literature?

My reply is, not that there isn't any such an animile, but that if there is, Dorothy Parker doesn't care. What maddens me most about her is that she could easily have a place in literature if she would only write. But she refuses to write. All she does every once in a while is to turn out something that is quite perfect in its way, but that is only an aside. All of her things are asides. Instead of accusing her of not having enough sympathy with a world that is all wrong, it ought instead to be insisted of her that she has such an enormous sympathy with it that it is the excess of this sympathy that compels her to write these, apparently cynical, asides. That is to say, she reverses herself. No human being can reverse herself in this manner without great innate capacities for human emotions. Dorothy Parker is in revolt over what Walter Lipmann calls "stereographs." She was sick and tired as soon as she was born, of repetitions and *cliches*. She doesn't mind the sun coming up every day in the same old way, but she objects to having it dinned into her. But the acid she treats you with is not the acid of a heart imbittered. It is the sanitary acid that brings out into bold relief some of the high lights of life. It is unerring instinct for the exposure of crudity, for sham, but more than all for slovenliness. Dorothy Parker hates slovenliness. And she writes of mentally and morally slovenly people, and especially of women, in a way to make your bobbed hair curl. I'll say she is immense!

Nature eventually levels all things, and can always be relied upon to counteract all tendency to extremes. We see this constantly illustrated in literature. The pendulum swings back and forth; the Victorian age is succeeded by the present age; later on the women will be wearing hoop skirts again, and gentlemen with the enormous talents of Robert W. Chambers and Rupert Hughes will clothe their thoughts in mother hubbards. And, in many minor ways, this is true. There were people who declared not so very long ago that no woman in America wrote anything clever. The age of Pollyana set in. A publisher's reader (I know who he was but refuse to tell) happened by chance on a manuscript in which a mushy female corresponded

with an equally mushy male, and he insisted on its
publication.   It was thereby discovered that nothing
was too banal, nothing was too reeking with edulcora-
tions, nothing was too flabby and googoogeyey to tempt
a public clamoring for sentimentality.   Thus there
succeeded a series of pop-eyed stories, each one worse
than the last, until all the changes had been rung and
any slobbering female whose head rose above the surface was in danger of her life.   The war came on; the
rough stuff sex-movement with it, and, to counteract
all the former mush, came Mrs. Parker, piercing below
the surface of woman and eating out her foibles.   All
she does is to voice what people think inevitably.   It
is a simple expedient, but, oh, how rare!

CHAPTER XXVII

HENRY A. SHUTE

("Brite and Fair")

MR. SHUTE'S "Real Diary of a Real Boy" was published in 1904, and attracted a great deal of attention, not only from lovers of boys but from lovers of humanity—this being pretty much the same thing. Mr. Shute is a comparatively young man; he was born something before 1860; he illustrates a great principle, however, which is to the effect that it is necessary to become fifty before you can become fifteen. What he says about himself follows:

I am not aware that I have had any conscious preparation for book or story writing. As a newly-fledged and not particularly well-fledged lawyer I was fortunate in having an office in an old brick building on Water Street in Exeter known as Ranlet's Block. In the third and top story, the *Exeter News-Letter* was printed. In the second story, the office of the Editor was next to my office.

The Editor was out of health and inattentive to business. The foreman, John Templeton, was a tremendous worker, and a veritable Poo Bah on the paper. As I had little, if anything to do in my office, I wrote up the locals and an occasional editorial in a spirit of pure altruism and to kill time. Templeton, who had a keen sense of humor, collaborated with me, and some of the description of local affairs that we produced would have secured our extradition from any state, and should have resulted in our banishment from any civilized community. It was not that we spoke ill of any one. We gilded lilies and refined roses that prior to our articles had been regarded, and perhaps justly, as thorns that "infest the ground."

But it was in the writing of obituary notices that I shone with a garish light. It is a pretty safe thing for an obituary writer of a country paper to observe the maxim *De mortuis nil nisi bonum*. I do not think an obituary writer ever so strictly observed the letter of the maxim as I did. Did an old curmudgeon die, who in all his business transactions had been a living illustration of cupidity and meanness, I eulogized him as a model of lavish generosity. Did a common scold pass beyond, who, in colonial days, would have been ducked as such, I drew a pathetic picture of her kindness, forbearance and Christian good will to all. Did a town rounder, who had, like Mulvany

> "Put his fut through ivery
> wan of the tin commandments
> bechune revelly and taps"

I spoke of him as a man of singularly blameless life, an *Integer Vitae, scelerisque purus*. Of course the friends and relatives of the deceased bought hundreds of the papers and sent them broadcast, while the rest of the subscribers snorted with disgust.

I wrote a few editorials of so complex a nature that nobody could understand them, which was just what I wanted, for I could not understand them myself, nor could John. In short we reduced the standing of the paper, in the brief time before the demise of the editor, to its lowest ebb as an uplifter of the public morals and as a literary organ.

Upon the death of the editor and owner, my friend bought the paper, and, very properly dispensing with my hitherto invaluable aid, succeeded in developing it to and maintaining it at a very high standard, which under his admirable management, it still maintains.

In April of 1883 I wrote my first story, "The Story of Josh Zack," a tale of the unexplained disappearance of a locally popular colored boy in the forties. The main facts of the story were true, but I invented a few characters and a great many particulars to embellish suitably, and to give color to the tale, winding up with a description of two stained and weatherbeaten tablets in the "Old Cemetery." On Saturday, the day after publication, and on Sunday the regular day for cemetery promenades, the ground was black with citizens of all ages and stations in life hunting for the tablets, which of course could not be found.

As a result I lost what little standing as a man and a brother my literary efforts on the *News-Letter* had left me. I should hate to write down just what some people said about me. It was years ago, and I have in a measure outlived it, possibly because I have outlived many of my detractors. And in the thirty-seven years since that time lots of things have happened in Exeter. The Goddess of Liberty has been taken down from the tower of the Town Hall, her crinoline readjusted and hand-painted, and the scales of Justice, which are supposed to be even, made so by skilled carpentry.

Then there have been several fires, a few embezzlements, several houses and barns have been painted, the first crocuses have appeared on the lawns of prominent citizens, the ice has gone out of Salt River every spring, the alewives have appeared with great regularity, the first dandelion has been duly plucked by our observant citizen, Mr. Blank, and duly embalmed in print, and really we have been too excited and busy to remember things.

A few years later I found, in a small box that dated to my early boyhood days, several articles of a most interesting nature, among which was a youthful diary which I published serially in the *News-Letter*. Very much to my surprise it excited rather more than a local interest and I received an offer by the Everett Press of Boston to publish it in book form.

"The Real Diary of a Real Boy" appeared in the fall of 1902 and owing to the fact that it dealt with actual occurrences and with characters under their true names, and that it contained an appendix furnishing the addresses of the characters, and a short history of their subsequent achievements, the book met with a very unexpected success.

This was followed by "Sequil," "Real Boys" and a dozen other books, in all of which the scenes were laid in Exeter, and the characters taken from our most worthy citizenry "naked and unashamed."

It is a curious fact that the supposedly useless fads I had as a boy and as a youth, and which still remain with me, a love for music and musical instruments, for farm and domestic animals, for woods, fields and country roads, and above all else for my own town Exeter and its citizens, have been the stimuli under which all my books and magazine articles have been written.

And which book do I like the best? That is difficult to say. I think the two last books published.

"The Real Diary of the Worst Farmer" and "Brite

and Fair" are the best. I like the chapter in the latter beginning "September 1" because it gives the best description of the utterly dissimilar but most delightful qualities of my father and mother.

I am particularly fond of the closing chapter of "The Youth Plupy or the Lad with a Downy Chin," as showing how much of a real hero my father was in my eyes.

If I have shown any talent for seeing the funny side of life and for describing it, I owe it, I am sure, to the wit, the optimism and the whimsicality of my father, which, in a very small degree, I have inherited or developed by delightful association with him. Any facility in writing is due in a great measure to my experience as a volunteer obituary writer for the *Exeter News-Letter* in the old days.

I have been frequently advised to quit the practice of law and to give all my time to writing. But no one but a lawyer, and a country lawyer at that, realizes the intense interest and the almost infinite variety of the general practice of law. And I hope that, for many years to come, I may sit in my office, and as the afternoons wear on and the shadows deepen, may look across our beautiful Square towards the west where the tall elms, the colonial houses and the church spires stand stark and black against the rose of the after-sunset, and watch them fade into darkness.

CHAPTER XXVIII

I WANTED to discover how "Dere Mabel" was written, so I wrote to the author, and this is what he sends me. It is a model autobiography. It contains no names or dates, but it does tell how he came to write. The dull and useless facts about Mr. Streeter are that he is a Harvard man, and was born in New York in 1891, and that he is an Episcopalian. He is the first humorist I know who calls himself openly an Episcopalian (except all the bishops and clergy of the Episcopal church). But what he writes about himself is interesting:

In view of the fact that this brief, autobiographical sketch may fall before the eyes of some young aspirant in the field of humorous writing, I approach the task with diffidence. By an indiscreet phrase I might draw into the shades some joyous, sunlit disposition, and the world, possessing too few, would never forgive the theft.

To any persons seized with a desire to whet their sense of humor on the General Public I issue a solemn warning. To those hardy souls who choose to disregard the signs I offer the few crumbs thrown me from time to time by experience.

Primarily, a successful career in any line of endeavor involves covering a certain amount of vertical distance measured from the bottom to the top. Now there are, obviously, two ways of covering this distance. One is by beginning at the bottom and working up to the top; the other by beginning at the top and working down to the bottom.

For some reason the ascending method is almost universally recommended. Personally, however, I favor the second, or descending, which I have found infinitely easier. As an example I can only refer to my first work, "Dere Mable." It could not have sold better had it been suppressed by the Anti-Vice Society. Following the Descending Theory in orderly sequence my publishers disposed of only half as many copies of the second attempt. The third never achieved the dignity of four numbers, and I refrain from giving data on the fourth lest it prejudice my future.

Thus you will see that, with four manuscripts, I covered the distance from the bottom to the top; only, by the simple plan of moving against the traffic, I avoided congestion and accomplished the journey with a quarter of the effort usually required. By moving down instead of up I made the law of gravity my friend rather than my enemy. In this case, gravity is a great aid to a humorous writer.

There is another point which should be impressed upon the serious-minded young humorist. The best way to insure the success of any book in lighter vein is to be unaware that you are writing it. When I wrote the "D. M." letters I had no idea that they would ever appear in book form. For that reason only did I escape the temptation to be funny.

In order to disentangle this paradox I must explain how the "letters" ever came into the light of day.

Their entrance was that of a hemp rope through the needle's eye.

In the fall of 1917 while I was serving with the 27th Division at Camp Wadsworth, South Carolina, I was assigned to the *Camp Wadsworth Gas Attack*— which I hasten to explain was a weekly paper, not a disorder. The task of editing a humorous page titled "The Incinerater" was foisted upon me. It was to be filled, according to orders, with "short, witty paragraphs on Army Life."

I could think of many short things to say about the army, but they lacked all other qualities except the profane. As a humorist I grew morose.

When the first number was assembled for press "The Incinerater" contained two senile jokes which were originally employed by General McClellan to depress the Confederate troops across the Potomac. The remainder of the page rivalled my mind. In desperation I wrote a letter from a soldier to his "sweetheart." It was a despicable trick, and only used as a last resort.

I handed this to Dick Connell, the editor. With his usual good taste he O. K.'d the jokes as having considerable historic value. His criticism of the letter was to crumple it up and throw it under his desk. Whereupon he went to mess.

Although I was unaware of it at the time, my future life hinged at this point upon Connell's appetite. Had he curbed it sternly and made up the dummy before he left, as was his duty—had he subordinated it to ordinary politeness and offered me the chance to eat first, I should not have been writing this article today.

He did neither of these things, however. He went out to mess, leaving the dummy and me in the office. I quickly discovered that we had much in common.

The rejected letter was smoothed out and shipped hastily to the printer with the rest of the manuscript.

The thing didn't look so bad in print, so, the following week, I repeated. Repetition quickly grew into habit.

Just before the Division sailed for France I received a five-day leave. It occurred to me that, while in the North, I might stumble on some editor optimistic enough to turn my manuscript into a book. So I stuffed the letters into a pair of extra putties and set forth.

I had a note of introduction to a publishing house which specialized in school text-books and dictionaries. Somewhat to my indignation they turned down my offering after reading the title. With thirty-five minutes to catch my train for the South I looked up the publishing house nearest the station. Throwing the manuscript and my camp address on the Treasurer's desk, I ran from the office, leaving the firm somewhat doubtful as to my sanity.

Fortunately for me the deal was finally closed. The book appeared a few days before my outfit sailed. For several months I dodged my mail about France. When it finally overtook me I learned that "Dere Mable" had grown to be a big, big girl. I began to feel more like her godson than her godfather. Writing looked to me like a glorious profession.

Since then I have had more opportunity to establish a perspective. After two years I have decided that humor is one of the most trying and elusive tasks in the world. But yesterday I heard a similar groan from a lawyer, a portrait painter, and a bond salesman —so I do not take my decision too seriously.

It is not a bad job if any one could ever discover how to do it. This little matter of humor has been analyzed, dissected and resolved into its component parts by scores of literary chemists. Yet nobody will ever be able to discover that mysterious drop which converts dead commonplace into warm, living reality —a reality which draws a reflex chuckle from the cross, busy old world. And it is the occasional sound of that spontaneous gurgle which repays so many days of unproductive labor, and keeps the alchemists bending over their phials.

CHAPTER XXIX

E. W. TOWNSEND

SUNSET COX, who used to be one of our most "compelling" humorists, has related in quite a charming manner how the reputation for being a humorist is likely to kill a man off in every other respect. There is no objection of course to a man displaying a sense of humor, say in Congress, but to write humor, to be known as a humorist—that is the difficult part. Elsewhere in this volume I have given some examples of this fatal tendency, and how it was parried—as in the case of Mark Twain and his "Joan of Arc."

Mr. Townsend, however, is probably the only humorist who lived down his reputation long enough to be elected to Congress. Although well known as the author of "Chimmie Fadden," this interesting fact lay in his past more like a bright and shining cloud than a shadow. I rather think that he himself deplored it. But, at any rate, it had no apparent effect upon his congressional career. His comrades, so far as I know, did not hold it up against him.

How he came to write "Chimmie Fadden" is told by Arthur B. Maurice perhaps better than I can tell it.

The star reporter on the *New York Sun,* Mr. Townsend, was one day sent to "cover" a newsboys' dinner at the Brace Memorial Newsboys Lodging House. There the idea of Chimmie Fadden first came to him. At the dinner was the woman, a slum worker, who was the original of Miss Fannie of the stories. After the first tale had been written Mr. Charles A. Dana sent word ordering the writing of the second story. Others followed, and began to be known and quoted. One day Mr. Chester S. Lord, then the managing editor of the *Sun,* said: "Can't you run up and find that little Bowery chap you've been writing about and get him to talk some more." "Oh," said Townsend, "he's purely an imaginary character." "Then imagine some more about him."

* * *

It was a very different New York that was reflected for us in those Chimmie Fadden tales of the early nineties. The Bowery was still the Bowery, and was almost as Irish in origin and flavor as it had been in the days of the "Bowery boys." As a companion in life, Mr. Townsend bestowed upon Chimmie a French lady's maid, whom Chimmie dubbed "de Duchess." Other characters of the tales were "de Duchess's" mistress, Miss Fannie. Miss Fannie's father, to whom Chimmie flippantly referred to as "His Whiskers," and Mr. Paul, who eventually became Miss Fannie's second husband. One of the drollest of the stories was that which told of the appearance of Chimmie and "de Duchess" at the festivities of the Rose Leaf Social Outing and Life Saving Association. When Mr. Townsend was in San Francisco he and a number of other members of the Bohemian Club spent most of their leisure time cruising about on a yacht. They adopted the humorous title "Rose Leaf Social and Outing Club." On one of these cruises they rescued

the crew of a boat that had capsized in the bay, and
the "Life Saving" was added in commemoration of
this event.

* * *

After the stories that made up the first Chimmie
Fadden book had appeared in the *Sun* Mr. Townsend
went to Mr. Dana to ask permission to have them
brought out in book form. Mr. Dana, in giving the
required consent, added, as he then thought extravagantly, "And I hope that you sell ten thousand
copies." A few months later, a close friend of Mr.
Dana gave Mr. Townsend a dinner to celebrate the
hundred thousandth copy of "Chimmie Fadden" sold.
The next morning Mr. Dana went to Mr. Townsend's
desk in the *Sun* office and, after referring to the dinner,
said: "Can you tell me why 'Chimmie Fadden' has
reached a hundred thousand?" "Because," replied
Townsend, "of the sentimental relations of Chimmie
Fadden and Mr. Paul toward Miss Fannie."

* * *

Probably most readers have forgotten that Mr.
Townsend was once challenged to a duel by no less a
personage than the late Richard Harding Davis.
About the same time that he was writing the "Chimmie
Fadden" stories Mr. Townsend was making a certain
"Major Max" series the medium of his passing observations on aspects of current life in general. In
Richard Harding Davis's "Our English Cousins"
there was described the changing of the guard at St.
James' in London. With the description, Major Max
found flippant fault to such effect as to provoke from
the creator of "Van Bibber" a challenge worthy of a
less hard-headed age. Soon after Mr. Davis's "The

Princess Aline" appeared and a San Francisco paper telegraphed Mr. Townsend for a fifteen-hundred word review of the book. The review—probably the only book review ever telegraphed—was, however, measured and laudatory, and contained no allusion to the narrowly averted "affair of honor."

What is so singular now, after this charming account of Mr. Townsend's creations, is that the man is so silent. Surely a genuine humorist like Mr. Townsend ought, in the maturity of his powers, to produce genuine satire of a high order.

Mr. Townsend's observations on Congress alone, written as he alone could write them, would be delightful reading.

CHAPTER XXX

J. A. WALDRON

By J. A. W.

I GO back to first principles in journalism. Impatient of school, I began active life as a printer's apprentice at my birthplace, Sherburne, New York, in the office of a country weekly. The "printing office" in a small town then was—as no doubt it still is—the most fascinating of local institutions. And a printer then was a man with a comprehensively practical knowledge of the Art Preservative, whereas now he is competent only in some special branch of the craft, for machinery has developed it to a manufacturing enterprise.

I entered journalism as a young man in Albany, on the *Argus,* when the late St. Clair McKelway was editor of that journal, Daniel Manning, later Cleveland's Secretary of the Treasury, owner, and Colonel Daniel S. Lamont political writer. I took up Colonel Lamont's assignment as reporter of the Senate and Capitol Hill, in addition to reporting the Court of Appeals, service for the Associated Press, and special work for several big out-of-town papers when Lamont went with Governor Cleveland as private secretary.

From the *Argus* I went to the *Albany Evening Journal* under the W. J. Arkell régime and the chief editorship of the late John A. Sleicher—I becoming city editor. My predecessor in that position was Charles R. Sherlock, now prominent in the United Cigar Stores administration. As city editor of the *Evening Journal* I had the early training in newspaper work of men who have distinguished themselves in that and other fields. Among them were John P. Gavit, remembered as Washington manager of the Associated Press, afterward managing editor of the *New York Evening Post,* then with Harper & Brothers; Henry I. Hazelton, for ten years night editor of the *New York Press,* associated with other metropolitan papers, chief writer and translator for the Italian Bureau in this country during the war, and now managing his own business in Chicago; Thomas N. Sammons, afterward prominent as a newspaper man in Tacoma, then in a senatorial secretaryship in Washington, and later consul-general at Tokyo, where, and in other cities in Japan he served this government under at least three administrations. Other men with me on the *Evening Journal* in whose early careers I had some influence were Amos P. Wilder, later a prominent editor in the West and a representative of this country abroad; Eugene Chamberlain, appointed Commissioner of Navigation by President Cleveland, and still holding the position; and Robert Fuller, afterward private secretary to Governor Hughes, then on the *New York Herald,* and now secretary of the Merchants Association of New York.

I came to New York primarily to secure publication of a manuscript on Shakespeare—indorsed as a notable literary discovery by the late Professor Dowden of Dublin University, and declared to be the most valuable addition to Shakespeariana in a generation by the late Professor William J. Rolfe, of Cambridge—but that is another story, and an amusing one. At that time—

some thirty years ago—a noted memorist, whose professional style was "Loisette," after successes the world over, had an office on Fifth Avenue, and engaged me to write a book on memory systems for him. That involved a lot of study, as it began with the ancients, but he paid me for it, and I wrote the book. He wanted, he said, to bequeath his system to the public, and by the book to show how superior his system was to any that had preceded it. His system was based on the association of ideas. The plates for the work were made, but the book was never published.

In Albany, in my newspaper time there, that city was, and long had been, a great dramatic center, as a history of the American stage will reveal. And there in those days the dramatic criticism was quite metropolitan. On the side, with my other work, I had been a dramatic critic there, and had some acquaintance with the contemporary stage. Thus naturally in New York I gravitated to the *Dramatic Mirror,* and soon became its managing editor. For a long period when I was with the *Mirror* it was recognized abroad as well as here as the leading dramatic journal. With me on the *Mirror* were such men as the late Albert Ellery Berg and Arthur Hornblow; and later I had a hand in training—for then they were by no means as well known as now—as staff men Townsend Walsh, since prominent in the business end of the theater as well as a writer; Whitman Bennett, well known in the better side of the motion-picture industry; Porter Emerson Brown, Channing Pollock, Jules Goodman, and others.

For eight years, while I was editor of the *Mirror* —a period during which her greatest successes were scored—I evolved the press publicity for Mrs. Fiske. Some of her plays during the time were "Tess of the

D'Urbervilles," "Mary of Magdala," and "Becky Sharp."

I wrote for *Judge,* when a young daily newspaper man, and when the late Isaac Gregory was editor. I have been editor and literary editor of *His Honor* for some ten years. If I have anything to be proud of, aside from my having had a hand in developing a number of good men, it is this: That, after many years in the very different fields, I have noted I happily developed new angles as a writer in a still different field.

CHAPTER XXXI

HARRY LEON WILSON

HARRY LEON WILSON had the distinction of being the editor of the old *Puck* during its palmiest days, from 1896 to 1902. After he left the paper it went through a long series of vicissitudes. It was finally bought by Mr. Straus, and he disposed of it to Mr. Hearst. Mr. Hearst, through his representatives, endeavored to put it on its feet, but *Puck* by that time—which was only a couple of years or so ago—was to all intents and purposes feetless. It was not, however, as its editor that Mr. Wilson achieved his distinction. He was destined to greater things. I tried to get him to write something for this book, but he was silent. Then, not wishing to break my rule that I myself must write as little of the book as possible, I got a friend of his to write the following biography:

Harry Leon Wilson is so modest that, if it weren't for communicative friends of his, we'd not know much about him. One of them who "knew him when he wore knee pants, and apparently had no other object in life except to read, chuckle to himself, and grow fat" vouchsafes the assurance that he is not English, as some folks think he must be from his "Ruggles of

Red Gap." His father came from New York State
to Illinois. Harry was born in Oregon, about one
hundred miles from Chicago. His home town wasn't
proud of him, for he wouldn't go to school. The
first money he ever earned, $1, was paid for the arduous
task of setting half a column of type. He studied
stenography, but he didn't do anything with it except
to keep it on hand when he went with the men sent
out to the wild Sierra Nevada country to write a life
of Fremont. Before any one knew it he was sending
stories to the East and getting them accepted. *Puck*
offered him a job on the staff—and he's just gone on
writing best-sellers, and jaunting off to Europe. With
Booth Tarkington he wrote that shekel-luring comedy
"The Man From Home." His early books were
illustrated by Rose Cecil O'Neil, the Kewpies' mamma,
who later became Mrs. Wilson. She isn't any more,
though. Mr. Wilson, with a new, charming, and
talented wife, is one of the colony of authors and
artists living on the coast a few hours' ride from
San Francisco.

Mr. Wilson has other qualities besides the talent of
writing humor. Indeed his humor may be said to be
a by-product. He is a novelist; he is a satirist. He is
one of the few humorists in America who have risen
above the personal pronoun "I" and given to his work
a lasting quality that will make it long remembered as
a part of the best literature of the time.

His last book, "Merton of the Movies," fully sus-
tains his reputation.

CHAPTER XXXII

CAROLYN WELLS

CAROLYN WELLS has so many books to her credit—or discredit, as she is so modest as to insist upon—that one is quite bewildered by their variety and extent. It may be said of her, as Portia said of Mercy, however, that the quality of her humor is not strained, but falleth like the gentle dew from heaven alike upon the just and unjust.

It was many years ago—it must have been near the beginning of this century that I recall quite vividly one day receiving a manuscript from Miss Wells. I am quite certain that it was the first manuscript she had sent to *Life,* of which I was then the literary editor. It consisted of some highly amusing verses about the wearing of hats by women at the theater. At that time this hideous custom was still in vogue, and Miss Wells undoubtedly performed a great service for suffering humanity by thus lampooning it. I considered the verses so good that they were duly illustrated by Mr. Allan Gilbert.

The joy of thus finding, or at least welcoming, a new contributor is one of the high compensations of being an editor. At that time I flattered myself that I was the only one that knew about Miss Wells. In this, however, I was undoubtedly mistaken. Miss Wells herself declares that her two guardian angels among mortals were *St. Nicholas* and the *Century Magazine,* and, among immortals, Oliver Herford and Gelett Burgess. It was to Mr. Burgess, at that time editor of the inimitable *Lark,* that she sent her first work.

She once said in an interview:

"I regard Gelett Burgess and Oliver Herford as my masters. From them I learned all I know about nonsense. It was they who taught me the technique of verse making and the science of silliness. Yes, silliness, to be genuinely funny, must be scientific. It's strange but people don't give us nonsense folks credit for one-tenth the gray matter we've really got to have in order to manufacture our particular brand of literary product. Now if we were to write sentimental stuff about love and the moon and the wind sighing in the trees we would get far more credit, though it isn't half so hard to do. Why, I don't mind saying that I had to work patiently learning my trade before I could write anything that the editors would so much as look at, though I am certain I could have trained myself to reel off love sonnets in much less time."

The Price of Success

"Unappreciated genius! Not a bit of it!" she echoed, laughing at the suggestion. "I don't believe in unappreciated genius, and besides, appreciated or otherwise, I am not a genius. I'm an honest, respectable working girl, and I couldn't be a genius if I tried. I know what my limitations are and they are very rigidly drawn. I work pretty hard, but I get a lot of fun out of my work, probably because I always try to infuse as much fun as possible into it. I am constitutionally fun-loving. I believe in having all the fun one possibly can. Writing nonsense came naturally to me, but, like most other things in their natural state, my faculty was quite worthless until I began training it. I kept sending things to the papers, and the stuff came back. It came back because it was trash. I knew it was trash, but at the same time I had faith in myself. I pegged away. I had made up my mind I was going to write nonsense verse. I was inspired by the genius and example of Lewis Carroll. Of course I didn't hope ever to attain his distinction; still I thought well enough of myself to believe I had some stray talents in that direction. All I needed was a trainer, a teacher, and I knew it. At last I found him in Mr. Gelett Burgess."

The chocolates in the little dish were all done now, and Miss Wells rose, crossed the room to another table and brought over a fresh, unopened, five pound box.

"Where did I leave off? Oh, yes, about Mr. Burgess. Well, that was in 1895. I got hold of a copy of the *Lark* one day. It was a San Francisco paper, devoted to nonsense, and Mr. Burgess was the editor. He was also, it appeared, the sole contributor. I supposed this was because nonsense-verse writers were so rare, but I afterward discovered my mistake. Among other literary gems I read in that precious publication was:

'The window has four little panes;
But one have I;
The window-panes are in its sash—
I wonder why!'

Miss Wells undid the string on the box and filled up the bonbon dish afresh. Then she laughed.

"It may not have been the most exalted ambition of which a young Christian lady of my bringing up should have been capable, but I must confess that, when I read those verses, I felt I would rather be the author of either one of them than to have written, let us say, 'Evangeline.' I immediately wrote to Mr. Burgess asking if he wished contributions for his somewhat erratic paper. The letter I received in reply was not encouraging—indeed, it was rather sarcastic. A less nonsensical person than myself would have voted Mr. Burgess a brute, and would have told him to go hang himself and his paper. But I, who never did take life, or men, or the things men say seriously, sent him instead a contribution. It came back very promptly, with the added information that the editor did not think me up to the mark, and that I had better stop trying to write nonsense stuff. I replied with still another contribution, and this time I met with a hurricane of ridicule.

"He not only rejected my poor verses, but he spurned them, he hooted at them. Nothing daunted, I even replied to this assault upon my vanity, and in his reply to this letter, which also contained another contribution, Mr. Burgess flattered me by pointing out in a score of ways just why and how I had failed as a poet of nonsense. That was the first encouragement anybody had ever given me, and thus encouraged I began to send him my stuff with systematic regularity, and he quite as systematically, and quite as regularly, rejected them, when they were worth rejecting. It usually happened, though, that they were tossed in the wastebasket, though the editor never failed to write me in criticism of them. I thus got into a spirited correspondence, and fourteen months after I had sent in my first contribution, and after submitting hundreds, only to have them rejected, at last I had one accepted. If I don't deserve credit for patience, I don't know who does. During this weary period of probation, while I was spending all my pin money in postage to San Francisco, I was learning a great deal about the technique of verse writing, and considerable, too, about the science, or rather the philosophy, of nonsense. One of the first lessons I was taught by Mr. Burgess was the ability to distinguish between silliness and nonsense. Silliness is chaotic, while nonsense—that is, nonsense manufactured for commercial purposes—has got to be organic, well ordered, and, you might say, almost mathematical in its precision, and in its certainty to hit the reader or listener straight between the eyes, as it were.

Philosophy of Nonsense

"In real genuine nonsense, there is always a most ludicrous, and, at the same time, a most logical surprise awaiting. Without the element of surprise nonsense fails to be nonsense. Not only must it be logical, but it must not be too obvious, and it must always be truthful, that is it must be truthful and convincing within the range of probabilities set forth in the argument and proposition. That is what I mean by the mathematical precision of a genuine nonsense verse. You see, we nonsense poets, like to think that the mechanism of our art rests on principles as unalterable and as fundamental as Greek tragedy."

In this account of herself, which relates to her earlier work, Miss Wells speaks of her friends. Being our chief woman humorist, and a quite ubiquitous argument against that foolish declaration that women have no sense of humor, her friends among men writers number quite a host in themselves, and many of them have written of her talents in the most engaging manner. Mr. Arthur Bartlett Maurice, one time editor of the *Bookman,* in an article has declared himself as follows:

If Miss Carolyn Wells has any grievance against life it is that she never receives credit for what she considers the best thing that she ever wrote. Some years ago a large business enterprise made her an offer of one hundred dollars for a suitable phrase to be used for advertising purposes. She sent back "The Smile That Won't Come Off." Its success was instantaneous. But the phrase was at once incorporated into the American version of the English language, with the quite natural result that Miss Wells' part in the matter was entirely forgotten. When Mr. Gelett Burgess first introduced the now hackneyed terms of "Bromide" and "Sulphite" he made the statement that there were only seven female Sulphites in existence. He placed Miss Wells at the head of the list. "She is a Sulphite of the Sulphites," he said. "You can never know what she is going to think, do or say. Sometimes she isn't even witty. But none of us could be witty if there were no Bromides to be made fun of." This opinion of Miss Wells' uncertainty is shared by a certain well-known theatrical manager. Miss Wells had written a book for an opera which had been submitted to the manager for consideration. As a whole it could not be used, but there was one lyric that the manager wanted to interpolate in another opera. He telegraphed, asking if he could have the Kitten

Song. Her reply was, "You can have the kitten, you can have the kitten." The next time the manager met Miss Wells he asked her why she had twice told him that he could have the kitten.

"Well," she replied, "I could send ten words for the same price as five, and I thought I might just as well get all that the telegraph company would stand for. I always did love bargains." Miss Wells considers her best bit of work to be her reply to Gelett Burgess's Purple Cow, modeled on Chaucer.

"A mayde ther was, semely and meke enow,
She sate a-milken of a Purpil Cowe;
Rosy hire cheke as in the Moneth of Maye
And sikerly her merry songe was gay
As of the Larke uprist, washen in dewe,
Like Shene of Sterres sperkled hire eyen two.
Now came ther by that way a hendy knight,
The Mayde espien in morwening Light.
A fair Person he was, of Corage trewe,
With lusty Berd and chekes of Rody Hewe:
'Dere Ladye' (quod he) 'far and wide I've straid,
Uncouthe Aventure in strange Countree made,
Fro Berwike unto Ware, Parde I vowe
Erewhiles I never saw a Purpil Cowe!
Fayne wold I knowe how catel thus can be?
Tel me, I praie you, of yore Courtesie!'
The Mayde her Milken stent. 'Goode Sir,' she saide,
'The master's mandement on us ylaid
Decrees that in these yclept Gilden Houres
Hys Kyne shall ete of nought but Vylet Floures.' "

But perhaps Miss Wells' really best bit of work was her poster girl parody on "The Blessed Damozel":

The blessed Poster Girl leaned out
   From a pinky-purple heaven:
One eye was red and one was green;
   Her bang was cut uneven;
She had three fingers on her hand,
   And the hairs on her head were seven.

Her robe, ungirt from clasp to hem,
   No sunflowers did adorn;
But a heavy Turkish portiere
   Was very neatly worn;
And the hat that lay along her back
   Was yellow like canned corn.

It was a kind of wabbly wave
   That she was standing on,
And high aloft she flung a scarf
   That must have weighed a ton;
And she was rather tall—at least
   She reached up to the sun.

She curved and writhed, and then she said,
   Less green of speech than blue,
"Perhaps I am absurd—perhaps
   I don't appeal to you;
But my artistic worth depends
   Upon the point of view."

I saw her smile, although her eyes
   Were only smudgy smears;
And then she swished her swirling arms
   And wagged her gorgeous ears.
She sobbed a blue-and-green-checked sob,
   And wept some purple tears.

Miss Wells is said to have a characteristically original rule for measuring the proper length of a book when she writes it herself. One of her many publishers asked her recently "Why do you always send us your book manuscript in a five-pound candy box?" "You see," replied Miss Wells, "when I feel that I am going to write a book I always buy a five-pound box of candy and a pint of ink. Then I begin to write. And when the candy is all gone, and the ink is all used up, I know that the book is long enough."

It is interesting to learn that Miss Wells numbered among her friends that fine American poet Joyce Kilmer, who gave his life for his country and the tragedy of whose death still lingers with those of us who knew and loved him. In 1915 Mr. Kilmer wrote for the *Times* an account of an interview with Miss Wells. Space forbids its completeness, but the following extracts are too good to omit:

"Then Americans aren't either humorous or serious?" I asked.

"Not in my opinion," she answered. "English humor, I think, is humor. But American humor is wit."

"Isn't that contrary to the generally accepted opinion?" I asked. "Isn't Mark Twain considered the greatest humorist of modern times?"

"Personally," said Miss Wells, "I never become wildly enthusiastic over Mark Twain as a humorist. He was a great novelist, a great interpreter, and he undoubtedly was witty. But I believe—and this is merely my own opinion, which is in this respect at variance with that of most of my friends—that much of the enthusiasm over Mark Twain's fun is merely a matter of tradition.

"People have been trained to believe that Mark Twain is a great humorist. So they laugh at his books and say that they are funny when as a matter of fact the fun has no real appeal to them. Much of Mark Twain's fun, like that of Bill Nye, is hopelessly old-fashioned; it belongs to a period wholly different from our own.

"I do not mean that Mark Twain was not a great writer. But if we look for a modern writer of Mark Twain's type we do not find a humorist, we find a novelist like Mr. Arnold Bennett, for example."

"And the English," I said, "are humorous?"

"The English humor," said Miss Wells, "is, I think, the best in the world. Now, I'm in no sense of the word an Anglomaniac. I am not saying that humor is better than wit or wit better than humor. But, as I said, I think that the English are humorous and the Americans witty."

"Who are the greatest of living humorists?" I said.

Miss Wells reflected for a moment.

"I think," she said, "that Sir Owen Seaman and Oliver Herford are the funniest men alive. Oliver Herford is English, and his work is thoroughly and definitely humorous, as is that of Sir Owen Seaman."

"But using the word 'humor' in its widest sense," I said, "what is the essential difference between the English variety and the American?"

"American humor," Miss Wells replied, "is finer than English humor, but it is often in bad taste. English humor is broader, and it seldom is in bad taste."

"How do you account for this difference?" I asked.

"It is a matter of national character," she replied. "There is the same difference between English and American social life, business methods and everything else. We are quick, deft, nervous, energetic; therefore our sense of fun finds its expression in the nimble exercise of wit. The English take everything much more seriously, therefore, their sense of fun finds expression in the more serious and dignified exercise of humor.

"Humor can be and generally is, dignified. Wit seldom is dignified. Only serious people can be really humorous, and Americans are not serious."

"What," I asked, abruptly, "is a sense of humor?"

Miss Wells did not hesitate or parry my question for a second.

"A sense of humor," she said, "is an appreciation of a happy misfit in the eternal fitness of things."

"And what," I asked, "is wit?"

"That is a harder question," she answered. "But sometimes wit is the verbal expression of a sense of humor."

The conversation drifted back to certain humorists, and Miss Wells again mentioned Oliver Herford.

"Did you ever hear the story of Oliver Herford and the Impressionist?" she asked. "The Impressionist painter was laying down the law to Oliver Herford, and objecting particularly to his making so many pictures of kittens.

" 'Of course you can draw,' he said, 'but why will you draw nothing but kittens? It's kittens, kittens, kittens all the while.'

"Oliver Herford listened patiently. At last he said, 'Yes, I do make pictures of kittens. But at any rate I call them kittens. I don't call them landscapes!' "

Miss Wells, who edited a few years ago a Satire Anthology, does not believe that America has produced many distinguished satirists.

"Satire is almost a lost art in the United States," she said. "We have no time for satire."

"Satire requires long and serious thought. We don't take things seriously enough to satirize them. The English take literature and life so seriously that they readily become satirical.

"The greatest of all satire is social satire. And to write social satire one must seriously regard social ranks and gradations. We don't do that in the United States, so we don't produce great satirists.

"I suppose that the most distinguished of our satirists was James Russell Lowell. Because of his 'Biglow Papers' some critics rank him with Thackeray as a satirist.

"Of course all our writers of light verse are satirists, in a way. Oliver Herford sometimes writes satire, but most of the best humor and wit of our time has in it a 'sweetness and light' that does not properly belong to satire. Gelett Burgess's 'Book of Bromides' is satire.

"Who was the greatest English satirist?" I asked. "Was it Shakespeare?"

"No," said Miss Wells. "Not Shakespeare. Shakespeare is the greatest genius, of course, but not the greatest satirist. Let's see, who was the greatest satirist? Carlyle was a great social satirist, but a satirist of the heaviest sort.

"Lewis Carroll and Edward Lear were not satirists, they were great nonsense writers. W. S. Gilbert was the greatest writer of light satire. But Thackeray— that's it, of course! Thackeray surely is the greatest satirist in the English language."

Miss Wells believes that the youth of the United States has much to do with the national attitude toward wit and humor.

"A young nation," she said, "like a young person, refuses to take things seriously. So the American people have a quick appreciation of wit and the English people have a deep appreciation of humor. As America grows older this will change.

"Rudyard Kipling is a good example of the English type of humorists. And nearly all English novelists show flashes of humor. On the other hand, nearly all American writers, novelists, essayists, even historians, show flashes of wit.

"And then, most of the American humorists are young, very young indeed, compared to the English humorous writers. When I was in London I saw the famous mahogany table in the office of *Punch*. Carved on it were the initials of the great contributors to *Punch*—nearly all of them men well on in years. Now, if an American humorous weekly were to have such a table, the initials carved on it would be the initials of young men."

Returning to the subject of the characteristics of English humor, Miss Wells said:

"Here is a joke that might stand as a type of British humor: A man who had dined very well indeed was unsteadily endeavoring to get to his home. He wavered up to a policeman and said: 'Is this Piccadilly Circus or is it Tuesday?'

"Now, I think that is a very funny story. But there are many intelligent Americans whom it does not amuse at all. There is nothing witty about it; but it is thoroughly humorous. It is founded on absurdity, like most English jokes.

"Nearly every picture and joke in *Punch* depends

for its effect on humor.   And nearly every joke in any American humorous weekly depends on wit."

Miss Wells, although she thinks that the general attitude toward humor changes with the age of a nation, believes that the greatest humor is ageless.

"The funniest things written to-day," she said, "would have been laughed at a hundred years ago, and will be laughed at a hundred years from now.   Humor has identity *per se;* it is not ephemeral.   The greatest humorists are accidents, splendidly independent of time and place."

In 1918 Miss Wells was married to Mr. Hadwin Houghton (since deceased) and took up her residence in New York.   Mr. George Horace Lorimer, editor of the *Saturday Evening Post,* having requested her to write the "Story of her Life," she gave this interesting account of herself:

Since reading the autobiographies of Henry Adams and Ella Wheeler Wilcox, I have been conscious of a strong desire to write my own.   Another pet ambition of mine is to appear in prose on the pages of the *Saturday Evening Post.*   And now, having been invited to kill these two birds with one stone, my cup of satisfaction is fuller than it was.

And yet, confronted with the longed-for opportunity, I can't think of a thing to say that would interest anybody.   For I was born and brought up in New Jersey, and, except for our ex-President, New Jersey never reared anybody very interesting.

I am not disparaging my native state.   It really has beautiful trees—but my soul is urban, and condemned to live under said trees.   I longed for city life "as the hart panteth for the water brook." Every other ambition was swallowed up in the desire to become an integral part of the population of New York City. Then I heard a story of a man who was in jail for twenty years, when a bright thought struck him and he jumped out of the window.

My bright thought was that by marrying I could live in New York! So I did and do.

I thought I'd give up my writing when I married; it seemed more proper so. But inexorable publishers insisted on my filling unexpired contracts that called for certain masterpieces of fiction, so I am still at it. Moreover, my husband proved a most satisfactory collaborator.

To write of myself is not so easy as I anticipated, for I am suffused with that extreme guilty feeling of egotism—and yet I have the smug satisfaction of knowing that in autobiography egotism is inevitable, even admirable. The kindly editor asked me to dilate on my outdoor sports. But I never go out of doors if I can possibly help it. Since the war made it impossible for me to take my walks abroad I don't take them at all. I am happy only among interior decorations, and truly blissful only when playing bridge or reading detective stories. The last time I was really out of doors was in Egypt.

Now, I dare say, I ought to write about my literary work. But it isn't work; it is only play. I can't bring myself to take it seriously. I think I am of the ilk of Mr. Pope's "mob of gentlemen who wrote with ease," and though I've been told what sort of reading easy writing makes, yet I incline to the attitude of Sentimental Tommy's Mr. Duthie, who said: "What's the need of being so particular? Surely, the art of writing consists in using the first word that comes and hurrying on." So I hurried on, until now I have over a hundred books to my discredit, and have most kindly relations with thirty-one different publishing houses. My subjects comprise all sorts—from thrilling detective stories to gentle girls' books; from humorous verse to grave essays. I follow any primrose path that I strike in the fields of literature—except *vers libre*.

No, I do not care for the new poetry—but I have influential friends who do—so it isn't entirely wasted.

I read all the new books by the best authors, the worst writers, and the mediums.

I have looked into spiritism lately, because when a new movement—or the recrudescence of an old one—interests me, I investigate it thoroughly, card catalogue it in my brain, and put it away.

And I have concluded that I agree with Hereward Carrington—there may be two per cent of truth in the matter of spirit manifestation, but there is positively ninety-eight per cent of fraud or self-deception. But, after all, we must admit that P. T. Barnum knew his public.

My life has been especially fortunate in the matter of friends. Stevenson said that, in a lifetime, one could not hope to meet more than twelve absolutely congenial spirits. I think that allowance far too liberal. I never met but one, and I married him. But friends, good, kindly, interesting, clever friends, have been as plenty as blackberries. As an alleged humorist, I have achieved friendships that might not have come to me otherwise.

Theodore Roosevelt became my friend, primarily because of my nonsense verse. In memory I see him now, walking up and down his veranda at Sagamore Hill, hands behind him, while I repeated ridiculous rhymes until he memorized them—and begged for more.

Similarly, my comic muse gained for me the friendship of such men as Sir Owen Seaman, editor of London *Punch,* and Sir William S. Gilbert, of "Pinafore" fame.

The latter said to me most kindly that he saw no reason why I shouldn't write light opera librettos for American audiences as successfully as he had done for the English people. I still treasure the compliment, but the only light opera I ever wrote graced the boards of the New Amsterdam Theater for but one short month. So I don't think I shall try that again, for I am always willing to accept my limitations.

Not long since a magazine editor invited me to write a serial for him, which could afterward be brought out in book form, and become a best seller.

It sounded attractive, and after inquiring carefully as to length of instalments and such details, I began it. I worked very hard over it and, with pride, I took him the first instalment for consideration. His verdict was that it fell so far below his expectations and desires it was really useless for me to write more of it.

I was disappointed, but bore the blow cheerfully and went back to my beaten tracks—and to beating a few new ones. And so my literary output has come to be remarkable for quantity rather than quality.

Having mastered the psychology of detachment, I can produce more copy in less time than any other writer in my class. I am more fond of achieving than striving. My ambitions must be realized—or dismissed as impossible. My theories must prove to be facts, or be discarded as worthless. My efforts must be crowned with success, or discontinued.

As for ideals, standards, aspirations—these are

chameleon words, and take color from their speakers
—often false tints.

One of our foreign ambassadors once told me that
he went a thousand miles into the desert to get away
from the word "uplift," and it was almost the first one
to greet his ear when he arrived at his destination—
and I cannot feel that I am quite alone in my in-
ability to enjoy the conversation of a class of people
in to-day's limelight who are, as Brander Matthews
expresses it, "educated beyond their intelligence," yet
I would not be considered as, in any way, intolerant of
the world or its denizens—a broad, sweet tolerance is
to my mind one of the greatest of the Christian graces.

But this is meant to be an autobiography—not auto-
introspection.   And I am constantly haunted by a
conviction that I ought to write of my "work."   They
all do.

Well, at present I am engaged in the compilation
of a volume of humorous verse.   It will be the largest
collection ever brought together in one volume, and
will be on India paper (since published).

Dr. Coates once said: "If you want to be happy
make a collection."

"What of?"

"Oh, anything; only make a collection."

I have collected all my life—from brass candlesticks
to old mahogany furniture; from authors' signed letters
to editors' signed checks; but the joy of collecting
humorous verse outweighs them all.   My only regret
is that I have but one volume to fill, big though it is,
and that I am forced to omit hundreds of wonderful
finds.

To work is decidedly educational too.   I've learned
that the real reason I can't care very much for Walt
Whitman is because he had no sense of humor.

Not that I would have wanted him to write humorous verse—though he did!—but I find that the most serious, exalted and sublime literature is the work of men whose sense of humor provides them with a mental balanced ration. A sense of humor necessarily endows one with a humor of sense—which sounds epigrammatic, even if I'm not quite sure of what I mean by it.

Perhaps George Eliot expressed it better when she said: "Hang on to your sense of humor. It'll carry you through when religion fails, and when money and friends are clean out of sight!" And, taken by and large, a sense of humor connotes happiness.

For happiness in this world is merely the ability to recognize it, and to it the humorless mind is often blind. Whereas the eyes of the soul filled with humor are blinded to many of life's unpleasantnesses.

My own attitude is that of Kipling's Tramp-Royal:

> Speakin' in general, I 'ave tried 'em all,
> The 'appy roads that take you o'er the world.
> Speakin' in general, I 'ave found them good.
>
> . . .
>
> So write, before I die, " 'E liked it all!"

CHAPTER XXXIII

THE professional wit is the peculiar product of America. It is true that there are paragraphists in all countries, but when one studies the newspapers of other countries, and sees the pitiful showing they make, one turns with a kind of subdued whoop of joy to the journals of the United States.

And especially to the country journals. The vein of homely philosophy, of deep sanity, of cutting satire and of genuine wit flows in a constant stream from the pens of our unknown humorists of the daily and weekly press. And, as will be seen, it is not confined to any one locality.

In a book that deals so largely with the makers of representative American humor, it would be an ungracious omission to refuse recognition to those men who are doing so much not only to entertain but to enlighten the great American public. I have, therefore, ventured to make this chapter about the one who is perhaps the greatest humorist among us, namely, U. S. Anonymous. And, inasmuch as this chapter is to be "different," it may not be out of place to say something about the making of epigrams—an art that goes back as far as we have any historical knowledge.

Cicero tells the story of a man who called and asked
for the mistress of the house. "She is not at home,"
said the servant. "Then," said the man, "tell her I
didn't call." This repartee, with a finished illustration,
appeared some few years ago on the cover of *Life*.
The humorous one or two line comment or epigram
turns almost inevitably on the change of a word which
shall produce a violent contrast. Beyond this, however, the art of the humorist is shown in his selection
of the right word in the wrong place, so to speak, so
that it will bring out his point. For example, it has
been a common saying that accidents will happen in the
best regulated families. But Mr. Oliver Herford, taking advantage not only of a kind of scandal that is
quite broadly known, but also of the sound of certain
words, declares that "actresses will happen, etc." There
we have the method. Your wit passes most of his
waking hours in the search of a phrase or a saying in
the hope that he can apply it to some condition.
Oscar Wilde was, in Great Britain, perhaps the most
notable example of the epigram maker. And yet he
fell far short of many of our own unknown paragraphists because his phrases were based not so much
on truth, as on any paradox that was clever without
regard to its accuracy. One instance is where he said
that he lived "in constant fear of not being misunder-
stood."

This, of course, is exceedingly clever. It almost
makes one gasp. But it is not true. Indeed, Wilde's
life was a passionate outcry against this sort of thing.
His "Ballade of Reading Gaol" and his "De Pro-
fundis" are both highly finished protests against this

very epigram. He belied himself. To be smart was always more important than to be truthful.

As a tribute, therefore, to Mr. U. S. Anonymous, I have selected from among many sources a few examples of what seem to me to be the best of the wit produced by these unknown knights of the quill. It is needless to say that I have made no attempt to be comprehensive. At this moment there are doubtless much better sayings floating about; but at least what follows is fairly representative of American paragraphic humor.

For every woman who makes a fool out of a man there is another woman who makes a man out of a fool.—*Lincoln Star*.

W. L. George, the English writer, says American children have no fun. Has he ever worn a top-hat down Main Street just after a big snowstorm?—*Little Rock Arkansas Gazette*.

The modern ladies should devote less energy to making permanent waves and more to making permanent wives.—*Chicago Journal of Commerce*.

The best way to honor our dead soldiers is to remember the living.—*Greenville (S. C.) Piedmont*.

We always thought the Irish wanted freedom until they began to insist on having a republic.—*Columbia (S. C.) Record*.

In the heart of the New York financial district there is an animal hospital.—*News Item*. We didn't know New York's financial district had a heart.— *Little Rock Arkansas Gazette*.

In 1916 Germany planned on making America pay for the war. Well, we are.—*Marquette Tribune.*

News Item: "Ford cars have taken another drop." Where'd they get it?—*Greenville (S. C.) Piedmont.*

Thrift is the art of buying a complexion to match a hat instead of buying a hat to match a complexion. —*Sioux City Journal.*

Free Verse: The triumph of mind over meter.— *Life.*

The world expects a financial revival. Billy Sunday should be hired to officiate, as he is about the best-known financial revivalist.—*Manila Bulletin.*

Many a bride sweeps up the aisle of a church who has never had a broom in her hand.—*Charleston Gazette.*

That Frenchman who says Americans can't appreciate tragedy should watch the grand stand when an outfielder drops an easy one.—*Cleveland News.*

Another thing that somewhat cheers the ultimate consumer on his weary way is the reflection that the shoe men have to buy coal and vice-versa.—*Columbus (Ohio) State Journal.*

That comet that was headed toward us took one good look and then kept on its way.—*Charleston Gazette.*

The Woman's Democratic League asks that a woman be named for Controller. Most any experienced married woman is qualified for the job.—*New York Morning Telegraph.*

We are burdened with excess prophets.—*Washington Post.*

The present tendencies in some nations are in the direction of self-termination.—*Asheville Times*

Our heart goes out to the soldier of Uruguay. The national anthem down there has seventy verses.—*Dallas News.*

There are 6,000,000 families in the United States who own their own homes. This is an anti-Bolshevik argument in a nutshell.—*Boston Shoe and Leather Reporter.*

If you will kindly buy your winter coal now, as the papers urge you to do, you may save some poor coal operator from the poorhouse.—*Labor* (Washington, D. C.)

The little red schoolhouse is better than the little-read citizen.—*Boston Herald.*

A news item says bagpipes are shown on a Roman coin of 68 A. D. History records that Nero killed himself the same year.—*Seattle Post-Intelligencer.*

What this country needs is less agitation about bobbed hair and more for bobbed government expenses. —*Kansas City Star.*

CHAPTER XXXIV

WRITERS OF HUMOROUS STORIES

Hugh Wiley, Octavus Roy Cohen, H. C. Witwer

THERE are a few writers of short stories who deal with tragic elements alone, who do not employ humor at all. But they are in the minority.

The majority of short-story writers make use of humor. Many of them employ it constantly; others use it as they need it. When we consider the number of short-story writers, it is plain that in a brief chapter like this, it would be impossible to treat of all of them. I can take only a few, mention a few others, and indicate in a general way what it is that constitutes a humorous short story.

As nine-tenths of all the writing done in America is on a commercial basis, it follows that the short-story market, on the whole the most prolific one, has been thoroughly plowed up. It is assumed for general commercial purposes, that any unintelligent person, who is willing to take any kind of a course offered in colleges—and it is getting to be a very poor college who doesn't have a professor of short stories—can write short stories, and thus raise a family, or possibly two. It is a fact, however, that, for some reason, writers of short stories don't seem to raise large families; some of them indeed don't even believe in living regularly with the people they marry.

The writing of short stories is, however, a great and noble sport. And if the story is a humorous one, the chance of selling it is thereby increased. Ever since O. Henry wrote, the country has been flooded with short-story writers. Many of these, however, have refused to adopt the method for writing short stories adopted by O. Henry, namely, of first serving a term in jail. They preferred to take the harder way of being instructed by some college professor, who "points with pride" to the fact that "Miss Holloway Smythe, after taking only three lessons in our great system, was able to sell a story to the *Saturday Evening Post* and the *Atlantic Monthly* in the same week."

But it would be churlish on my part to criticize the short-story schools. They have no doubt been useful in stimulating a lot of writers with real talent to write good short stories. Without these schools, these writers might not have written. That is all the schools have done for them. You cannot add a cubit to the stature of any writer; but if he himself has within him the capacity for growth in a particular direction, you may start him. We have produced, and we are now producing, a whole group of standardized story writers. But, on the whole, this may be the only way to get the best results because, when a whole lot of people are working according to a method, among them there are geniuses who are certain to break away. What astonishes any one who will take the trouble to

read our short stories to-day is their enormous cleverness.   Many of our best story writers have got the
thing down so fine that it is actually painful to read
their work, it so well done.   Not a single effect is
missing; one feels towards them the same confidence
that one feels towards a skilful juggler in a vaudeville.
It is quite apparent from the start, that, no matter how
many balls are in the air at one time, every one of them
will get back to the manipulator.   One begins to long
for the quaint old tales of yore, in which everything
was disorderly, and there were no clever sayings, no
epigrams, nothing but people who moved about and
said the most ordinary things.

Let me advise any reader to make this experiment:
Let him read, say, four or five short stories from our
leading magazines in any one month, and then let him
take up Jane Austen's "Pride and Prejudice" or her
"Sense and Sensibility" and read either one.   The contrast is indescribable.   It becomes immediately apparent
that, in the case of our periodical literature, the whole
affair is strained and artificial, but at the same time,
that it is incredibly more intricate, that it bears the same
relation to Jane Austen's time that a motor car does
to a sedan chair.

On this account alone it should not necessarily be
disparaged.   But when I say "artificial" I mean this:
it is almost wholly a matter of vocabulary.

To "market" a short story in these days is largely
a matter of vocabulary.   For example, take the case
of Harry Charles Witwer, one of our most prolific
humorous short-story writers.   When he first began
writing stories, he had, he says himself, no success

at all. Suddenly it was suggested to him that he write
as he talked. His success was immediate. The reason
was that he had been associating with a kind of people
whose vocabulary, to put it mildly, was "unique." All
he had to do was to sit down and reel off a short story
in the language he knew and he could sell it at once.
He has been accused of copying Ring Lardner. Very
likely. But at the same time I doubt if any one could
have the remarkable success that Mr. Witwer has won
merely as a copier of another man's work. Mr. Lardner, who has much greater depth than Mr. Witwer,
declares—as I have already stated—that he "learned
how to listen."

Now we may say this of Jane Austen, that she faithfully reproduced the more or less dull talk of her own
generation, and because she was a great artist, preserved for us this generation. That is true. Why then,
is not the same thing true of young men like Mr.
Witwer who, going about among race-track touts and
prize-fighting gentlemen, succeeded in translating this
atmosphere for us? The difference of course lies in
the profoundity of the one and the artificiality of the
other.

In estimating, therefore, our humorous writers and
particularly our short-story writers, we must remember that in many cases their success has depended upon
the fact that they were able to seize the vocabulary of
a particular group of people and translate it into money
just because a whole body of readers like to hear how
such people talk. Thus because the American people
are, above all things, lovers of sports, sporting stories,
stories concerning themselves with all kinds of ath-

letics are uniformly popular.   If any young man, with a moderate talent for writing, and a good memory, will go about for four or five years with any group of athletic people, and acquire their language and atmosphere, and will then write short stories based on any one of the well-known models, I will guarantee him a respectable income for ten years or more, when he ought to be willing to retire.

In spite of all I have written, however, the fact still remains that the story writer who must inevitably reap the greatest reward is the one who remains true to the principles of literary art.   Thus we shall find that Booth Tarkington, take him all in all, is our best humorous story writer, not alone because he has mastered the vocabulary of his characters, but because he has studied, he knows his characters, he gets under their skins: not always, but enough to show that he is an artist.   Mr. Witwer, for example, takes the prize-fighter first and the human being afterwards.   Booth Tarkington takes the boy as a boy, and afterwards as a human being.   His vocabulary is true to nature, but so is his boy.   With him, the plot is of no consequence, because it must inevitably grow out of his characters; and this is something that the tyro rarely learns.   Atmosphere and character are the two guardian angels of the short story.   And the method must be one of restraint.

Now let us get back to Mr. Witwer for a few moments.   Fortunately there is preserved for us the story of how he made his entry into literature!   The story appears in *Success* and is written by Thomas Thurs-

day. With some omissions—for which I hope **Mr.**
Thursday will forgive me—it is as follows:

New Success, June, 1921

Evidently H. C. Witwer and enthusiasm are twins.
And Pep is his private secretary. He radiates energy,
optimism, and pluck—a trinity that is guaranteed to
land a man on top when properly directed, or on
bottom when misdirected.

When I called to interview Mr. Witwer on how
he dared to climb to the high rungs without the aid of
a college education, I found him busily engaged in
putting the finishing touches to his latest short story,
which will bring him $1800. He was pounding the
periods, smashing the commas, and banging the ex-
clamation points in such a manner that I marveled that
the typewriter lasted more than a day without falling
apart.

During a pleasant hour, I succeeded in getting his
own story. It is a story better than anything he has
ever written.

Born at Athens, Pennsylvania, March 11, 1890.
Attended grammar school for several years and learned
everything but grammar. He seemed to be born with
a natural antipathy toward anything pertaining to
correct English. But don't pity him! His ignorance
of the proper correlation of Messrs. Verbs, Adjective
& Co., has made him approximately $125,000. In
other words, he has earned that sum by writing what
has been termed "the most perfect specimen of slang
ever propagated." And what Blanche Bates, the
famous actress, says is "full of pep, fun, of sporting
spirit, of the joy of youth."

Perhaps a sample, taken from his Ed Harmon stories, may be of interest. By the way, Harmon, is his most noted character—and most profitable—having realized more than $60,000. Herewith a sample— Ed Harmon doing the writing:

Well, yesterday mornin' I am up in my flat, Joe, engaged in the innocent pastime of playin' with my baby whilst Jeanne looks on with a lovin' smile on her equally lovin' face and a book by the name of "The Whole English Language in One Lesson," in her hand, when they's a ring at the bell. Our imported maid from Yonkers trips lightly over a rug into the room and exclaims that they's a guy outside by the name of Mac which wishes to see nothin' better than me. I give permission for him to come in.

"Well, well," he says, lettin' forth a grin. "The happy family, hey? How is everybody this mornin'?"

"What's the use of kickin'?" I says. "What d'ye think of my child?"

"Fine!" says Mac. "What is it?"

"What d'ye mean what is it?" I hollers. "It's a baby—think it was a giraffe?"

"I mean is it a boy or a girl," says Mac. "Save that comedy for the club house."

"It's a boy," I says. "Some kid, hey?"

"I'll say he is!" says Mac, approachin' carefully like he was afraid my baby was gonna bite him or the like. "Looks just like his mother, too. Got them navy blue eyes, hey?"

"Never mind tryin' to get in solid with the wife!" I says, whilst Jeanne presents him with a dazzlin' smile. "D'ye want to hold him a minute?"

"Well—eh—let's start with something else," says Mac, backin' away. "He seems all right where he is, I'll let that part of it go for awhile, hey?"

"*Cherie,* say '*bon jour*' to *Monsieur* Mac!" remarks Jeanne to my baby.

"Ump—goof—waugh—gunko!" returns my baby with a sarcastical grin.

"Don't mention it!" says Mac. "Say, that kid's a wonder! Talks as plain as I do. How old is it by now?"

Needless to say, such pummeling of the King's English did not escape the keen eyes of the language authorities. Far from it. Mr. Witwer has received countless letters from enraged grammarians informing him that he is a menace to the country, *et cetera.* With all of which, the modest author agrees. He invariably replies to the peeved professor that he started out to write literature but the editors claimed that his stories were entirely too weird. So he started to write *illiterature.* And went over big!

At the age of sixteen, he decided to conquer New York City, and landed therein with ten dollars in his coat pocket and a straw hat with a six-color ribbon surrounding the same.

That night he rented a room on Forty-Second Street for $1.50 a week.

After tramping around, young Witwer finally obtained a job that was both a delight and a gastronomic success. He was to be paid six dollars—count 'em!— a week for serving unsuspecting folk with various kinds of sodas. He was happy; he was en route to success!

Up to this point, it should be mentioned in passing, that he had had no thought of becoming a writer. This fact is stated for the benefit of the young and old who are constantly told that writers start off at infancy by composing sonnets on their bibs and employing their nippled milk-bottles for fountain pens.

That night, Witwer wrote home to his aunt and informed her that he had conquered the world and points west at one fell swoop. After which he decided to cut down expenses and become wealthy. Hitherto, he had been squandering large sums for meals. So he decided to cook his own meals over his gas jet—which was strictly against the landlady's pet law.

He made his first attempt that evening when he arrived home with two eggs and a frying pan under his arm. Coaxing the gas to do its best, he dropped the eggs neatly into the pan and held it over the flame. A short while after—about forty minutes—the eggs were finished. "Finished" is the right word. On investigation the eggs showed that they had turned to either concrete or marble. He threw them out the window into the back yard. Which was poor diplomacy, indeed. For, be it known that friend landlady was just emerging from the basement. Exit Mr. Witwer!

Let us now consider his advent into the story writing game—the game that has made him fame and fortune, friends and enemies:

During the next few years, he tried his hand at every job that either man or mammal has ever devised. For instance, after being fired—he claims that he was never "discharged"—the word is too genteel!—from his soda-jerking position, he was once more on the high seas of vagrancy and youthful glory. Since then he has held—anywhere from two hours to two years—the following positions: bell-hop, hotel-clerk, private secretary, salesman, cub reporter, sport writer, editor, copy reader, press agent, collector, and about fifteen other positions that have escaped his memory. The collection of ideal positions are not listed in the order of merit or in the order that he tried them, but they serve to show that he has had a splendid background for the profession of letters. What a wonderful experience for an embryonic writer! No college could possibly inculcate or approximate the things he observed and stored away in his subconscious mind. And it seems safe to remark that, had he not had such experiences, he would now—provided that his bent was authorship—be writing the pedantic, dull essays that no live person cares to read.

Finally, he found himself. He had often wondered, during the years that he had skipped with gay abandon from job to job, what was his object in life, what was he created for? He was intelligent enough to understand that, before being a success at anything, he must first have a purpose, a plan of life, something to concentrate on.

He chanced to meet a newspaper reporter. And it was this reporter who initiated him into the newspaper game—known to most everybody except reporters themselves, as journalism.

After having had his fair quota of news-gathering positions, he got the idea that he should be a successor to Shakespeare and write for the magazines. So he spent his spare time in concocting weird yarns that were supposed to be salable. No sign of the humorist showed itself in a single line. Sad stuff, sob stuff, dreary stuff! He made the mistake of writing about Newport and "The 400" when he should have written about Times Square and "The 4,000,000." He also lacked a knowledge of how a story should be constructed; its technique, and the rest that makes a story valuable to the editors. In his enthusiastic ignorance, he wrote three short stories a week. Three stories a week were duly sent to the magazines. Three stories a week were duly returned with the editors' printed

regrets. In fact, his yarns came back so quickly that
he now believes that he must have mailed them attached
to a rubber band.

He sold his first story March 26, 1915. He was paid
five dollars! He raved as only a true author can
when a deathless masterpiece is insulted in such a
manner. Five dollars! For the moment, he thought
seriously of quitting the game and angling for better
fish.

It was his wife who gave him the suggestion that
set him upon the right road. She suggested that he
stop trying to be literary and highbrow, and be himself. To write of things he *knew* about. To his
friends he was really funny, decidedly humorous. So
Mrs. Witwer suggested that he write as he talked.
He did. And he sold the first two stories—written in
his inimitable slang—to a magazine that paid him real
money. It was the beginning of real success, the start
of his remarkable climb from $5 a story to more than
$1800. To date, he has made approximately $125,000
from his work, most of it within the past two years.
He has also established a record for work that has
never been equaled in story writing. In a single year
he wrote and sold eighty-five stories, averaging 9000
words each!

In conclusion, it might be well to mention that his
path to success was not laid entirely with thornless
roses. Far from it. Ill health has been his most constant companion. In fact, he has spent about three
years in hospitals, sanitariums, and so forth. Chief
trouble is nervous disorders. He has undergone two
major operations, and was told, on each occasion, that
he had only a fifty-fifty chance of surviving. Pleasant
outlook!

Many a man would have complained about the luck

of life, the ways of fate, and given up whatever ambitions he had, notwithstanding pep.

If I had a mountain to move, I'd call upon H. C. Witwer for assistance.

This moving tale about Mr. Witwer reminds us somewhat—although in Mr. Witwer's case the current moves more swiftly—of the experience of Fannie Hurst, who passed some twelve years in New York striving for a mastery of style and action, until she finally made good.

And she was helped by Bob Davis, that genial guardian angel of all young authors. But her story does not belong in this book, although without doubt she possesses humor—genuine humor because it consists of an accurate characterization of life, made with the painstaking art of the true artist.

It is very difficult, indeed, to separate the purely humorous story from its fellows. For example, "The Outcasts of Poker Flat," by Bret Harte, undoubtedly contains humor, but it cannot be considered a humorous story. Mr. Alexander Jessup, in his extremely interesting collection of the "Best American Humorous Short Stories," put in it "The Angel of the Odd," by Edgar Allan Poe. Very likely. Yet I am not at all certain that Mark Twain's "Jumping Frog," which he also includes, can be considered strictly as a short story. It is undoubtedly a great piece of humor. Then again, I should be inclined to include more of Bunner than "Nice People." Naturally Mr. Jessup was limited or he would also have included more of O. Henry. He omits "The Lady or the Tiger." Mr. Jessup also omits from his volume a lot of stories that, in his opinion, do not measure up to certain literary standards, and he is undoubtedly right in this. His volume, he says, does not aim to contain all of the best humorous stories, but on the whole, it is so well done, that, even if this book of mine does not make any claim to perfection, I am tempted, as a kind of historical aside, to give the list of stories in his volume; because, on the whole, they are probably the best humorous stories published up to the beginning of the war. The list is:

"The Little Frenchman and His Water Lots," by George Pope Morris.

"The Angel of the Odd," by Edgar Allan Poe.

"The Schoolmaster's Progress," by Caroline M. S. Kirkland.

"The Watkinson Evening," by Eliza Leslie.

"Titbottom's Spectacles," by George William Curtis.

"My Double and How He Undid Me," by Edward Everett Hale.

"The Celebrated Jumping Frog of Calaveras County," by Mark Twain.

"Elder Brown's Blackslide," by Harry Stillwell Edwards.

"The Hotel Experience of Mr. Pink Fluker," by Richard Malcolm Johnson.

"The Nice People," by Henry Cuyler Bunner.

"The Buller-Podington Compact," by Frank Richard Stockton.

"Colonel Starbottle for the Plaintiff," by Bret Harte.

"The Duplicity of Hargreaves," by O. Henry.

"Bargain Day at Tutt House," by George Randolph Chester.

"A Call," by Grace MacGowan Cooke.

"How the Widow Won the Deacon," by William James
  Lampton.
"Gideon," by Wells Hastings.

How we have progressed since this collection was
made!

Among the writers of stories that can be termed
purely humorous are Hugh Wiley and Octavus Roy
Cohen, both of whom are familiar to the great public
that is read by the *Saturday Evening Post:*

Mr. Wiley has kindly supplied me with the following data about himself:

The Wildcat was born in Zanesville, Ohio, February 26, 1884. Seven or eight years later he began to
look around him. He discovered that he was in an
interesting world. At this time he was living at Cascade Locks in the State of Oregon where his father
was engaged on the construction of a canal around the
rapids of the Columbia River.

Engines and derricks, concrete mixers, locomotives
and the varied phenomena of construction work lay
before him, but his keenest impressions came from the
glittering brass on the surveying instruments used by
the civil engineers. Before he left Cascade Locks he
faced one of life's serious problems. The highway
had branched. On one hand was an adventurous career
with an Indian tribe that infested that part of the
country. Indian life had an appeal. On the other
hand was civilization and an engineer's career.
Parental influence, and the glittering brass on the tran-
sits and levels won the day. The Wildcat's Indian
associates bade him farewell. Thereafter, for three or
four years, he submitted to school in St. Louis and in
Chester, Illinois. The school business did not bite very

deeply, and when the Wildcat was fifteen years old, he achieved his freedom in a job on the Mississippi River which afforded him unlimited opportunity to play with surveying instruments. During this year, the Government of the United States bestowed upon young Huck Finn a monthly pay check amounting to thirty dollars. When he was about sixteen years old he returned to the family hearth in Chester and was again slammed into school without any serious results. He began a side-line of reading, apart from his school work. One thing led on to another. A copy of an East Aurora publication fell into his hands, and with an accomplice whose father owned two or three country newspapers, he began the publication of a rival magazine. Back of this activity was something of an ambition to show the local smart set that the sixteen-year-old river rat in their midst was not quite a complete social outcast. In butcher paper covers, the *Pariah,* which was the magazine's name, made its bow. This first greeting was a duplex affair. The bow served as salutation and farewell. The *Pariah* blew up, and with it, all of the Wildcat's hopes of ever joining Main Street's dancing classes, and the other gentle groups of the younger set about him.

For the sum of two bits a small but gratifying flask of whisky could be obtained in any of the river saloons "under the hill" in Chester, and now and then, the Wildcat would shoot a quarter on the hootch. There followed a year or two of hard-boiled life on railroad surveys. A casual adventure in a conflict between two competitive railroads resulted in some wholesale killings, and with this background of blood to serve as a standard the Wildcat went into the hills of Mexico seeking silver and gold and adventure. He found some of each. He stayed in Mexico two years, and then jumped north into the Cobalt country in Canada on the trail of native silver.   When he hit the district, it was fairly well crowded, so he continued his journey into the north.

Somewhere along in 1906, he resolved that the business of working for another man had its serious defects.   Thereafter, whenever he could he mixed up in construction work as a contractor.   Now and then, when he would go broke, he would take a job long enough to get a stake and then, once more his own boss, he would bid on some work and land a contract that would pile up into big money or big trouble.

Throughout this time all thoughts of the world of letters were swamped under the press of affairs and, from 1902 until 1916, the bug of literature was inert in its chrysalis.   Incidentally, not a lot has happened since then, but after a few successes and a few failures in the business of building bridges and railroads, the Wildcat, a little tired of the show, turned to memories of his earlier days for relief from the stress of the present.

In 1916, some of these bridge contracts piled up into both money and trouble.   A quiet hour of serious reflection induced an attempt to escape from the tentacles of business.   In his office, which was just then in Seattle, he sat down and wrote a story of a shipwrecked circus boat.   Without any knowledge of technique or form he wrote the adventures of three old Mississippi River men combating the combined terrors of a flood and a menagerie that had drifted down upon their little floating domain.   This story, which included the massacre of a young camel for eating purposes, was mailed to *Scribner's Magazine* in October, 1916.   It made the riffle.

The title of this first story was "On the Altar of

Hunger," and, in the manuscript, the word "altar" was spelt "alter" which should have been enough to discourage any editor. The story was followed by two more Mississippi River stories and a story of Mexico, all of which went to *Scribner's*.

In 1917, seeking a more congenial environment, the Wildcat left the Northwest and established himself at San Francisco. Now the stories were coming too fast for one magazine and so, while *Scribner's* were reading two of them, he sent a third to *Collier's*. The story was accepted and was followed shortly after by another one.

At this point, the affair with Germany broke in on the gentle business of arranging cheap words into expensive groups and, for more than two years, the Wildcat lived abroad with the 18th Engineers in the A. E. F. He continued to live. After the armistice was signed he wrote the first story of the Wildcat series and mailed it to the *Saturday Evening Post* from France. On the ship returning to the United States, the second story of the Wildcat series was written.

To the Wildcat, the whole thing seems to be an accident. Sometimes he thinks that the fifteen years of running around were wasted, and then he knows that all of the old wild days serve as a background of raw material for his fiction factory.

The one general difference between men and the other animals is that man can laugh. The Wildcat gets his greatest kick out of life when he discovers now and then that he has taught some member of the human family how to smile.

And Mr. Cohen, who comes so close to Mr. Wiley in the same field, has this to say about himself:

All About I

By Octavus Roy Cohen

Previous to my earthly advent on the twenty-sixth day of June, 1891, American literature had managed to make pretty fair headway—all things considered. And I have not yet decided how much it has suffered under the impact of my breaking-in.

Having been asked for my autobiography for inclusion in a volume which is to be entitled "Great American Humorists"—or something like that—I have settled myself to the job with corrugated brow and a literary expression. Until the arrival of the urgent request I doubted my right of representation in such a collection. If the truth be known, I still doubt it. But I've figured out that, once I do get in, the publishers can't push me out without destroying the plates —and I'm not worth that expense.

Matter of fact, my autobiography is about as passionate as the eighth book of geometry. It will not prove particularly inspiring to other young men nor cause anguish to any beauteous damsel who might, had she so desired, have obtained me for a matrimonial partner.

It was in Charleston, South Carolina, that I first emitted an infantile wail—which might be taken as a study in cause and effect. Existed in New York a while during my boyhood and then the family moved back to the South Carolina home. I wasn't educated. But I did attend prep school at the Porter Military Academy (Charleston) and took three-quarters of an engineering degree at Clemson College, South Carolina.

Following a series of disagreements with the faculty relative to my desirability as a student, I departed suddenly and completely from the zone of higher learning and went to shoveling coal in Alabama. Lovely existence—shoveling coal. Romance of the mining camps, and all that sort of thing.

Then a series of misadventures, each embarked upon with the idea of securing the wherewithal for the next meal. I wound up as a newspaper reporter on the *Birmingham* (Ala.) *Ledger,* now happily defunct. That was in 1910. I continued in newspaper work—principally as a sport writer—in Charleston, South Carolina; various New Jersey papers . . . with a bit of a space assignment, now and then, from New York journals.

Returned to the old homestead and entered my father's law office, where for many long and dreary months, I puzzled over legal phrases and legal forms. During that period I amused myself by hammering a typewriter. I judge that I amused a good many editors, too. Finally, in the obvious effort to exterminate me by shock, one of them—Mr. Ray Long of the *Blue Book,* now of the Hearst organization—bought a story from me for which he paid the entirely too lavish price of $25.

His acceptance did not have the hoped-for effect. I laid down a story barrage around his desk. Occasionally one of the things took, which accounted for my lack of wild enthusiasm when I passed the South Carolina bar examinations in 1912 and started in to practice.

Thereafter it was a hot contest between the law and literature. The latter lost. I became a writer.

In 1913 I became engaged. In 1914 I married the girl to whom I was engaged—Miss Inez Lopez of

Bessemer, Alabama. She is now the mother of one child, to wit: Octavus Roy Cohen, junior—age five, and persistently growing older.

At the time of my marriage, I made a momentous decision. Coming to the conclusion that no hazard was quite so desperate as matrimony, I dropped my law practice and dedicated myself to a writing career. The first month after that marriage my total receipts from the literary field amounted to $15. I had just about decided that a mistake of judgment had been made when the stories—I had seventy of them in circulation —commenced to sell.

Since then I've been pretty fortunate. But it was hard sledding for awhile.

For several years I tried to make up in story-quantity what I lacked in story-quality. And finally, back in 1918, I conceived the idea of fictionizing the ultra-modern city negro of the South.

I started something when I did that—particularly as that first attempt—and all that have followed it up to the date of this writing—sold to the *Saturday Evening Post*. And I suspect that, because the negro lends himself so readily to a humorous portrayal, I have taken a sort of rank as a humorist. Certainly, if that doesn't explain the inclusion of this autobiography in this book, then nothing can.

And so, for three years, I have devoted myself to negro stories, to an occasional outside short story that demanded to be writ, and, by way of variety—detective novels. And plays of various sorts.

I was also seduced one year into doing moving pictures. Other—and abler—writers have expressed themselves on this subject more aptly—and profanely —than I shall ever succeed in doing. So I will not touch upon it save to say that I made several vitally important discoveries during my movie experience. For the benefit of the uninitiate I catalogue them herewith:

1. The movie queen does not hate herself nor look down upon her art.

2. The male star doubly ditto.

3. A story is meant to be first bought, then butchered, then forgotten.

4. A continuity writer is a better author than the person who wrote the original story—or play. If this statement is doubted—ask any continuity man.

5. A scenario reader—meaning the person who rejects good manuscripts and accepts poor ones—is neither as good an author as an author, nor so poor a one as a continuity man.

6. All directors immigrated from Heaven—but will never visit their home town.

My stage experience has been infinitely more pleasant. There was a melodrama, "The Crimson Alibi," written in collaboration with George Broadhurst, with a six months' Broadway run, and the present continuance of its—now—two-year period in England. Then "Come Seven," a negro comedy, which appeared to amuse Broadway for a while—not half so long a while as I wished. And two other plays, which have been more or less successful on road tryouts, and which are due in New York before long.

And books: five of them to date, and my publishers have the manuscripts of three more on hand—the contracts stuffed snugly away in my box at the bank.

To finish with all such tiresome data—my home is in Birmingham, Alabama. I am married to the same wife I wedded originally, and am called "Daddy" only by the single child hereinbefore mentioned.

It being always necessary in such an article as this

to chronicle one's personal tastes—and weaknesses—
I hasten to oblige.

Regarding other writers, I rank Ring Lardner as the
greatest humorist ever produced in this country.   I
think that George Fitch runs Lardner a close second—
and I grab for everything published under Stephen
Leacock's name.

I think the three best American novels I have read
are Sinclair Lewis's "Main Street," Booth Tarkington's "The Turmoil" and Corra Harris's "Happily
Married."

I think Hugh Wiley's negro stories are wonderful,
but his Chinese yarns are even better.   Wiley I regard
as the master of the staccato style of story-telling.   I'd
write in the same style—but I can't get away with it.

I am not unusually eccentric.   I am the worst golfer
in the world—and play oftener than most.   I am also
the worst saxophonist—but I love the instrument.
There is, to me, nothing quite so enthralling as to
harness oneself to a saxophone, stand before a full-
length mirror, toot wildly and watch the little keys
jump.   There are so many of them—and they wiggle
so unexpectedly.

I despise New York—and prefer Birmingham to any
other city in the country.   And still maintain that I
am ·not eccentric.   I have no temperament, save a
chronic before-breakfast irritability.

I would rather be Jack Dempsey than Rudyard
Kipling, and would love to see my son become a champion pugilist—*nom de guerre:* Killem Reilly!

I'm crazy about football—and have carried a game
knee for the past thirteen years as the result of my last
scrimmage.

If my wife were not a slender brunette, I'd frankly
confess a preference for plump and amorous blondes.

When we consider more recent writers of short stories, we are confronted by the same difficulty of discriminating between those that are purely humorous and those that are not. The work of Thomas Beer, of Ben Ames Williams, of Lawrence Perry, of Frances Noyes Hart, of Elizabeth Alexander Heerman, all notable story writers, is characterized by much humor, but it appears to me that, in each instance, the humor is subordinate to the other elements. Probably L. H. Robbins would be considered as a writer of humorous stories, pure and simple. He has contributed for many years to the *Newark News,* to *Life* and other papers, but his short humorous stories have appeared mostly in *Everybody's,* and have deservedly won the commendation of the O. Henry Memorial Committee. His "Mr. Downey Sits Down" was included in their last volume of Prize stories of the year.

Among the latest arrivals in the humorous short story field is Richard Connell, who, as the author of "The Sin of Monsieur Pettipon," has sprung into almost immediate fame. Mr. Connell has written numerous short stories for American and English magazines. He was born in Poughkeepsie, New York, and is under thirty. His father was editor of a daily newspaper there and, at a tender age, he wrote police court and other news stories. While attending college he did some newspaper work and, after his graduation from Harvard in 1915, he was a reporter on a New York daily. Later, he wrote copy for an advertising agency. He enlisted in the army and was a soldier for two years in the 27th Division A. E. F. and saw active service in Belgium and France. He is now devoting his entire time to writing. He is married and lives in New York in the winter, and in Connecticut in summer. In an article published in the *New York Tribune,* entitled "Taking Humor Seriously," Mr. Connell says about his own art:

Taking Humor Seriously

By Richard Connell

"Sir," said an editor of *Punch,* "I'll have you understand that our jokes are not to be laughed at!"

That *Punch* editor is typical of all makers of laughter from the first Neanderthalian man who sent his mate into guffaws by slipping on a discarded bit of dinosaur blubber, down the centuries to our own Dunnes, Adamses, Lardners and Benchleys. He is protesting against the attitude of the mass of mankind toward his art. From Aristophanes to Ade, humorists have desired to be taken seriously; that is to say, they have wished to be acknowledged by more than the few to be the men of intellect, penetration, weight and philosophy that in fact they are.

Now, between the simple mechanics of slipping on a bit of blubber and the keen shafts of Mr. Dooley, are some millions of years of development. However, the humorist can't help realizing that the making of laughter to-day is still regarded, pretty generally, as a low form of human endeavor, at its best, less praiseworthy, let us say, than the composition of etudes for beginning pianists, or the manufacture of motor cycles or tooth paste, and incomparably lower, in the artistic scale, than the incubation of fifth rate sonnets, beginning,

"Oh, Death, upon thee oft I ponder deep."

* * *

The humorist's protest against this false estimate of his art is more than self-justification. It is a protest against the larva state of our civilization, against the emotional moronism that appraises tears above laughter, and the dull ore of solemnity above the golden coin of wit.

* * *

What is the state of the national humor to-day? Low. Higher than it was, perhaps, but still much too low. Who is to blame? The makers of laughter themselves are partly to blame for they have been maneuvered into being on the defensive about their art, and, indeed, I regret to say, sometimes a little ashamed of it.

Take such an artist as Charlie Chaplin. How slow the dwellers on our artistic Parnassus have been to admit his genius. Isn't the real reason because he makes them laugh at themselves? Well, Charlie harbors a desire to play Hamlet. I have no doubt he could do it. But why should he want to? The reason seems to me to be this: He is the victim of the inferiority complex that is forced on all makers of laughter by an essentially dull and humorless age. Chaplin has a scientific attitude toward his work and a complete mastery of his medium. In brief, he is a genius. In Max Eastman's new book, "The Sense of Humor," Chaplin answers the question, "What do you do to people to make them laugh?" as follows:

"I tell them the plain truth of things. I bring home to them, by means of a shock, the sanity of a situation which they think is insane. When I walk up and slap a fine lady, for instance, because she gave me a contemptuous look, it is really right! They won't admit

it, but it's right, and that is why they laugh. I make
them *conscious* of life. 'You think this is it, don't
you?' I say, 'Well, it isn't, but *this* is, see!' And then
they laugh."

Tears are noble; laughter vulgar. This is the accepted formula. Thus we find Mr. Henry B. Fuller,
in a recent paper on Chicago novelists, giving columns
to the latest piece of sordid "egg on the vest" realism,
and dismissing two of our foremost humorists in this
lofty manner, "Such popular character sketchers as
George Ade and Peter Dunne." He has used the second most deadly epithet in the vocabulary of the
contemporary critic, "popular." The most deadly, of
course, is "humorist." Why he did not make a thor-
ough job of it and utterly annihilate the creators of
Dooley and of the "Fables in Slang" by calling them
"popular humorists" is one of the mysteries of the
critical brain which I am unable to solve with my
microscope.

Tears are noble; laughter vulgar. And here we en-
counter a paradox that must be shocking to such as
Mr. Fuller. Man seems to prefer laughter to tears!
Can it be that man is inherently vulgar? Or can
it be that the formula is wrong and should be reversed?

Everywhere is evidenced that man is eager to laugh,
pathetically eager. Consider the things he will laugh
at. I grant you he is often cheated by shoddy goods,
and this may be a contributory cause why laughter is
not more highly esteemed. There is nothing poorer
than poor humor. And we have a deluge of it.

Many men have gone into the business of manufacturing what passes for humor, not because they
have any equipment or any sense of the comic, but because it pays. Of course, it pays. Humor is the most

precious commodity in the world; diamonds are dirt beside it. One celebrated editor says, "I can get twenty, yes, forty good 'serious' stories for every good humorous story." Man wants so earnestly to laugh that he will deal with bogus humorists. They can continue to exist only because of the low ebb in our taste. You know the men I mean. They are like the Irishman, who, when asked if he played the trombone by note or ear, replied, "Neither. By main strength." We have men who are humorists by main strength, the "go getters" of literature.

Now, poor humor deserves no more critical consideration than poor painting, music or poetry. But good humor deserves fully as much critical attention and appreciation as any of the arts. It does not get it. Why?

Humor does not get its due because of the greatest fault in mankind. I mean fear. The simple truth is that most men, including the critics, are afraid to laugh. That is because they cannot laugh at other men without at the same time laughing at themselves.

Man seeks to cover his nakedness, i. e., his true self, with various garments—dignity, self-importance, solemnity, sentimentality, hypocrisy. Along comes humor, a lightning flash of the truth. It strips off his dignity, tears aside his sentimentality, pierces his hypocrisy. Therefore, he fears humor. Humor is truth. If it is true that the truth shall make you free, it is equally true that the truth shall make you uncomfortable.

We need humorists. It is a shame to see the younger writers going astray. Let them remember that Bergson has said, "A humorist is a moralist disguised as a scientist" and "a comedy is far more like real life than a drama is." Let them remember that laughter has concerned all men who have thought deeply about life.

By way of encouraging the younger writers to develop into humorists, I should like to offer, as a glorious example, a sort of all-literature football team, composed exclusively of humorists, and I hereby challenge all champions of solemnity in literature to produce a team that in weight, force, influence and scoring power could possibly stand up against my team.

Right end—Aristophanes.
Right tackle—Cervantes.
Right guard—Juvenal.
Center—Shakespeare.
Left guard—Voltaire.
Left tackle—Lucian.
Left end—Swift.
Quarterback—Molière.
Right halfback—Thackeray.
Left halfback—Dickens.
Fullback—Rabelais.
Substitutes—Twain, Gogol, France and Shaw.

Such a team would soon convince any other you can name that in the words of Professor James Harvey Robinson, "Humor must be taken seriously, but not solemnly."

There is, in conclusion, just one thing more to be said about the humorous short story, and that is that it must deal with characters that are essentially comic in themselves, and are, therefore, limited. Thus we have Mr. Wiley and Mr. Cohen depicting the negro, and Mr. Robbins depicting a character that is limited to a particular perspective, and we have Mr. Connell

creating out of a barber a series of adventures that
might be easily classed as burlesque.

All this, of course, is not the highest kind of humor.
Much of it is very funny; but it is rough stuff. It is
intended to be rough stuff. When we get to the finer
shades of humor we find it invariably mixed with other
elements. It is much like the veins of gold in quartz.

"It is a truth universally acknowledged" begins Jane
Austen in the opening chapter of "Pride and Prejudice" "that a single man in possession of a good fortune must be in want of a wife."

Mrs. Bennett asks Mr. Bennett if he has ever heard
that Netherfield Park is to be let at last. He replies
that he has not.

"But it is," returned she; "for Mrs. Long has just
been here and she told me all about it."

Mr. Bennett made no answer.

"Do not you want to know who has taken it?" cried
his wife impatiently.

"*You* want to tell me, and I have no objection to
hearing it."

This is precisely, of course, just what Mrs. Bennett
would have said and it is precisely what Mr. Bennett
would have replied. Such delicate touches as Jane
Austen delivers, the whole effect being to bring out
into comic relief the realism of certain types, would be
utterly lost on indiscriminative readers. It is precisely in this delicacy of treatment, however, that the
genuine humorist is revealed. As a matter of fact, I
cannot quite see how there can really be such a thing
as a sense of humor, considered by itself alone, apart

from other faculties, and this term has always seemed to me absurd.   Humor and satire are closely allied; they run into each other.   Fidelity to nature, an almost acute sympathy with the subject under consideration, a sensitiveness to violent contrast, and all this united with restraint and a feeling for words—these are some of the necessary qualities.

And it is in the field of our short stories that we see these qualities more in evidence to-day than in any other form of our literature.   If it lacks the clarity of vision of a Jane Austen, and the enormous comprehensiveness of a Dickens, it often has the fine finish, and the fidelity to life that come only from those who are striving in their work and, under their limitations, to do their best.

CHAPTER XXXV

THE COLUMNISTS

Bert Leston Taylor, Keith Preston, Ted Robinson,
H. I. Phillips, Roy K. Moulton

GIVEN a set of morning papers," says F. P. A.,
"any child able to frame a coherent sentence and
to rime in simple couplets, can begin to write
a column. In a day or two, the public will begin to
help him; then he is an editor and a conductor, and
the public does most of his work for him. Thus his
task is the pleasantest of all jobs in a newspaper office
and out of it."

This quotation (I trust without protest) is taken
from a very pleasant little book entitled "The Gentle
Art of Columning" by Charles L. Edson. The reader
is referred to this book for specific information. I
am not going consciously to entrench upon Mr. Edson's
playground, and, for a long time, I have thought that
there should be more confraternity among authors anyway. This book itself, as the reader will perceive if
he has not already done so, is mostly written by the
people themselves who are in it. All the other thoughts
in it have also been provided by others, in many cases
without due credit, because I cannot remember the
authors.

I have purposely avoided reading any more of Mr.
Edson's book than the quotation I have given to start

this chapter, for fear that, even unconsciously, I might appropriate his ideas. Some of his headings, however, are suggestive. One of them is "The Punning Paragraph," another "Contribs" and still another, "Comic Verse." I shall try to avoid therefore, anything but the slightest reference to these intimate details. Mr. Edson, however, writes entertainingly in an article which he published later in the *New York Tribune,* and which was reprinted from Brentano's "Book Chat":

"No one really can tell how hunches come," wrote a reviewer discussing the chapter under that heading in "The Gentle Art of Columning." In that chapter I had said that every paragrapher has a definite system of wooing the spark of inspiration, just as every old barn has a system of lightning rods to pull the electric flashes down out of the clouds.

I then briefly stated the systems used by F. P. A., Christopher Morley and Don Marquis. A more detailed account is here given of the systematic search for hunches. Jim Smiley, paragrapher of the *Kansas City News,* an evening paper, sits down at his desk and begins reading the Morning Sheet. He is looking for hunches.

* * *

After Jim had red penciled all the promising ncws stories, he took his writing pad and wrote a brief summary of the stories, thus:

Von Moltke has been dropped from the German staff.

The French army has ceased retreating and is advancing.

French soldiers wear red pants. Etc.

He had a score of such items all written on one sheet of paper. Then he sat down to pump jokes out of them. He wrinkled his brow, stared fixedly at the twenty items and said to himself: "Come on, Concentration, come on." Within two minutes he was in a trance and the ideas began hopping about in his brain like rabbits jumping in and out of hedgerows. Von Moltke had quit. "The Kaiser's backers are quitting him Von by Von." The French army in red pants suddenly turns with the first frost of autumn and drives the olive-colored Germans back. "The Germans camouflaged themselves in green and had all the best of it until frost turned the forests red. And then the green uniforms were easy marks for the French." And so it went with every one of Jim's twenty news items. Concentration yielded a wheeze out of every one of them.

* * *

Such is the system of the paragrapher. These are the fruits of his seeking after inspiration. The ideas that he selects are governed by his personality. One man is fond of parody and jeers. His hunches will come when he reads a good thing and writes a parody of it, or when he reads a feeble thing and writes a "hot roast" or jeer. This is F. P. A.'s column. Don Marquis is fond of satire, burlesque and epigram. Morley likes puns. But they all work by blue print and by plan. With their chart before them they daily sit at their desk and, offering a prayer to the god of concentration, they go into the silences.

The fashion of having a column in a newspaper written by a humorist, or at least a pleasant person (all humorists are not pleasant) was, for aught I know, started by Ben Franklin, who seems to have started more things in this country than any other individual, or any group of people that could be named—including a post office, good roads, stoves, electricity kite flying and whistling.   Such, however, is the temper of the American people that columns of comment in papers would have started spontaneously everywhere sometime or other if, for any reason, their coming had been delayed.   There have always been local humorists on our country papers.   Many of our big humorists started in that way.   Years ago 'Gene Field's column in the *Chicago News* was famous.   Robert J. Burdette had one in the *Burlington Hawkeye* and later in the *Brooklyn Eagle*.   Now every considerable paper has one.   They are all pretty good as the world goes.   I think that probably Bert Leston Taylor and F. P. Adams have done more to make the average column better than any others.   Richard Atwater (RIQ) of the *Chicago Post* should not be overlooked—one of the most promising writers we have.   Although Bert Leston Taylor has passed away from us, I personally cannot feel that he has gone, and I shall assume that he has not gone, but is still here.   The real fact is that he is still here, because his work and influence keep on.   When preparing this book, in 1921, I wrote to him in February of that year, and, under date of February 26, 1921, I received the following letter from him.

MY DEAR MASSON:
        Perhaps you can get what you want out of the enclosed sketches.
    As for my "best book" I have always had a sneaking fondness for "The Well in the Wood," written to entertain a six-year-old daughter.   It was published by Bobbs-Merrill, and must now be out of print.   I am getting out a couple of small volumes for next Christmas time.

I feel that I ought to remind you that I am not a humorist, nor ever claimed to be.

With all good wishes,

Sincerely,

B. L. TAYLOR.

P. S. In the *American Magazine* for last October is an article on "The Colyum."

A few weeks later (March 20) Bert Leston Taylor passed away. Now the material that he enclosed was a short autobiography of himself that was published in his column, "A Line o' Type or Two," in the *Chicago Tribune* in August, 1919. I wish it might be possible for me to reproduce it all here, but at any rate, I must quote from it. Mr. Taylor is telling about his visit to his birthplace, Goshen Hill, where his father was born, and *his* father before him. Then he himself quotes from Anatole France:

People are sometimes blamed for speaking of themselves. Yet it is the subject that they treat of best. They are interested in it themselves, and they often make us share in that interest. There are, I know, wearisome confidences, but the bores who plague us by telling us their own histories completely overpower us when they relate those of other people. A writer is rarely so well inspired as when he talks about himself."

Mr. Taylor now goes on:

"The home of my parents was really New York City, whither I was removed a few weeks after my introduction to the world."

He declares that his childhood was very dull and that his school days were exceedingly commonplace.

My most notable feat of reporting was done for the *Chicago Journal,* but I have never said much about it. I was told off to keep account of a libel suit that involved two prominent citizens, and I visited the courthouse faithfully for ten days or more. The trial ended abruptly in favor of the defendant, and I met the plaintiff coming away from the courthouse. I tarried to discuss with him the miscarriage of justice, and completely forgot my newspaper, which went to press with no word of the trial's end. The managing editor was so annoyed by my dereliction that he took me out of the local department for a fortnight, and set me to writing editorials. A few weeks afterwards "The Colyum" was born. But that—as we used to say before the phrase was worn to ribbons—is another story.

The many tributes paid to the memory of Bert Leston Taylor would, in themselves, make a large volume. I am tempted to quote however from one of them, written by Al Weeks, who wrote of him:

For nearly twenty years, with a few interruptions, Bert Leston Taylor had been a conductor of a department of wit, wisdom and nonsense entitled "A Line-o'-Type or Two." Making the Line came to be one of the most popular of indoor sports, not only in Chicago, not only in Illinois, not only in the Middle West, but all over the country, with now and then a devotee in Europe and Asia.
    B. L. T. may be considered the first of the columnists, for although Eugene Field and Bill Nye and Mark

Twain preceded him with newspaper niches, Taylor set the style, so to speak, for such men as Franklin P. Adams (F. P. A. of the *New York World*), Don Marquis of the *Sun,* Christopher Morley of the *Post* and H. I. Phillips of the *Globe,* and for Richard Henry Little, who succeeded him on the *Chicago Tribune.*

It was Taylor who first gathered to him a hard-working group of assistants whose remuneration was nil but whose industry was prodigious—the band of contribs who labored for him. It was Taylor who first abbreviated old-fashioned to o. f., and well-known to w. k. It was Taylor who gave the traveling sales-men a forum with his reports from what he called the gadders. It was Taylor who founded a mausoleum for conventional phrases, for bromides, which he termed so felicitously the "Cannery." It was Taylor who first featured striking examples of nomenclature and filed them in the Academy of Immortals, over which the deathless Jet Wimp presided.

Nor was Taylor's column always given over to levity alone. Now and then he struck out a paragraph that was rich in philosophy and observation. He was ever eager to praise the best in literature and in music, and he was an ardent golfer.

The first posthumously published volume, "A Penny Whistle," was issued last year. Now comes a collection of bits from the column entitled, "The So-Called Human Race," and it is delicious reading. Just to show the variety of his mind and the antic quality of his humor, read these, chosen at random from the new book:

"Since prohibition came in," says the Onion King, "Americans have taken to eating onions." As Lincoln prophesied, this nation is having a new breath of freedom.

There are many definitions of optimist and pessimist. As good as another is one that the Hetman of the Boul Mich Cossacks is fond of quoting: "An optimist is a man who sees a great light where there is none. A pessimist is a man who comes along and blows out the light."

The Wetmore Shop, on Belmont Avenue, advertises "Everything for the baby."

One lamps by the advertisement that the Fokines are to dance Beethoven's "Moonshine Sonata." The hootch-kootch, as it were.

The manufacturer of a certain automobile advertises that his vehicle "will hold five ordinary people." And, as a matter of fact, it usually does.

Spring Has Come

The trees were rocked by April's blast;
  A frozen robin fell,
And twittered, as he breathed his last,
  "Lykelle, lykelle, lykelle."

The headline, "U. S. to Seize Wet Doctors," has led many readers to wonder whether the Government will get after the nurses next.

"For sale—1920 Mormon Chummy."—*Minneapolis Tribune*. Five-passenger, at least.

A Kenwood pastor has resigned because some members of his flock thought him too broad. The others, we venture, thought him too long.

And now let me give space to some of our leading columnists who have in each instance kindly supplied their own text. Within my limits it would be quite impossible to publish them all. The three leaders, whether by common consent or by critics' dictum, appear to be Don Marquis, F. P. A. and Christopher Morley, all writing in New York. These three writers have all been treated elsewhere in this volume. It should be noted, however, that their great reputations have been gained quite largely for other qualities quite apart from their columns. All are authors on their own account.

KEITH PRESTON

(Chicago News)

I was born September 29, 1884, in Chicago, within easy walking distance of the Union Stockyards. My formal education was in local schools, beginning with Appleton's first reader, and ending with an oral examination for the Doctorate in Classics at the University of Chicago. From this experience I retain a deep admiration for the Greek and Latin masters, and, in English literature, a taste for eighteenth century prose and the poetry of Milton and Marlowe.

Outside academic walls, I came under various influences, some of which I now recognize as of lasting importance. A book that influenced my child mind was "Forging His Chains," by George Bidwell, the Bank of England robber. As a youth, I attended the Methodist church, and sat under the preaching of Dr. Frank Crane, whose homilies made an indelible impression, which nothing that either of us has been able to do since could entirely eradicate. While teaching at the University of Indiana, I met some of the best people on earth at the local Elks' lodge, and got my grounding in the works of the Indiana literary school. A year's teaching experience at Princeton under Dean Andrew West taught me the intellectual importance of luxurious surroundings. The genial influences of the Princeton and Nassau Inn bars deserve passing mention. From the lush pasturage of Princeton I passed to the Northwestern University at Evanston, where such lax tendencies as the *Indiana Elk* and the *Princeton Tiger* had encouraged have been gradually corrected.

My entry into journalism was not premeditated. I began writing as one of the moths that fluttered round the brilliant light that Bert Leston Taylor kept burning in "Line o' Type" column in the *Chicago Tribune*. Under his discerning eye, I learned to distinguish *vers libre* from poetry, good puns from bad, and how to detect plain and fancy piffle. The next step was transplanting to a corner of the Wednesday book page of the *Chicago Daily News,* where I was encouraged to set up shop as a critic of modern literature, a full-fledged critic who had read nothing much since Alexander Pope! To my surprise and delight I discovered matter for laughter, matter for tears, and even stuff for serious admirations in the work of living writers. Mingling the methods of the laughing and weeping philosophers with an occasional whole souled blurb in the best modern style, I have battened for four years on the creative writers of the day. Lately, I have been presented with a daily column in which to vent such puns and doggerel as cannot plausibly be strung upon literary leaders.

The result is a professor turned columnist, rueful at times over the lost teaching which he found good fun, but enjoying the give-and-take of journalism. Like any old dog that has learned new tricks, he envies the technique of columnists bred from cubs to the chase. He continues a humble student of the art of

columning. As a critic, of course, it is a different
story, for here the professorial ego flourishes unchecked
over defenseless poets, novelists, and publishers.

TED ROBINSON

(*Cleveland Plain Dealer*)

Edwin Meade Robinson ("Ted Robinson") was
born in Lima, Indiana, in 1879. He was educated at
Howe School and Wabash College, receiving his degree from the latter institution in 1900. After a year
of teaching English in the Attica High School, he
entered the newspaper business in Indianapolis. He
was editorial writer on the *Indianapolis Sentinel,* and
later on the *Indianapolis Journal;* on each paper he also
conducted a weekly column of verse, humorous and
serious. In 1904, he went to the *Cleveland Leader,*
where he conducted a column called "Just By the Way"
for six years. From the *Leader* he went to the *Plain
Dealer,* where he has conducted "The Philosopher of
Folly" ever since.

For particulars concerning his method of column
conducting, see *Everybody's Magazine* for March,
1920; article, "The Columnists' Confessional."

Robinson was secretary-treasurer of the American
Press Humorists' Association in 1913-14 and President in 1914-15. His book of more or less serious
verse, "Mhere Melodies," was published by David
McKay, Philadelphia, 1918. A book of humorous
verse, "Piping and Panning," by Harcourt, Brace &
Co., New York, 1920. A novel, "Raw Material," is
in course of preparation by The Macmillan Company.
Married. One son.

H. I. PHILLIPS

(New York Globe)

I was born in New Haven, Connecticut, November 26, 1888, schooled there; took a job on the *New Haven Register* with the idea of earning enough to go to Yale; fell hard for the newspaper game and never got up again. I was made managing editor of that paper when I was twenty-three and thought myself a bigger man than Ochs of the *Times*. Held that job some six years, vainly trying to get an increase over the original M. E. salary; then came to New York and went to work on the *Tribune* under a managing editor by the name of Pope or something like that. I remember he munched peanuts all the time and held his hands clasped in back of his head; also that he told his assistant to tell his assistant's assistant that I would make an excellent stevedore. Somehow, I never could get down to working there: I was always so fascinated by watching Pope eat peanuts. My job was copy-reading, by the way.

I told Pope he'd have to stop eating peanuts or I'd have to stop working on the *Trib*. He kept on with the peanuts. Then I came to the *Globe,* where George T. Hughes put me to work as a make-up man. One day, in 1919, I wrote a column and left it on the desk of Hughes. He used it. It has been running ever since and is now syndicated by the Associated Newspapers. Now I eat peanuts myself and am quite cocky about it. My folks are quite upset about me. Father wanted me to be a sign painter, and mother is afraid writing is hard on my head. My readers think there is something in what they both have in mind.

ROY K. MOULTON

(New York Evening Mail)

When I was a very young sap, back in the old home town, St. Joseph, Michigan, my father conducted a hardware store. It is one of the pleasant privileges of a hardware man's life in a small town, to polish stoves. My father did not avail himself of this great blessing but passed it on to me, and for some years, to all intents and purposes I belonged to the Ethiopian race.

I finally tired of masquerading as a negro minstrel, although I believe that, while I did masquerade as such, I developed a sort of sense of humor. I could not look at myself in the glass without smiling. I suddenly decided to get into the newspaper business, and after scrubbing for several weeks, I applied at the home paper and got a job, and the honorarium as I remember now was $6 a week. I worked at this for about a year, when I had saved up $18 out of my salary and I went to Detroit, where I went to work for the *Detroit Free Press.* It was on the *Free Press* that I wrote my first column.

That was in 1900, and so I have been writing columns steadily for 21 years and have not amassed great wealth. I was discharged from the *Free Press* four times, and finally I got very angry and quit. I went to the *Grand Rapids Press,* where I wrote a column for ten years. It was there that I began syndicating my work. I went from there to the *Grand Rapids News* for a short spell, when I came to New York and immediately went to work for the *Evening Mail,* succeeding Franklin P. Adams, when the latter went to the *Tribune,* or shortly afterward.

I shall always believe that the stove-polishing business made a sort of humorist out of me, although I could never convince my father that I could not have done much better in the stove profession.

I have contributed to many magazines, and have, for eight years, contributed a line of special articles to the Hearst newspapers which have been given wide circulation. My most successful work with these papers has been a special article weekly called "Quincy Todd," being the adventures of a red-blooded American.

There is nothing distinctive to any extent in column writing. One takes the news as it comes and comments on it and then he spends the rest of the day reading contributions which, in my case, often run up to one hundred a day. I have stuck to column writing all these years for the reason that I don't know how to do anything else, and then, I have a sort of secret love for the profession.

I have always told my young son that if he ever adopted the writing profession I would shoot him before he got a job, but probably I would not, at that.

I have been asked what influence guided me most in my profession. I don't know. Perhaps the fact that when one gets printers' ink on his fingers he never gets it off. Perhaps it was the stove blacking. Even now, occasionally, I find a bit of it on me. I have also been asked to give a sample of my best work. It has not yet been written.

I expect to spend my declining years writing jokes for dear old Dr. Hostetter's Almanac which, to say the least, is a pleasant outlook. That is all I know about myself except that I am forty years old, still have a full head of hair, and wear a belt, but no suspenders.

I like to spend my summers in New York and ride in the subway. If that does not indicate, at least, a slight sense of humor, I will get up and give my seat to somebody else.

CHAPTER XXXVI

THE YOUNGER SET

*Heywood Broun, Lawton Mackall, Clarence Day, Jr.,
Don Herold, George Chappell, Donald,
Ogden Stewart, and Others*

SPEAKING from the commercial standpoint
alone (and in this benighted country why should
any one engaged in literary exploitation expect
to speak from any other standpoint?) the business of
raising incipient humorists is fraught with tragedy.
The incubator for new humorists is the university.
In every principal college, and in many of the minor
ones, and also among the private and high schools,
there is likely to be a humorous paper. The *Harvard
Lampoon,* the *Yale Record,* the *Princeton Tiger,* are
familiar names to most readers. Indeed, out of Harvard alone, have come a large proportion of our present day young humorists.

Much of this college humor is better than the humor
published in regular comic weeklies and periodicals.
It is fresh (sometimes altogether too fresh) and often
has a spontaneity denied to maturity. Much of it is
extraordinarily bright. Thus, through all of these
papers, any talent likely to be lying around loose in

any college or school is at once preëmpted, and made
to serve.   And, when these boys leave college, if they
have made good on their papers, they immediately seek
a market for their wares.   The tragedy lies in the
fact that there is practically no market.   The columnists pay nothing.   Humorous stories, running up to
seven or eight thousand words, if good, are eagerly
grabbed up by the magazines.   But your young humorist is unable to make this grade.   He therefore depends
upon getting into *Life* or *Judge* or *Vanity Fair,* or
else drags out his vaulting ambition until it leads him
into the bond business, or in fact, anywhere he can
make a living.

Another embarrassment about the young humorist
is that, if he does make good, he is quite likely to make
good in some other way than as a humorist pure and
simple.   For instance, there is Mr. Marc Connelly, a
delightful writer of humor, who has succeeded in
becoming a successful writer of plays, and, associated
with him, is Mr. George Kaufman.   Both of these
young men have extraordinary talents, demonstrated,
for example, in a play like "Dulcy."   Their talents have
gone out in that direction, doubtless to the envy of
many of their young compatriots—for it is needless
to state that to be the author of a successful play is
the high water mark of any young writer's ambition.

The gap between the humorous and serious writer
is closing up more and more.   There is much humor
in the work of Sherwood Anderson, yet it is not as a
humorist that he is known, but as a new American
writer of distinction and originality.   The same thing
is true, perhaps, however, from another standpoint in

the work of Heywood Broun. Mr. Broun has a true
sense of humor. For one thing, he never loses his
temper, a necessity for any humorist. But his main
abilities lie in the direction, not of straight literary
criticism, but of something beside. I should say that
Mr. Broun was always in danger of becoming a critic,
and always being saved by his sense of humor. It requires a great deal of sanity not to be a critic when
one is under the ban of being one. Mr. Broun is older
than some of the other members of this younger set.
He was, in fact, born in 1888, but he has so far survived being what he is commonly supposed to be by
suburban societies and woman's clubs, not from any
special direction of his own, but because he didn't
know how to be. Thus far, he seems to have been
incapable of being ruined by any of his own defects.
For example, he is undoubtedly a very careless writer,
but his instincts are so admirable, and his capacities
are so enormous, that this never seems to matter, the
main point being that he is interesting. He has a
kind of modesty that acts as a gyroscope, even when he
is leaning over towards himself and his son, who figures quite largely as Heywood 3rd—all of which is
admirable, but not to be copied by any one else. Mr.
Broun is a Harvard man. He was formerly on the
Tribune, but is now on the *World.* He writes about
books and the drama, and other things. He exercises
quite a marked influence over first books and, as a rule,
does it very well and with great justice and clarity,
with an astonishing scent for the good thing by the
new author. He appears to be utterly without any
rancor. His first book, "Seeing Things at Night," is

much more than a book of book reviews.   It is charming in places.   So is his second, "Pieces of Hate."

By a singular coincidence, for which I am unable to
account, Lawton Mackall was also born in 1888.   I
was much more fortunate with him than with Mr.
Broun, who promised but didn't perform for me, and
I have been obliged to write this notice of Broun
myself—something that I shrink from doing in such an
admirable affair as this volume, which is supposed to
be done by all those that are in it.   However, here is
what Mr. Mackall says about himself:

LAWTON MACKALL

Early I learned to take humor seriously.   When I
was about seven years old (born 1888), the only child
in the household of my grandfather, General A. R.
Lawton, I used to spell out diligently all the jokes in
each week's issue of *Life*, but my particular treasure
was an old copy of Joe Miller's "Joke Book."   I knew
it was humorous, because it was called a joke book.
The fact that I could understand few of these jokes
by no means lessened by admiration of them.   I
felt that they were benevolently designed for
the entertainment of mankind, so I memorized
them and repeated them on all occasions, as a
sacred duty.   It was my earnest social contribution.
For example, one evening at dinner when there
were guests at table, in a pause in the conversation, I piped up with: "I read a joke in *Life* to-day.
It said, 'There was a drunken man walking along the
street and he said to a policeman, "Officer—hic—will
you please tell me—hic—where the other side of the
street is?"   And the policeman said, "Right over there,

sir." And the drunken man said, "Hic—I was over there—hic—and they told me it was over here."

"What do those 'hics' mean?" queried my grandfather with a twinkle in his eye.

"I don't know," I answered stanchly. "But they're in the joke."

Since which time the humor I have been permitted to dispense has been, if not funny, at least uncompromisingly conscientious.

In my undergraduate years at Yale I tried vainly to "make" the *Record* board. By the end of my senior year I had scored exactly two jokes. Then the great change occurred. As a graduate student I lodged not on the campus, but in a boarding house five blocks away, where there happened to dwell also a girl of scrumptious appearance. To her I introduced the then chairman of the *Record* Board, and forthwith I became a steadily successful contributor to the magazine. The acceptance of my manuscripts was not uninfluenced by the fact that they were usually handed to him at the same time with notes of a possibly intimate nature from the young lady. Now they have two boys, two girls—and a Ford. The gold Owl Charm which I was awarded for my distinguished service is now worn by my wife.

A woman's smile, which confers glory upon aspiring manhood, was quiet in comparison with the contagious laughter of a certain young lady at the Century Company where I was an office boy. The solemn industry with which I carried refilled inkstands, and later served as clerical assistant to female taskmasters (long and privileged in service) seemed to cause her much amusement. When, a year afterward—I was then toiling with a music publisher—I appeared in the office with a manuscript for the "In Lighter Vein" department, her laugh won the day. Frank Crowninshield, at that time one of the editors, to whom I handed the manuscript, read it aloud dubiously. My queen of cachinnation made audibly merry, so that Crowninshield asked suspiciously "Is this a conspiracy?" But he accepted the manuscript and published it in the Christmas Century. It was the thing called "Those Symphony Concert Programs."

When it appeared in print Oliver Herford and Stephen Leacock made kind comments on it, which so reassured Crowninshield that he asked me for more.

This encouragement, coupled with the loss of my job with the music publisher, made me a professing professional humorist. Little did I dream that, before long, anxiety over household and doctors' bills would make me a humorous editor; for two years I was managing editor of *Judge*. During the war I organized and conducted a department in that magazine devoted to amateur contributions, text and pictures, from men in all branches of the service. That was really a lot of fun.

My total published work in book form consists of a tome less than half an inch thick entitled "Scrambled Eggs," written entirely in fowl language.

My one claim to distinction is in the fact that I have never lost a collar button. My back collar button I have worn for twenty-five years, and my front one for twenty-one. Explanatory note: My early cape-collars, which I wore as a child, required only one button, and the one now serving as a rearguard then graced my youthful Adam's apple.

CLARENCE DAY, JR.

Clarence Day, Jr., deserves a much better biography of himself than the one he has furnished. This is it:

Clarence Day, Jr., was born in 1874 in New York. He is a graduate of Yale University, and the author of "This Simian World."

Since this brief note was written, Mr. Day has published another book entitled "The Crow's Nest." I am tempted to quote something from it, with Mr. Day's permission, which, I make no doubt, he will grant, but before doing so, it would be well to make note here that Mr. Day is a special kind of humorist. Indeed, I would hesitate, in one sense, to call him a humorist at all. I have put him in the younger set, and, quite possibly, this is a mistake; not that his years are so many, only that he has a vein of real wisdom, a kind of deep spiritual insight that is not so likely to come to youth, but is rather the result of certain forces, reluctantly and slowly, working upon one. I am only guessing at Mr. Day—am only trying to express about him certain things that I feel quite vaguely. I do not suppose that he would ever be popular—at least not until some years after he had passed away.

In this respect, indeed, there are two classes of writers, each of whom is unable to understand the point of view of the other, and yet there is justification for both. The first class is very small in numbers. They are the ones that shrink from publicity; they have reserved minds. They seek for perfection. They do not stoop. They are quite unable to develop any sort of skill in doing that common thing known as "advancing your interests." It isn't that they would not like to be known—only that they don't know how to make themselves known, except by doing things that they cannot do. They have no self-advertising power. I may be mistaken, but I rather get it that Mr. Day belongs in this class. His work has extraordinary merit—all very quiet, but highly artistic and effective.

Now the other class of writers is composed of those that can not help doing the other thing. They are sometimes despised for doing it, but this is a mistake. Mr. Broun, for example, undoubtedly belongs in this class. It is natural for him to write carelessly, and to write about himself, and to give his own opinions. Those horribly offensive people—the ones that have every one's "interest at heart" have occasionally remarked to me that they thought Mr. Broun wrote too much. But that is what everybody does—either writing or talking. That is to say, Mr. Broun may do a little bit more of what everybody is doing too much of. But that is not the way to find out about him, or to find out about Mr. Day. There is, in short, no standard that I have been able to discover, whereby a writer can be judged, except whether he is interesting to you, personally. And, in each case, the man himself should be quite separated from his work.

For a long time, I didn't believe this, rebelled against it, but I am coming to see now that a man's work is what counts, not what the man is or what he does.

About Mr. Day, I think it may be said of him that

possibly he is more of a satirist than a humorist. He is really both. His "Simian World" is a fine satire on the human race. And here is the thing I promised to quote, a little thing about Cows in his "Crow's Nest"—and I quote it, not because it is necessarily his best thing, but because Mr. Broun, when the book came out quoted it in his column.

On Cows

I was thinking the other evening of cows. You say why? I can't tell you. But it came to me, all of a sudden, that cows lead hard lives. It takes such a lot of grass, apparently, to keep a cow going that she has to spend all of her time eating, day in and day out. Dogs bounce around and bark, horses caper, birds fly, also sing, while the cow looks on, enviously, maybe, unable to join them. Cows may long for conversation or prancing, for all that we know, but they can't spare the time. The problem of nourishment takes every hour. A pause might be fatal. So they go through life, drearily eating, resentful and dumb. Their food is most uninteresting, and is frequently covered with bugs; and their thoughts, when they dwell on their hopeless careers, must be bitter. In the old days, when huge and strange animals roamed through the world, there was an era when great size was necessary, as a protection. All creatures that could do so grew large. It was only thus they felt safe. But as soon as they became large, the grass eating creatures began to have trouble because of the fact that grass has a low nutritive value. You take a dinosaur, for instance, who was sixty or seventy feet long. Imagine what a hard task it must have been for him, every day, to get enough grass down his throat to supply his vast body. Do you wonder that, as the scientists tell us, they died of exhaustion? Some starved to death, even while feverishly chewing their cud—the remoter parts of their bodies fainting from famine, while their fore-parts got fed. This exasperating fate is what darkens the mind of the cow.

DON HEROLD

The first time I ever heard of Don Herold was one day when Oliver Herford came to me in a state of feverish excitement and declared that Herold was the best humorist we had, or other feverish words to that effect. For days, Herford (who is that way) would talk of nothing else but Herold. Then he kept referring to something Herold had written about Noah Webster, and that it was very funny. And so I met Herold and got him to write something for *Life,* and afterwards got him to write his biography. He hedged. This was all I could get out of him:

Birth: Yes. Usual birth; at Bloomfield, Indiana, July, 1889; only relatives and friends. *Education:* No. None whatever, including A. B. Indiana University. *First Began Literary Work:* Yes. *Where Has Work Appeared: Life, Judge, Collier's, Harper's, American Magazine,* Newspaper syndicates. *Best Price:* $50 a word. In college, wired father: "Send fifty."

But with it he sent me a copy of his famous piece on "Noah Webster" (from *Judge*), and here it is:

Noah Webster's Cleverness

"Need 250 more words, or book is going to be too thin," was the telegram that Noah Webster received from his publishers, The Cast Iron Dictionary Pedestal Company.

Noah Webster was seldom madder in his life. "Oh shoot! I'm sick and tired and disgusted with the whole proposition," he said to himself.

Then he sat down and wrote them a stinging telegram: "Impossible to think up any more words."

He wondered why he had ever tied himself up with these people. No doubt it was his passionate anxiety to get his book published. None of the regular publishers would take it, and it was only as a last resort that he placed it in the hands of The Cast Iron Dictionary Pedestal Company, which was really nothing but a branch of The North American Bridge and Structural Iron Corporation.

As he sat thinking it all over, in the room in which he usually sat and thought, he received an answer to his telegram. There were fewer telegrams in those days, so they moved faster.

"Agreement was that book was to weigh at least 75 pounds. Otherwise people are apt to hold it in their laps. We cannot publish hand-book or lap-book. Must have at least 13 pounds more."

Noah Webster could of course understand their point of view, and then again he couldn't. The entire success of the plan was based upon the weight of the book. The publishers did not care about what was in it. There would be no profit to them in the book itself. In fact, they had told Noah Webster that they would actually lose money on the book. All that they wanted was to sell a lot of cast iron pedestals at a good profit.

But it made Noah angry to think that his publishers cared nothing about the *art* of the thing. Already he had put in several thousand unnecessary words, and still they called for more. They were ruining his dictionary.

"Darn, but us authors always have a hard time of it!" he mumbled. Then he had an idea, and he wrote another telegram:

"Lift all pictures out of text of book and repeat them in special illustrated section in back of book." A good stroke.

"I'd like to bust their old cast-iron, three-legged pedestals." Then he wrote another telegram: "Am writing pronouncing gazetteer. Will fill 168 pages."

The dictionary and the cast-iron stand were already widely advertised and prices were quoted on each. A demon thought came into Noah Webster's fertile brain. "I'll write such a thick book that they will have to make the pedestals so strong they won't make a cent on either the stands or the books."

Then he scraped up about 1500 new words and defined each of them until he was black in the face. In a few days he mailed the manuscript, with the note: "Must go." The next day he mailed another bunch of manuscript, "Beginner's Guide to Pronunciation" and he wrote about 50 pages of "History of the English Language."

It was in the contract that the book could be as thick as he pleased. They were not to restrict him. The mistake the company had made was in quoting a price in full page advertisements in all the newspapers on their dictionary and pedestal.

"There ought to be several thousand obsolete words. I'll dig them up and send them in." And in a few days Noah Webster mailed in a few hundred feet of

these. The next morning he received a telegram:
"Stop. Book already 16 pounds overweight." He
chuckled, and sat down and wrote a reply: "Run
pictures of flags of all nations on extra heavy paper in
front of book."

Well, the result was, as those of you know who recall
the bankruptcy of The North American Bridge and
Structural Iron Corporation, that the book was so thick
the publishers had to put a great deal more material
in the stands than they originally intended, and they
lost money not only on the books (as they planned)
but also on every stand they sold. And this is the
story of how *one* author got even with his publishers.
It is the only instance of its kind on record.

Burlesque

While humor itself is never so popular as it seems
to be, the public is eager to grasp anything that is new,
and, owing to certain circumstances, the great reputations achieved by two young men during the past year
have been quite remarkable. One of these young men
was a newcomer. The other was, or had been, a writer
of great success in certain fields. Both published first
books. Both books were seized upon by the public.
The whole affair was so extraordinary that it is worth
while recording briefly, not only as an example of
publishing enterprise, but also as establishing the fact
that real merit is sure to be recognized. The first book
was the "Cruise of the Kawa," by George Chappell,
the second was "A Parody Outline of American History," by Donald Ogden Stewart.

When these young men started their respective endeavors, burlesque was undoubtedly in the air. The period of reckless abandon immediately succeeding this was at full swing. Everything, mentally, was wide open. On the one hand, Frederick O'Brien had published his book entitled "Mystic Isles of the South Seas" a mingling of sex appeal and realism, and, on the other hand, there had been some agitation about American history text books. Here was an opportunity for burlesque. Both of these young men, doubtless unknown to each other, seized upon it. Mr. Chappell, an architect, had discovered for himself a talent for writing, which he employed to good advantage in some pieces that first appeared in *Vanity Fair,* under the tutelage of the polished Frank Crowninshield. He became a member of that group of writers, some of them old, more of them young, who hung about "Crowny" as he is affectionately called, and, with an extraordinary talent, proceeded to build this book, figuring himself as Dr. Traprock. The affair progressed with great skill. The book, admirably covered and printed, contained a long and, in places, some tedious account of Dr. Traprock's adventures. Mr. Chappell got some of his cronies to pose as South Sea Islanders, the photographs being taken, if I remember rightly, somewhere along Long Island Sound. A dinner was given to usher in the book. Don Marquis, in his column, and Heywood Broun, in his, nobly came to the rescue. Dr. Traprock was exploited day after day by these respective writers. The book was issued. The suburbs took it up. Knowing ladies nudged one another and asked each other if the other had read it.

Mr. Chappell, in the guise of Dr. Traprock, is still lecturing about the country.

Mr. Donald Stewart's method was somewhat quieter, but none the less successful. He began publishing his parody of American history in the *Bookman*. It attracted the attention of the keen Mr. Broun, who gave it a deservedly fine notice. When the book was published it "caught on." Thus two smart young men, by a set of circumstances that seemed, from start to finish, to reek of commercialism—of that kind of successful publicity which, when it is successful, excited the envy of everybody concerned, were able to achieve these results. The question remains whether they were simply lucky, or whether their respective books, if published without any preliminary notices or "business," would have been taken up by the public.

It is impossible to answer this question with any accuracy. But one thing is quite certain. Both books would have fallen flat as pancakes if they had not had extraordinary merits. Undoubtedly the authors were lucky in getting them out at a moment when that sort of thing was possible—when all the circumstances were favorable. And yet no one can read these books, with a critical eye, without seeing in them things that we may be in America "proud to own." Both Mr. Chappell and Mr. Stewart are young men of great promise. They need now only to deepen their work to make it more lasting.

It was about this time that another burlesque success must be recorded in the field of comic journalism by a young man named Robert Sherwood, who came out of Harvard, who had been through the war, who had been associated with "Crowny," and who finally landed in the office of *Life*—as it happened at the time —as one of my own assistants. Sherwood undoubtedly belonged to the younger group. He had met Robert Benchley and Mrs. Dorothy Parker in the office of *Vanity Fair*. With them was another young chap named William Henry Hanemann, and many's the time we grieved for him to think of his carrying about a long name like that. It was this group of writers that conceived among them the idea of getting up what possibly was almost the most famous number of *Life*— namely—the "Burlesque Number." Their methods were secret and mysterious. Bob Sherwood headed the gang. They had clandestine meetings with the printer, and they regarded Louis Shipman (now editor of *Life*), Oliver Herford and myself, all of whom belonged to a prehistoric age, with suspicion and contumely. They were obliged to consort with Frank Casey, the art editor, because he had charge of the plates. The fatal day arrived when the number was to be made up. Never before in the entire history of *Life* had there been such secrecy. But, at last, the complete proofs were spread before us, and we pronounced them good. The result is known to all lovers of burlesque. Afterwards, a stream of telegrams and letters poured into the office in all directions, everybody agreeing that this number of *Life* well deserved its name. The following year (September, 1922) Mr. Sherwood and his trained band of burlesquers issued another burlesque number, a take-off on the Sunday papers, admirably done.

This first number, however, was not without its pathetic side. One picture published in it was a doctored photograph of an old man. A letter was received from a young woman who declared it her father's picture (her father was deceased), and that she couldn't understand how we could have obtained it. Several others wrote in, in answer to some of the seeming advertisements. As a matter of fact, I do not believe that one-half of the readers of *Life* understood what the number was all about. But among the small proportion of literary elite, the intellegentsia and advertisers, this number is now a classic. But I don't think that Bob Sherwood ever recovered from it. Since then, he has become so seriously involved in the movies that his great and growing reputation as an international humorist is sadly threatened.

How many others there are among the younger set who deserve an account of their talents! They are coming up all the time—an increasing body of joyous souls. I recall among them the names of Frederick L. Allen, Isaac Anderson, Arthur Bugs Baer, Fairfax Downey, Morris Bishop, Mabel H. Collyer, James Dyenforth, Katherine Dayton, Caroline Duer, Elmer Davis, Foster Ware, Corey Ford, Lauren S. Hamilton, McCready Huston, E. J. Keifer, Neal O'Hara, Charles G. Shaw, Nate Salsbury and Joseph Van Raalte. Of these Mr. Allen writes for the Lion's Mouth, *Harper's Magazine*—a charming essayist. Mr. Anderson writes jokes, Mr. Baer writes for Hearst's *American* some of the funniest things printed. Mr. Neal O'Hara is on the *Boston Post,* and quite celebrated as an after-dinner speaker, and both

Nate Salsbury and Mr. Van Raalte display talents that will give them greater prominence as time goes on. Mr. Salsbury writes under the name of "Baren Ireland," a remarkably versatile young man, with a decidedly nice touch, and a splendid vein. As for Mr. Van Raalte, who writes for the *World,* I predict for him a great reputation. He is good, very good. Frederick W. Van De Water has also been making an enviable reputation as a columnist, his work on the *New York Tribune* showing very fine literary quality and Newman Levy's work in the *Saturday Evening Post* is astonishingly clever.

Then, there are young Battell Loomis, son of a famous humorist, and Gregory Hartswick, son of a splendid mother and writer. Both of these young men are coming on. And so, *au revoir* to them, and good luck!

AMERICAN PRESS HUMORISTS

(*Membership List*)

Franklin P. Adams	*New York Tribune*
Grif Alexander	*Philadelphia Evening Public Ledger*
Mrs. Darrah Aldrick	Minneapolis, Minn.
Berton Braley	New York
George Bingham	Mayfield, Ky.
John Nicholas Beffel	New York
Clare A. Briggs	*New York Tribune*
James H. Birch, Jr.	Burlington, N. J.
John W. Carey	*Review,* Rock Rapids, Ia.
Arthur Chapman	Care *New York Tribune*
Will Levington Comfort	Santa Monico, Calif.
Paul Cook	*Age-Herald,* Birmingham, Ala.
Edmund Vance Cooke	Cleveland, Ohio
Marjorie Benton Cooke	*American Magazine,* New York

Homer Croy	Forest Hills, Long Island, N. Y.
Irvin S. Cobb	Rebel Ridge, Ossining, N. Y.
Thomas A. Daly	*Record*, Philadelphia, Pa.
Jay N. Darling	*Register Tribune*, Des Moines, Ia.
Walter Juan Davis	*Morning Telegraph*, New York
J. H. Donahey	*Plain Dealer*, Cleveland
George Douglas	*Chronicle*, San Francisco
Robert J. Dean	New York City
John I. Flinn	*Christian Science Monitor, Boston*
J. W. Foley	Hotel Oakland, Oakland, Calif.
Strickland W. Gillilan	Roland Park, Baltimore, Md.
Richard Graves	Tulsa, Okla.
Edgar A. Guest	*Detroit Free Press*
L. H. Gingles	Waukesha, Wis.
Chi H. Gamble	*Journal*, Peoria, Ill.
Kin Hubbard	*Indianapolis News*
William Herschell	*Indianapolis News*
J. U. Higginbotham	San Francisco
Don Herold	New York City
Stanley Horn	*Southern Lumberman*, Nashville, Tenn.
Grant E. Hamilton	New York
Dr. John Hutchinson	New York
F. Gregory Hartswick	*Judge,* New York
Ray I. Hoppman	*Telegram,* New York
M. H. James	Harrisburg, Pa.
Will. J. Johnson	*Register Gazette*, Rockford, Ill.
Al. C. Joy	*Examiner,* San Francisco
Burges Johnson	Vassar College
William E. Lowes	*New York American*
S. E. Kiser	Thousand Oaks, Berkeley, Calif.
Peter B. Kyne	*New York Tribune*
Ring W. Lardner	*Telegram,* Youngstown, Ohio
Charles A. Leedy	New York University
James Melvin Lee	*Houston Post*
Judd Mortimer Lewis	*Denver Times*
Battell Loomis	New York
Orson Lowell	B. & O., Baltimore, Md.
John T. McCutcheon	*Chicago Tribune*
Clarke McAdams	*Post-Dispatch,* St. Louis, Mo.
Douglas Malloch	Chicago, Ill.
R. P. McPhee	*Union,* Springfield, Mass.

Don Marquis	*New York Tribune*
Walt Mason	Emporia, Kans.
W. Kee Maxwell	*Evening Times,* Akron, O.
A. U. Mayfield	Denver, Colo.
Dixon Merritt	Dept. of Agriculture, Washington, D. C.
Edward W. Miller	Chicago
W. H. Miller	*Republican Times,* Ottawa, Ill.
Roy K. Moulton	New York
John J. Mundy	*Star,* Ashtabula, Ohio
Charles H. Musgrove	*Times,* Louisville, Ky.
Folger McKinsey	*Baltimore Sun*
Christopher Morley	*New York Evening Post*
W. D. Nesbit	Chicago, Ill.
Newton Newkirk	Boston
Ralph Parlette	*Lyceum Magazine,* Chicago
Arthur L. Price	*San Francisco Examiner*
Robert L. Pemberton	*Oracle,* St. Mary's, W. Va.
H. L. Rann	*Press,* Machester, Ia.
J. W. Raper	*Press,* Cleveland
Lowell Otis Reese	Auto Rest, Calif.
Leonard H. Robbins	Newark, N. J.
Kenneth L. Roberts	Kennebunk Beach, Me.
Edwin Meade Robinson	*Cleveland Plain Dealer*
William Ganson Rose	Chamber of Commerce, Cleveland
Grantland Rice	*New York Tribune*
John E. Sanford	Detroit, Mich.
Fred Schaefer	Brooklyn, N. Y.
James T. Sullivan	*Boston Globe*
Charles Sykes	*Philadelphia Evening Public Ledger*
E. Tracy Sweet	Scranton, Pa.
Maurice Switser	New York
McLandburg Wilson	New York
Will R. Rose	*Cleveland Plain Dealer*
Duncan Smith	St. Paul, Minn.
A. J. Taylor	Los Angeles, Calif.
Miriam Teichner	New York
Bert Thomas	*News,* Detroit, Mich.
Robert D. Towne	*Philadelphia North American*
A. Walter Utting	Woodhaven, L. I., N. Y.
Henry Edward Warner	*Baltimore Sun*

James A. Waldron	*Judge*, New York
H. T. Webster	*Globe*, New York
Harlowe P. White	*Leader*, Cleveland, Ohio
Waldemar Young	*San Francisco Chronicle*
Treve Collins, Jr.	Brooklyn, N. Y.
Ed Howe	*Atchison Globe*
Ralph Bingham	Philadelphia
Leslie Van Every	Kalamazoo, Mich.
C. L. Edson	New York
Mrs. Elizabeth Sears	Chicago
Jay E. House	*Philadelphia Public Ledger*

CHAPTER XXXVII

THE COMIC POETS

Walt Mason, James J. Montague, Arthur Guiterman, Tom Daly

I F it is difficult, with people that have no sense of humor, to make them understand what humor is, think how much more difficult it is in the case of humorous poetry. There are subtle cadences in much comic poetry, especially if it be of the more delicate type, which are so far beyond the ears of most people, that even to tell them that here is something they will never understand is, in itself, a waste of time. Not only does it bewilder them, but it may infuriate them. Nobody, no matter how ignorant he may be, likes patronage of that sort. If I understand much in poetry that is delightful, and you do not, it doesn't mean that I am intellectually superior. In many other ways you may be superior to me. It does mean, however, that we should all of us be tolerant of those who seem to be enjoying something that does not afford us any enjoyment. The philistine attitude, which is so objectionable, is the attitude of dismissing anything because one doesn't understand it, of declaring that it cannot be of any consequence merely because one has

no ear for it.   There is, of course, a like danger at
the other end—the danger of assuming that, because
one does understand a thing, and takes a particular delight in it, all other people are fools or ignoramuses
when they don't take a similar delight.   Thus the term
intellectual, and after it, *intelligentsia,* have come to
mean certain things that are peculiarly offensive to
the majority of wholesome and sensible people, who
readily recognize, under the pretensions of certain
poets, writers and artists, nothing but the most blatant
hypocrisy.   People with defective apparatus, who cannot maintain themselves by the ordinary rules, are very
likely to resort to tricks; they rapidly discover that
they can fool some of the people all of the time, and
as there are plenty of people, they move about from one
set to another.   This country is peculiarly susceptible
to such creatures.   It is a stamping ground for fakers.
Thus, an art movement based upon some particular
piece of impudent decadence, and that receives but scant
attention in Europe, may be started there merely for
the purpose of gathering in a crop of dollars here.
America lends itself to this sort of thing more readily
than other countries, because of its bigness, and because
of its polyglot population, there being no fixed standard of taste in any field.   Not having any standards of
our own, we are obliged to accept what we can get
from the outside, and, as these are offered to us in the
guise of the classic, or the "genuine," and we have no
means of determining the genuine from the false, it
necessarily follows that we are constantly imposed
upon.   The situation is not helped any by the fact that
our moneyed classes are so occupied, either with making

or squandering money, that they have no time for culture. They are, therefore, even more readily imposed upon than simple people, whose instincts keep them guileless. For example, the head of a fashionable girls' school told me that she could not employ a music teacher who did not have a European certificate because her wealthy patrons would not think they were getting "their money's worth" if a man was employed who received his musical education in America. She was thus obliged to dismiss a young man who was well equipped to teach, and employ one who was inferior.

I shrink from making general statements not based upon accurate facts, but rather close observation of American life for many years has convinced me that the higher up one goes among the alleged intelligent classes in this country, the lower becomes the standard of genuine culture. That is to say; if it can be proved that we have any standard of art, of literature, or of music at all, I believe that it exists among the common people rather than among the most highly educated. The so-called educated people of this country may be divided, roughly, into two classes: those that have their education from others, and those that have acquired it in order to sell it to others. In between these two classes is a very much smaller class, those that have dug in for themselves, that have sacrificed mere material things for the sake of teaching themselves. These are the real people among the whole mass of the educated. But, on the other hand, when you leave the educated and get down among the so-called common people, there is where you get genuine art, genuine music, genuine literature, because it is fundamental, and it is essentially the foundation upon which the whole structure rests.   There is where you find people really singing—singing at their work.   Our darkey melodies are fundamental.   You don't hear college professors singing at their work—if you did they would be mobbed.   A boy I know, seventeen years of age, rose one morning very early in a preparatory school to look at the sun rise; the head master discovered him in this heinous act, and demerited him; he ran away from school.   Do you blame him?

Now, it may be asked, if what I say is true, why are there so many terrible abortions in the shape of art and literature being inflicted upon the masses of common people?   Why does sentimentality run riot in the movies, and why do the works of Harold Bell Wright and others of the Pollyanna school meet with such wide response?   The reason is because, even as bad as we think these may be, they are much better than the "higher up" stuff.   Where any particular work is taken hold of by the public, be assured that there is something to it.   That does not mean that it is necessarily good art—it may be quite bad—but it does mean that it is much better than what *precious* people are giving us.   Take the question of sex, or of downright indecency.   Is it not true that neither of these things exists to any extent in our newspapers, more widely read than any other form of typography?   Our newspapers, sensational as some of them may be, are generally clean—they make no sex appeal.   They know that the people do not want indecency, which is usually confined to the occasional periodicals—those of more limited circulation. Indeed, the periodicals among us that have the widest circulation are absolutely clean, knowing that they would be ruined if they made sex appeals. And this has always been true. Indecency is only a form of decadence, and the instincts of healthy people are all against it.

Now, one of the peculiar qualities of all poetry is that it can never serve as a medium for sex appeal. There is, of course, prurient poetry, but it has no thrill. It has no other trait but nastiness, and of this there is very little. All this seems strange, because the foundation of all poetry is feeling, and certainly love has never been so well expressed as through the medium of poetry. It is almost impossible to indicate the delicacy with which certain thoughts and feelings we have may be expressed through poetry, execept by giving actual examples. But take this bit by Anthony Munday (1553-1633). Would it be possible, through any other medium, to convey the restraint, the suggestion of quaint humor, the absolute fidelity to that admixture of animal and spiritual that we call human nature?

Beauty sat bathing by a spring,
   Where fairest shades did hide her;
The winds blew calm, the birds did sing,
   The cool streams ran beside her.
My wanton thoughts enticed mine eye
   To see what was forbidden:
But better memory said Fie;
   So vain desire was chidden—
     Hey nonny nonny O!
     Hey nonny nonny!

Into a slumber then I fell,
  And fond imagination
Seemed to see, but could not tell
  Her feature or her fashion:
But ev'n as babes in dreams do smile,
  And sometimes fall a-weeping,
So I waked as wise that while
  As when I fell a-sleeping.

It would seem almost as if poetry, in its province of portraying our emotions, was incapable of using itself for the purpose of soliciting our baser passions, from which it ever holds itself aloof. Yet what power it has to move us to better things!

Most of us now know that, in manipulating a wireless receiving station, we are first forced to tune our instrument to the right wave length of the sending station before we can hear anything from that station. We know also that we can readily go from one station to the other, receiving from each in turn, and sometimes a part of two, merely by changing to the wave lengths of the sending stations we want to listen to. Is this not a perfect illustration of our varying appreciation of poetry? Unless our particular station is equipped with an accurate auditory receiver it will be utterly impossible to understand poetry. One of the most singular illusions entertained by some people is the belief that they can write poetry. In every community there is some poor soul who inflicts his verses upon the readers of the local paper and, encouraged by the editor, acquires a reputation that often stands by him to the grave, so that he dies in the belief that he is a poet. One or two of my own newspaper friends, whose names I charitably withhold, have been guilty in thus fostering fictitious reputations, by reprinting horrible verses from some obscure "singers" and helping them on their path of illusion. May it not be right after all to do this, and what is the difference, so long as the result is secured? Many people have reputations for respectability who, within, are quite hollow —and if a man thinks he is a real poet all his life, he is, so far as he is concerned.

I think it was William James who, some years before he died, made an attempt to define a standard of literature, so that any given production could be judged, not precisely by an "efficiency" chart, but by certain accepted rules agreed to by competent judges. Such attempts of course are not new. So far as poetry is concerned, the most blatant experiment to reduce poetry to a science was made by Hudson Maxim in his "Science of Poetry"—a perfect illustration of the futility of reducing any form of art to a formula. It seems to be true, indeed, of all scientific minds, that they are utterly incapable of understanding anything that is not material. The fine frenzy of the poet, the search for reality of the mystic—all these spiritual things escape them. This is the more strange because all that is finest and best in life, all those invisible things—God, and Reality, The Self, The Universe, Brahma, The Tao—call it what you will, are based upon Law, and Law is based on mathematics, on numbers, as Heraclitus pointed out so long ago. Thus it would seem as if all intelligent minds, working in restricted fields, would come rapidly to understand that it may not be given to them to grasp the perfection that has been achieved by others: or to put it in another way, it would seem as if all intelligent minds would tend to become more humble, instead of more self-assertive. Should the reader wish an example of what I mean, let him turn to an essay on George Eliot, by Edmund Gosse, in his "Aspects and Impressions" (Scribner). Mr. Gosse gives a bit of poetry written by George Eliot which is he declares "the best piece of poetry that George Eliot achieved." He then quotes the poem (a sonnet) and observes: "How near this is to true poetry, and yet how many miles away!"

The first four lines are as follows:

His sorrow was my sorrow, and his joy
    Sent little leaps and laughs through all my frame
My doll seemed lifeless, and no girlish toy
    Had any reason when my brother came.

Those that know poetry when they read it, and those that do not, are widely separated. Nothing can be done about either. And poetry itself cannot be put on any basis of so-called "efficiency."

I have friends who are incited to fury by the very mention of Amy Lowell. Yet there is a certain quality about her work that is often charming. Our best poet is considered to be Edwin Arlington Robinson; yet, in England, he is thought to be dull by the best critics. There is naturally a difference of opinion about him over there, his adherents being enthusiastic. Yet it is undeniably true that his poetry is not received there with the same acceptance accorded to that of Vachel Lindsay.

So far as the comic poets are concerned, practically our whole school of comic poetry is derived from the English comic poets. Without Calverly and Locker-Lampson, without Tom Hood, or Thackeray even, or at present, Sir Owen Seaman of *Punch,* and a number of others, where would our American versifiers be? Few of them have succeeded in breaking loose from the British tradition. Without W. S. Gilbert and his "Bab Ballads," not to mention his masterpieces in comic opera, it is doubtful if half our American comic poetry to-day, would be in existence.

Yet this, in itself, should not be taken as condemnation. On the contrary, pattern is essential. Undoubtedly the English writers got much of their inspiration and their form from the classical poets, particularly Horace. Shakespeare was only the best of a long line of contemporaries. Mahaffy, if I mistake not, says that, in Athens, there have been discovered over eight hundred fragments of comic operas. Perfection comes only through a great number all working for the same end. The real criticism to be made against our American comic poets is not that they copy the form of the British poets, but that they have so little else of genuine soil-inspiration to show. We are constantly looking for some poet of the people, who it is hoped will voice the native longings. Thus we had Walt Whitman, acclaimed by many foreign critics as a genuine poet; we have Whitcomb Riley, and latterly we have Vachel Lindsay and Sherwood Anderson. There is humor in much of this—sometimes very grim, but unmistakably there.

During the past few years there has been a tremendous outburst of poetry on both sides of the Atlantic. And while it may be true that, in verse writing pure and simple, we fall behind our British cousins who excel us in the finer cadences, in the more delicate word meanings, yet we often come closer to nature in our more boisterous efforts.

In his preface to "Poems from *Punch*" Mr. W. B. Drayton has this to say about the Comic Spirit:

If our comedy is the golden roof we raise, the shining triumph of the small matter of man's spirit over frowning great difficulties, something must be exacted of the builders who, if it is reared at all, must rear it. True comedy is essentially social. It reflects truth, and its servants, building it constantly and immaterially, must be servants of the truest social good. Satirists and cynics, tragedians and *farceurs*, may be as remote from life as they please and as individualistic. The servant of the Comic Spirit knows his kind, moves with them and loves them. He could be strong without this love no more than Antæus without earth. It puts him in possession of the strength of the whole. Allow for the necessary semi-detachment of the artist, and it gives to all who serve the Comic Spirit that sense of more than equalness to the task which makes men sing as they work, and of that work, otherwise perhaps uninspired, makes the true *domus aurea*.

It is precisely this note of remoteness that distinguishes the Comic Spirit, and it is just in this respect that, on this side, we fall short because our poetry is more commercialized. Where we excel, as I have tried to point out, is in directness, is in downright *unerring-*

ness, that is to say, in occasional flashes of racial humor, in the getting at the heart of things in a practical manner, as one hews down a tree. The humor of our baseball fields for instance is untranslatable,— swift, fleeting, exact in its terminology, unmistakable in its meaning. And it is precisely this genius for saying the direct thing that does such good service in our comic singing, marred as it is by the circumstance of earning out of it, not only a decent, but very often a luxurious living. Consider, for example, those poets who syndicate their verses, and, thus writing them in advance, who have them appear simultaneously in hundreds of papers all over the country! That is what Walt Mason does—spreading the gospel of joy to millions of people daily from his Kansas emporium of Pegasus. The late W. D. Howells set great store by Walt Mason's poetry, and praised it very highly—deservedly so. It is clean and wholesome, and fulfills a useful purpose. Personally, I believe that it has helped greatly in getting people, over a widespread area, to read poetry: by luring them first to his province, Mr. Mason has introduced them to other poets.

"Don't be afraid of us," he has said in effect. "We are gentle people; it will help you to sing with us."

The basis of all poetry is rhythm, and rhythm is music, and music is vibration, and vibration is mathematical and depends upon the laws of the universe. When we speak of getting "close to nature" we little realize that it is not so essential for us to send our physical bodies into the deeps of the forest, highly desirable and recreating physically as that may be, as it is to get what Mr. Trine calls "into tune with the Universe"; and this can be done only through self-discipline, and self-discipline is only tuning up. All this is a personal affair. Those that have taken the trouble to teach themselves, even imperfectly, any art, come to realize the new accretions in spiritual and mental power they receive through the avenues thus opened up. It is not in the finer gradations of scholarship that education or culture lies, but it consists almost entirely in that rhythmic quality that comes from training. Therefore Walt Mason's contribution to his period has been, and is, very considerable. He has introduced the American public to rhythm. He has helped them unconsciously to see what poetry is, what pleasant thoughts it may stir up.

From what Mr. Howells has written about Mr. Mason I am taking the liberty to quote as follows (*Harper's Magazine*):

The great Mr. Pope, indeed, made his money mostly, if not quite entirely, by the subscription publication of his *Homer;* for it was not Homer's *Homer,* though so polished and charming. Whereas we understand Mr. Riley's income has been from the sale of his books "in the trade." Has it been as great as Mr. Mason's? We have no right to ask this question, for it is not Mr. Riley whom the *Kansas City Star* has been interviewing, and, as we divergently began by saying, we are not clear as to the real sum of Mr. Mason's gains. "What is your annual income from poetry?" the interviewer promptly asks, and Mr. Mason answers with apparently the same frankness: "My lowest price a rime is fifteen dollars when I sell in carload lots.

The Adam Syndicate, for which I furnish a daily rime
all the year 'round, pays me twelve dollars each. I
often receive as much as twenty or twenty-five dollars
for a magazine poem. The most I ever earned with my
trusty typewriter was $875 in one month." One
would think that this was a definite statement, but
these are the months of the year—we are writing four
or five weeks before the 1st of March—when all good
citizens are trying to keep to the leeward of the United
States Revenue Collector, and we would like to know
whether Mr. Mason is swearing to $3758, or there-
abouts, as to his annual income. We do not say it is
not, but if Mr. Mason's poems are syndicated to, say,
perhaps two hundred newspapers every day, does he
mean to tell us that he gets $12 a day from the entire
group, or $12 from each paper, and $2,400 from all?
Is his annual income, therefore, $3700 or, more ac-
curately, $751,820? We think he will agree with us
that the last figures would more truly represent the
worth of his output, but we will not bring his modesty
to the blush on this point, and will rather leave him
to his conscience with the Revenue Collector. If his
annual income is actually $751,820, he can richly afford
to say so.

Yet this is a point where we prefer to turn from the
question of money and follow Mr. Mason in his replies
to such questions as the interviewer afterward asks:
"How does the poetry business compare with the
grocery business? Would you advise a young man
ambitious for a career to take up poetry? Has the
present-day poet any other mission than making
money? Are poets born or made? What do the people
want? Do you expect to make poetry your life work?"

From his response to the first of these demands, we
think that the large, affectionate following which Mr.

Mason's verse has won him throughout this fair land of ours will be sorry to learn that he does *not* expect to make poetry his life work, but hopes some day "to own a covered wagon and travel over the country trading horses. When I have earned enough to buy a string of ponies," he said, "I expect to send my lyre to the junk-man." This reply may represent the exhaustion of the over-interviewed rather than the real intention of our beloved laureate; but it is important to know that he believes versing a better business than grocering, so to speak. "I have no bad customers," he says; "and I don't have to stand and argue for three hours to sell forty cents' worth of goods." An editor, when Mr. Mason sends him a poem, "doesn't insinuate that I am giving short weight or that my poetry contains benzoate of soda." Yet he is not quite ready to advise any one to take up poetry as a career. "If I had a stepson who suffered for a career, I would advise him to secure a patent right on some good washing-machine. I wrote poetry for twenty years before I made any money at all out of it, and when moderate success did come, I was too old and feeble to enjoy blowing in the money as money should be blown. . . . If an able-bodied man would sell poetry now he must write poetry that the tired business man can understand at one reading," Mr. Mason says; and he says in answer to the crucial inquiry, "What do the people want?" "They want poetry easy to read; poetry with a jingle in it; poetry that treats of the things and conditions that they are familiar with, and they want their poetry clean and wholesome." And this is exactly what Mr. Mason's own poetry is and does, and has been and done since it began. *Horse Sense,* no more and no less, responds to this long-felt want in the average American than the firstlings of Mr. Mason's Muse, which we hope is not a disrespectful way of putting it. In answer to the question whether the present-day poet has any other mission than making money, he declares "that the modern newspaper poets are doing more to brighten the world and make it a good place to live in than all the extinct poets in the Hall of Fame or Westminster Abbey ever did. The poet certainly has a mission, and he will go ahead mishing whether the returns are large or small." As to whether the poet is born or made, he holds that he is "Both," and he goes on: "Unless one is born with a poet's ear he will never produce good lines, but if he has that equipment he has to be whipped into shape before he can accomplish anything, and the whipping process means travail of spirit and great bitterness; yet all this training is necessary to him if he would make good use of his gift."

Here we have the whole matter in a nutshell; true, a cocoanut nutshell in size, but full of the milk which somehow gets into the cocoanut, and is one with that of human kindness, as Shakespeare (or "Bill," as Mr. Mason calls him) calls it. Music, light, heart, horse sense—these are the vital elements of verse and are the component parts of the best modern poetry. Their blend cannot be too richly paid, whatever the publishers may grudgingly hold, and we never shall cease to rejoice if Mr. Mason earns $751,820 a year by his particular brand of it.

It is notable that Walt Mason was originally born in Canada, although he was undoubtedly reborn in Kansas —not an uncommon thing to happen. Indeed, it would seem as if Kansas was a special state set apart for Americans born elsewhere to be reborn in. The kind of inspiration that Kansas has on tap comes even more readily to those that move there than to those that are born there. The business of Kansas is to stimulate human beings to renewed efforts. Walt Mason's muse seems to be immortal. He was born in 1862, and is still as youthful as when Kansas gave him re-birth.

Another so-called syndicate poet is James J. Montague, whose fame as a humorist is well nigh equal to his fame as a comic poet. Indeed, one hesitates in which class to place him, but, after deliberation, I think his metrical qualities outweigh his more sober practical prose self. He writes me that he was born in Iowa and that, beyond this fact, there are no important events in his life. He has, he declares, been guilty of only one book, the name of which is "More Truth Than Poetry," and that he has been a managing editor and has lived in California, Oregon, Missouri and New York. Mr. Montague has so many qualities that it would be difficult to analyze them all, but, in the main perhaps, it is sufficient to say that his work is characterized by hard sense plus astonishing riming technique, which enable him, perhaps above any of his contemporaries, to maintain a constant level of highly humorous verse. Nothing that he writes, that I have seen, has been poor; almost all of it is so good that he is a constant marvel, especially when it is considered that he writes a poem every day. Back of his pen, he has integrity and accurate information. His satire is never biting, but always effective and sanitary. Take at random an example of his comment on the controversy raging about evolution. It will be recalled that Mr. Bryan had many things to say on this subject, and

provoked much criticism from the intellectuals. Note
that Mr. Montague disposes of Mr. Bryan in a wholly
kindly, but none the less thoroughly efficient manner:

"I wanted my descendants
To be bullfrogs," said the newt.
"A frog has independence,
He's crafty and astute.
He needn't dwell forever
In one unending groove—
But Mr. Bryan never
Would approve.

"The families I've founded,"
Observed the jellyfish,
"I hoped might be surrounded
By all a fish could wish.
But there is no use tryin'
To give the kids a lift—
For William Jennings Bryan
Would be miffed."

"I haven't the ambition,"
The wombat used to whine,
"To better the condition
Of progeny of mine.
My soul it much embitters
To think they have no chance—
But Bryan says us critters
Can't advance."

And so these timid creatures
Emotionless and mute
Retained their ancient features
And didn't evolute.

The newt might be a lion,
The jellyfish a trout—
But William Jennings Bryan
Scared 'em out!

Mr. Montague, it will be seen, has the true comic touch. His sympathies are universal, and being so, he may easily use himself as a medium in which to express his universality, as witness:

RENDERING A REASON

Although there is no end of cash
   In writing screen scenarios
(Which are unmitigated trash,
   As every movie author knows),
Could I, think you, demean myself
   To make the future more secure,
By writing things like this for pelf?
   Why, sure!

Although I know full well it pays
   To scrap one's literary art
And write the sort of sugary plays
   That move the honest low-brow's heart,
Could I produce this sort of thing,
   Though well assured it wasn't good,
For all the wealth that it might bring?
   I could!

Although there's coin in writing books
   Which are not true to life a bit,
In which detectives hunt down crooks
   By using superhuman wit,

Could I be made to use my pen
  For all the money it would get
In faking such unheard-of men?
  You bet!

I do not write scenarios;
  I do not fashion sugary plays,
Nor do I pen ecstatic prose
  In any smart detective's praise.
It's not my art that gives me pause,
  It's not that I am adamant
Against poor stuff; it's just because
  I can't!

If it be asked who writes the most accomplished
verse at present, I think the palm would be awarded
by the majority to Arthur Guiterman, although Newman Levy and Nate Salsbury, both newcomers, have
extraordinary metrical charm.   Asking Guiterman
upon one occasion how it was that his work was so
uniformly good, he replied that he had never written
anything of which he himself did not approve, and that
he had never attempted to write beyond his means.
Would that his example were followed by many others!
It was he that originated the book review in rime,
and his "Rhymed Reviews" have for many years been
one of the features of *Life*.   Here is an example of
his verse, taken at random from his book "The Mirth-
ful Lyre":

The Savage

The savage has the best of it
In Africa or west of it!
    Whatever meat
    He finds to eat
His stomach can digest of it.

His conscience isn't troublesome;
Of joy he has a double sum:
    Unvexed by frills
    And social ills
His mirth is free and bubblesome.

No business ever hurries him;
And when a varlet worries him
    He takes a club
    And smacks the cub
Then fricasees or curries him.

His fancy weaves him airy tales
Of monkey-folk with hairy tails;
    He never saw
    A play by Shaw
Nor read Dunsany's fairy tales.

The Savage has the best of it;
The world—he is possessed of it!
    He loves and loafs
    And laughs at oafs
Like us, who spoil the rest of it.

I want my wisdom frivolized.
My faith and creed unsnivelized,
    And life a sort
    Of sport—in short
I wish I wasn't civilized!

Among the very best of our newspaper poets is Tom
Daly whose Italian poems are many of them classics.
He writes as follows:

I am asked to confess how and when I began to be-er-funny; how I got that way. With apologies to Locker-Lampson I might say:

> I recollect ere I could creep
> I tumbled from my trundle bed
> I landed in a little heap
> Upon my elbows and my head.
> I shook with mirth in every section
> Thinks I "Ochone!
> I seem to be all funny bone"
> And that's my earliest recollection.

Later, with much labor, I dug out of my cranial bone thousands of jokes, which I exchanged for money; not much money to be sure, but probably more than they were worth. I did this first for the *Philadelphia Record,* because the city editor who was my boss at the time, asked me to do it. Then when I became general manager of the *Catholic Standard and Times* I started a little column in that paper of my own free will, for the double purpose of taking my mind off my business cares and of getting the paper quoted for its original humor. Both purposes were achieved.

My funniest quip? It's hard to pick *e pluribus unum,* but this, at which many have smiled, may be it:

The Tides of Love
*** * ***

> Flo was fond of Ebenezer
> "Eb," for short, she called her beau
> Talk of tides of love—Great Cæsar!
> You should see them "Eb" and "Flo."

But I know better. I'm sure the funniest thing I ever wrote, was perpetrated while my amateur standing was inviolate. It was unconscious humor, and it proved to be inimitable, a thing that cannot be said of later, and deliberately professional efforts. I was a clerk at the time in the business office of the *Record*. In those days, when the proletariat screwed up its courage to ask for a raise in wages, it invariably consulted the complete letter writer. But I was ignorant of this. So, in breathless interval of a busy day, I stole one-sixtieth of an office hour to write:

Mr. James S. Mc Cartney, Treasurer.
DEAR MR. MC CARTNEY:
    I have an idea that I am worth more to the *Record* than six dollars a week. Has that idea ever struck you?
                        Respectfully yours,
                              T. A. DALY.

The next morning I was called to the front, and Mr. Mc Cartney handed my letter back to me. But at the bottom of it he had written:

"It's a good idea, and worth a dollar a week."

The humor of it, the good intentional humor was all his, and it cost the *Record* $52 a year. I got a good smile out of it, and so did the chief clerk and one or two of the others to whom I showed it. A week or so later Mr. Mc Cartney called me to the front again.

"That letter of yours," he said, "did you show it to anybody?"
"Why, yes," I stammered, "I thought what you wrote was funny."
He handed me a letter sheet upon which was written in the neat penmanship of a brother clerk:

Mr. James S. Mc Cartney, Treasurer.
DEAR MR. MC CARTNEY:
I have an idea that I am worth more to the *Record* than six dollars a week. Has that idea ever struck you?

Respectfully,
MORRIS H. CANARY.

Not knowing quite what to say I looked at the boss quizzically. He shook his head, and taking the letter from my hand, dropped it into the waste paper basket. For once my writing was inimitable.

The number of our really accomplished lighter versifiers is much greater than appears. In the beginning, I suspect that they have been largely inspired by the work of Eugene Field, who undoubtedly created a school. It would be impossible in a book of this kind, intended more particularly for the writers of prose, to give extended notices to each one of our lighter poets. Among them may be mentioned Clinton Scollard, whose graceful lines for so many years have adorned the pages of *Life* and other periodicals, Jennie Betts Hartswick, Theodosia Garrison, Charlotte Becker, J. W. Foley, S. W. Gillilan and S. E. Kiser.*

* The writings of Arthur Guiterman, Tom Daly, Theodosia Garrison and a number of other humorous poets are also discussed in the third and revised (1922) edition of "Our Poets of To-day," volume 2, in *The American Writers* series by Howard Willard Cook.

CHAPTER XXXVIII

OUR COMIC ARTISTS

IF the really good humorist is rare, consider how much rarer is the comic artist. It would seem as if no country could raise more than two or three at a time. The best one in England at present is H. M. Bateman. Probably the best one in this country is T. S. Sullivant, whose drawings of animals have for so many years appeared in *Life*. And then again, Mr. Sullivant is an Englishman, just as the versatile Oliver Herford is an Englishman.

As a rule, those that begin life with a talent for drawing lack ideas; or at least their knowledge of life in general is too meager. Thus the satirist is almost, if not invariably, a mature person. He has first informed himself, and has then pondered upon his information. He is thereupon struck with the absurdity of the whole affair that we term "Existence," and turns his experience into ridicule. All this naturally takes time; one may not be, either an artist, or a satirist, over night.

It seems to be essential that an artist, to be successful, must have ideas, whereas anybody can *write*. Perhaps this accounts for the scarcity of artists, that is, of artists with a genuine sense of comedy. On the

other hand, there are any number of artists who, with
a moderate sense of fun, manage to grind out a vast
quantity of slap-stick pictorial humor, the recipe for
which appears to have been reduced to a science. The
formula is to develop a set of characters, usually two,
and to carry them through a series of adventures, most
of these exceedingly dull, for the reason that the artist
is obliged to turn out a new adventure every day. One
artist of this school confided to me that he discovered
a method whereby he could draw the whole weekly
series in one day, thus leaving the week free for other
matters. The so-called "strips" are then sent out to
a belt line of newspapers, and appear daily. They are
generally prepared weeks in advance. There is a constant demand for new characters, and a constant failure
to supply the demand. Many years ago, when Mr.
Bennett ran the *New York Herald,* Foxy Grandpa
and his adventures occupied the attention of vast numbers of children. Many of those children thus influenced are now, doubtless, taking their share of
responsibility in affairs. It would be curious to discover what real influence Foxy Grandpa had over them,
or still has over them, just as we may say to-day that
the adventures of Mutt and Jeff may influence the
coming generation. If any one doubts that the influence of pictures is not great, let him consider their
effect. There can be no doubt that the drawings of
Charles Dana Gibson changed quite radically the gait
and carriage of the girl of his period, just as the
movies have had their effect upon the flapper of to-day.
"Art," says Vivian, in Oscar Wilde's "Decay of Lying," "begins with abstract decoration, with purely

imaginative and pleasurable work dealing with what is real and nonexistent. This is the first stage. Then Life becomes fascinated with this new wonder, and asks to be admitted into the charmed circle. Art takes Life as part of her rough material, recreates it, and refashions it in fresh forms, is absolutely indifferent to fact, invents, imagines, dreams, and keeps between herself and reality the impenetrable barrier of beautiful style, of decorative or ideal treatment. The third stage is when Life gets the upper hand, and drives Art out into the wilderness. That is true decadence, and it is from this we are now suffering."

Oscar Wilde wrote these words some years ago, but they are more true now than ever, and they are truer here in America than in England. From this it ought to be evident to the simplest mind among us that any man that has talent—that is, any kind of creative talent —is taking on an enormous responsibility when, for the mere sake of making a great deal of money, he invents characters that, becoming fixed in the public mind, really affect the public, both mentally and physically. The artist must have his ideal clearly before him; it must be something better than he himself is. The temptation of the comic artist is ever to degrade human nature by catering to the lowest element in us, which is our enjoyment of the misfortunes of others. To me characters like Mutt and Jeff are more pathetic than amusing, and I never see them without a shudder. One may well ask however, whether it is possible to amuse without exaggeration, and, in reply, I feel tempted to paraphrase what Fielding has said about burlesque, in the preface to Joseph

Andrews—that he had discovered that it was only necessary to portray men as they are in order to make them ridiculous.

Thus, Mr. Robert Dickey, unquestionably one of the best dog artists in America, told me that he resolutely set his face against caricaturing dogs; that he discovered, by keeping as accurately as possible to nature, that he could produce the most comic effect. The result bears out his contention, and he has made a permanent contribution to Art by keeping true to his ideal.

We must, however, begin to temporize almost immediately, because, just as exaggeration in humorous writing is essential to produce certain effects, so it is in drawing. It depends altogether on how the thing is done. Mr. Sullivant's animals, for example, are grossly exaggerated—it is their very nature and essence to be thus exaggerated; one expects it of them. A Sullivant hippo is a sublime being, only, in this instance, the artist, instead of degrading, has produced an entirely new gallery of animal portraits—one might even say that he has succeeded in investing them all with the very spirit of Falstaff. Their incredible virility constantly fills us with awe.

When we turn to the drawings of A. B. Frost, we discover, at once, quite another quality. Mr. Frost, above all things, is American in his treatment; one gets from his work no suggestion of any foreign school. His calves are American calves, such delightful, rollicking creatures that the mere thought of them sends one into thrills of delight. His fidelity to nature

is again in evidence. He does not depart from truth,
yet how admirably he does it!

What is recognizable in the work of Mr. Gibson,
Mr. Frost and also Frederic Remington (long since
passed away, and, in no sense, a comic artist) is the
native quality of their genius. Latterly, there has crept
in among us, perhaps I should say there has flaunted in
among us, the *Vanity Fair* school of art, smart to the
last degree, without the slightest native appeal, but
nevertheless valuable in the lesson it teaches and in its
admirable technique. I have no quarrel with this sort
of thing, so long as it is healthy; much of it no doubt
is unhealthy, but we can stand a good deal even of that
if it is well executed. The main trouble with us heretofore is that nothing among us has been well executed
except our business deals and the people we lynch.
The British critics shout with applause whenever anything American that is sufficiently raw comes among
them. They welcome our vulgarities—which is all
very well—but we must not forget that to learn how
to do anything well has so far been quite beyond us.
For instance, take the matter of clothes. You will
notice, if you happen to wear what is known as a
custom-made suit, that the button holes in the sleeves
are false—that is, you cannot unbutton them. But if
your coat is made by a first-class tailor, you will notice
that the button holes are real—that is, they can actually
be unbuttoned. Our best tailors, in other words,
have taken their cue from Great Britain. America has
an enormous amount of raw material in art and literature, but our technique is rotten, and the reason why it
is rotten is that we have never had time to perfect

it. We have always been in a hurry. Therefore, we should not despise the lessons in doing things well that come to us from abroad; we should take them to heart, and learn from them that attention to detail so necessary to produce masterpieces. Everybody is an unconscious plagiarist. It is quite easy for example to despise Editors like Mr. Frank Crowninshield of *Vanity Fair,* and to say that he belongs to a limited circle of decadents. But that is nonsense. In his own manner, he has done good; he has made a lot of people very particular; he has created a school of artists and writers who care how they do a thing, and that is important. The substance rarely matters anyway. Personally, if I get him rightly, he is concerned almost entirely with the technique of his job. He has taste. I would much rather trust this job to him than to Mr. H. L. Mencken—who perhaps is too anxious for it.

It is to men like Mr. Crowninshield, Mr. Gibson and to many other editors and proprietors of papers and periodicals that our comic artists look for their sustenance, and therefore these men have a double responsibility. Recall the point I have been making, namely, that the creative mind is rare; that when it does create, it creates things that sway whole masses of humanity; that a single picture may change the physique of a people. Bear this in mind, and you will see that these gentlemen must not only support and develop our comic artists, but must help them to develop themselves in the right way; must offer them a proper medium for their wares; must give them the right setting.

In doing this, it would be a mistake to be too finicky, to be too fearful of consequences. Above all, one must have freedom. The comic supplements are not so bad. Foxy Grandpa and Buster Brown probably helped a lot. It is necessary to have people rough things out for us as we go along, and so I say, let us have anything at all so long as it is well done—and it is undeniable that things are being much better done than they were. The number of our comic artists who are doing their work supremely well is constantly on the increase. I would invite the reader who is at all interested in pictures to look at this work, as it is spread out for him in our periodical literature, with a more critical eye: he will discover in it things that he never suspected. It has always seemed to me a crying shame that a drawing, over which the artist toiled, and which, for technique and general excellence, is perhaps his high-water mark, should be almost ruined in the plate-making and printing, and then be glanced at hurriedly and thrown carelessly aside by thousands of people who have not the remotest idea of the long years of work the artist put in to perfect his technique.

I trust that the average reader, if there be such a person, will not think me a bore if I insist upon his using more discrimination hereafter in his observation of pictures. The pleasure that one derives from a growing capacity to know good pictures, when seen, is something scarcely to be measured until one has made progress, and it fortunately happens that it requires little time. Spread out before us every day are a great variety of pictures, the majority of them very bad, but a few worth while. Let one study the comic artists and discover their particular merits. Perhaps our best cartoonist is Rollin Kirby of the *New York World,* but Mr. Darling of the *Tribune* ("Ding") has his own high merit. To compare the two would be wrong; each belongs to a different school. Among the purely humorous artists, there are James Montgomery Flagg, whose versatility is a constant matter of surprise, and whose talent is almost equal to his enormous conceit, although one is bound to admit that this, like the reports of Mark Twain's death, has been exaggerated. One of the best artists, considered for his technical merits or his sense of humor, is Rea Irvin. His flow of genuine humor seems endless, and he has the merit of never, under any circumstances, being commonplace or tiresome. Then there are Ralph Barton, Gluyas Williams, John Held, Jr., Ellison Hoover, Herb Roth, T. S. Shaver, and a host of others.

The one who did more for comic art in America than any other man was John Ames Mitchell, the founder of *Life.* When Mr. Mitchell started *Life* in 1883, our comic artists could be counted on the fingers of one hand. He himself, an artist of great originality (I think his cupids still hold their own), drew for *Life,* made its cover, and did some of its best early cartoons. His astonishing quality of attracting to himself all kinds of talent, and then of making that talent better, enabled him during the period that he edited *Life,* literally to create a school of comic artists, and, through his paper, to support them so that the habit of looking at humorous pictures became more or less of a public necessity. Without his quiet influence and his astonishing capacities as an editor, many of the men who have made great reputations would not be here to tell the tale. He made comic art in America stand on its feet.

Comic Artists

Herewith is given a representative list of the principal
newspaper comic artists of this country, together
with features that are syndicated.

Gene Byrnes, "Reg'lar Fellers"
H. A. MacGill, "Percy and Ferdie"
Stanley McGovern, "Dumbell Dan"
Marion Farley, "Mrs. Contrary"
Percy L. Crosby, "Crosby's cartoons"
Jack Wilson, "Radio Ralf"
Clare V. Dwiggins, "School Days," "Ophelia's Slate,"
    "Tom Sawyer and Huckleberry Finn"
Harry J. Westerman, "Sketches from Life"
C. W. Kahles, "Hairbreadth Harry"
Lang Campbell, "Uncle Wiggily's Adventures"
Arch. Dale, "The Doo Dads"
Dudley T. Fisher, Jr., "Jolly Jingles"
Chas. P. Plumb, "When I Was a Kid, I Thought——"
Frank Wing, "Back Yonder"
Walter Bradford, "Radioitis"
Richard Cutler, "Among Us Mortals"
Jim Barnes, "Weekly Golf Lesson"
Claire A. Briggs, "Mr. and Mrs.," "Among Us Mortals"

Thornton Burgess, "Burgess Bedtime Stories"
Harrison Cady, "Peter Rabbit" book, "Caleb Cottontail"
J. N. Darling, "Ding"
Grantland Rice, "Spotlight" and "Tales of a Wayside Tee"
Charles Voight, "Petey" and "Betty"
Charles Wellington, "Pa's Son-in-law"
H. T. Webster, daily cartoons
George Chappell, "Pastimes for Old and Young"
Hungerford, "Snoodles"
Ad Carter, "Just Kids," "Our Friend Mush," "Mr. George," "Finheimer Twins"
Ed Wheelan, "Minute Movies"
Edwina, "Cap Stubbs"
Wood Cowan, sport cartoons
Francis Gallup, rural character illustrator
J. H. Donahey, human interest and humorous cartoons
Albertine Randall, "In Rabbitboro"
Paul Pim, "Baby Mine"
Hy Gage, "Gay and Glum" series
Glyas Williams, book, "In Pawn"
Wallace Goldsmith, "Two Boys in a Gyro Car"
Reginald Birch, Judge Shute's books
W. E. Hill, "Among Us Mortals"
Martin Justice, "Rebecca" and various books
Mrs. Lucy F. Perkins, "Twins" series
Clara Atwood, "Bunnikins" series
Milo Winter, "Billy Popgun"
Maurice Day, "Book of Fables"
Morgan Dennis, "The Real Diary of the Worst Farmer"
E. Boyd Smith, "Noah's Ark" series
A. I. Keller, "The Courtin'"
Ross, "Children's Munchausen"
Clifford L. Sherman, The Dot Books
Frank A. Nankivell, "The Book of Fairy Tale Bears"

Herbert Johnson, human-interest cartoon
A. R. Momand, "Keeping Up with the Joneses"
L. E. O'Mealia, "Wedlocked"
W. J. Sinnott, "Dicky Dippy's Diary"
K. C. Casey, "Yesterday and Today"
Billy De Beck, "Barney Google," "Bughouse Fables"
J. E. Murphy, "Toots & Casper"
Rudolph Dirks, "The Katzies"
Tom Powers, "Mrs. Trouble" and cartoons
E. C. Segar, "Thimble Theatre," "The Five-Fifteen"
Dok Willard, "Outta-Luck Club"
Russ Westover, "Tillie the Toiler"
George McManus, "Bringing Up Father"
Harold Knerr, "Katzenjammer Kids"
Fred Opper, "Down on the Farm" and cartoons
James Swinnerton, "Little Jimmy"
Jean Knott, "Eddie's Friends"
Walter Hoban, "Jerry on the Job"
Harry Hershfield, "Abie the Agent," "Kabibble Kab-
    eret"
T. A. Dorgan, "For Better or Worse"
George Herriman, "Krazy Kat"
J. P. Arnot, "How Do They Do It?"
Tad, "Indoor Sports"
Jean Knott, "Just Like a Man"
Tom McNamara, "Us Boys"
J. P. Arnot, "The General"
Fred Faber, "Then the Fun Began"
W. G. Farr, "Embarrassing Moments"
Hal Coffman, cartoons
Cliff Sterrett, "Polly & Her Pals"
R. F. Outcault, "Buster Brown"
A. C. Fera, "Just Boy"
Rube Goldberg, "Boob McNutt"

Winsor McCay, cartoons
Harry Murphy, cartoons
O. P. Williams, cartoons
Joe McGurk, cartoons
Fred Locher, "Cicero Sapp"
Rudolph Dirks, "The Captain and the Kids"
Gus Mager, "The Hawkshaw" strip
Maurice Ketten, "Can You Beat It?"
Vic Forsythe, "Joe's Car"
Bud Counihan, "The Big Little Family"
R. M. Brinkerhoff, "Little Mary Mixup"
Ken Kling, "Katinka"
Gene Carr, "Metropolitan Movies"
Milton Gross, "Help Wanted"
Zere, "Man the Master," "Will Somebody Explain This,
    Please?" "Ever Been Through This?"
R. L. Goldberg, "I'm the Guy"
Fontaine Fox, "Toonerville Trolley," "The Powerful
    Katrinka," "The Terrible Tempered Mr. Bang"
H. J. Tuthill, "Home, Sweet Home"
Harold Probasco, sport comics
E. P. Hughes, sport cartoons
E. A. Bushnell, editorial cartoons
John C. Terry, cartoons on Washington political life
Frank Beck, "Gas Buggies," "Down the Road"
Walter Berndt, "That's Different"
Chester I. Garde, "Never, Never News"
Mel Cummin, children's cartoons
H. Landing Smith, "Sleepy Time Tales"
Nelson Harding, editorial cartoons
Sidney Smith, "Gumps"
J. P. McEvoy, "The Potters"
Frank King, "Gasoline Alley"
Carey Orr, "The Tiny Tribune"

Carl Ed, "Harold Teen"

M. M. Branner, "Winnie Winkle, the Bread Winner"

John T. McCutcheon, editorial cartoons, etc.

Gaar Williams, political cartoons

Merril B. Blosser, "Freckles and His Friends"

George Swanson, "Salesman Sam"

W. E. Hollman, "Billville Birds"

Gene Ahearn, "Our Boarding House"

A. D. Condo, "Everett True"

Walter Allman, "Doings of the Duffs"

J. R. Williams, "Out Our Way"

Lee W. Stanley, "The Old Home Town" and "Gassaway Miles"

R. W. Satterfield, "The Bicker Family"

Leslie Elton, "Children's Stories in Pictures" and "Jack Daw's Adventures"

Edgar Martin, "Nut Bros."

Dorman H. Smith, political, etc., cartoons

J. R. Grove, sport cartoons

Louis Hanlon, "Follies of the Passing Show"

Sykes, daily cartoon

A. E. Hayward, "Somebody's Stenog"

Geo. W. Rehse, "Children of Adam"

Jack Collins, "That Reminds Me"

Dunn, "And Then He Changes His Mind," "Dumb-Bells"

John Bache, "The Crossing Cop"

Mr. W. Hanny, cartoons

Harry O'Neill, "Us Kids"

Frank W. Hopkins, "Noozie" The Sunshine

A. Y. Hambleton, "Smiles"

Al Posen, "Then Days Is Gone Forever"

H. M. Talburt, "Casey the Cop"

Vance De Bar Colvig, "Life On the Radio Wave"

Johnny Gruelle, "The Adventures of Raggedy Ann and
    Raggedy Andy"
Bud Fisher *
C. Frueh †

* Mr. Fisher is probably the most successful syndicate artist in
the country.
† Mr. Frueh does work almost exclusively for the *New York
World.* He ranks very high.

CHAPTER XXXIX

OUR AMERICAN HUMORISTS SINCE THE WAR

IF we assume the possibility of the inauguration of an Academy of American Humor, somewhat similar to the American Academy of Arts and Letters, but necessarily confined to the field of humor alone, who would be eligible?

Let us first make a preliminary list, subject to additions, and then discuss it on its merits. In this way we shall be able to get a fair idea of who our present humorists are, why they are humorists, the distinctions among them and other matters relating to this subject.

AMERICAN ACADEMY OF HUMOR

1. Finley Peter Dunne.
2. George Ade.
3. Harry Leon Wilson.
4. Will Rogers.
5. Irvin Cobb.
6. Montague Glass.
7. Franklin P. Adams.
8. Don Marquis.
9. Robert Benchley.
10. Donald Ogden Stewart.
11. George Chappell.
12. Corey Ford.

13. Simeon Ford.
14. George Kaufman.
15. Christopher Morley.
16. Clarence Day, Jr.
17. Amos (Freeman F. Gosden).
18. Andy (Charles J. Correll).
19. Ring Lardner.
20. Chic Sale.

It is immediately obvious that objections will be raised. A lot of people will raise their hands and want to know why others have not been included. Also, some will have forgotten all about Simeon Ford and even the immortal Finley Peter Dunne, just because these two real humorists have stopped writing humor. Then there is Simeon Strunsky, one of our most talented humorists, hiding his light in an editorial office.

They will doubtless all agree that George Ade should head the list (and the list I have made is not in any order of precedence) ; but some of them will think, if Harry Leon Wilson is included, why not other story writers, as for example Richard Connell.

Again somebody will object to Amos 'n' Andy, not because they aren't funny, but because they cannot be classed as literary.

I agree to every objection raised. My object is not to make an ironclad list, and get into an argument, but to start something so that, after it has been threshed out, a vote can be taken.

And all I propose to do is to give such information and observation as occurs to me, in order to shed light on this melancholy subject.

First then, it is practically impossible to define a humorist, as such, without having to admit that his humor, whatever it is, is a by-product, a fraction of his personality, just as a ham bone is only a flavoring part of a rich soup, which consists of a great number of other ingredients.

But still, broadly speaking, there are some men who, when we think of them, we think of them as humorists. Going back into literary history, we think of Artemus Ward and Bill Nye only as humorists. We think of Mark Twain as our chief humorist, and a good deal more. While his humor colored almost everything he wrote, he was also a story teller, a traveler, and his Joan of Arc gives him some standing as a biographer.

Similarly, today, we think of Will Rogers as being only a humorist. This does not, or should not, detract from his reputation as a wise man, but rather adds to it. Yet if you attempt to say why he is only a humorist, and thus are compelled to tell what a humorist is, you are in difficulty at once. Charles Dickens, among other things, was a humorist. But you cannot say of him that he was *only* a humorist. We think of Will Rogers more in that way, simply because we don't think of him particularly in any other way.

Similarly also but in a diminished manner, we think of Stephen Leacock as only a humorist, because we are but dimly acquainted with his other activities: that he is a professor of political economy. Thus Queen Victoria, thinking that the immortal author of "Alice in Wonderland" was only a humorist, wrote to him for "more" and was rewarded with some abstruse works on mathematics.

Those of us who are familiar with A. A. Milne's delightful child verses ("When We Were Very Young" and others) and his work in *Punch,* know that he is a humorist, but a broader public knows him as a playwright and novelist.

And if we are willing to admit that Amos 'n' Andy are real humorists only, what is the objection to including them in our proposed Academy? Indeed how can they well be omitted?

This leads me to ask: What are the qualifications to the Academy? Without wishing to force my views on the voters, I should say that the qualifications on the part of any member should be, first, that his work should be purely American, racial, springing from the soil, untainted by foreign influences; second, that it should be universally American, by which I mean that it should not be exclusive to any one section—this means that it should deal with those qualities of human nature which are common to all men and women; and third, that it should be pleasant, not unpleasant, sweet, not bitter, constructive and not destructive. No one can doubt that Amos 'n' Andy have fulfilled these requirements, in creating two characters who, in addition to displaying all the foibles of Americans, add to this the foibles of the negro, who is deeply rooted in the American soil. And their work is distinctive in that they are known only for this. Indeed it is a great achievement for these two men that they should have been the single exception to succeed as radio humorists, for of no other broadcaster can this be said. That this may be the one thing they have done, that it may fall of its own weight of repetition, does not detract from the dramatic qualities of this achievement.

Chic Sale is another instance of singularity. He told me he had created his humorous characters for vaudeville out of the original little red schoolhouse he attended as a boy. There he absorbed the universal elements which are the basis of all real comedy. It was this elemental atmosphere which enabled him to write "The Specialist," a best seller, running well over fiction best sellers, which—in a work of humor—is extraordinary, for it is rare that a work of humor becomes a best seller. In this instance, the fact that his subject was one not referred to in parlor conversation undoubtedly helped. Yet, as a matter of fact, there was certainly nothing destructive about it; it was mainly constructive. In a way it was vulgar but not unmoral—a pure American product.

Another soil humorist, one hundred percent American and humorist only, is Kin Hubbard of Indianapolis, who passed away from us so recently. He was rated very high, and deservedly so. His last books were "Abe Martin's Town Pump" (1929), and "Abe Martin's Broadcast" (1930). The first of these bears the dedication "To my friend George Ade." His work was almost exclusively gnomic, consisting of sententious sayings, as for example: "The life of a June bride an' a three-dollar straw hat seems to be about the same, both looking purty well done fer by September."

Kin Hubbard never wandered very far from Indianapolis, his philosophic temperament having absorbed whatever urge for fictitious fame might have been his had he gone out for it.

Bugs Baer, who writes much in the same vein, but has achieved a broader popularity, because of his syndicated material in the Hearst papers, is also a soil humorist, a master of humorous epigram, which, without the story-telling quality, has reaped him a large reward, but not as a fiction writer.

In strong contrast to what may be termed these human-nature humorists, there is a small group of highly sophisticated writers—strange to say, most of them coming from the interior—who, more satirists and burlesquers than humorists, have brought about a school of enormously popular vogue. This may be called the *New Yorker* school, as it has been fostered and developed by that astute journal, whose creator, Harold Ross, himself came from the interior. These ribald writers and artists, stopping at nothing in their fearless exposure of the idle rich, of eroticism and other forms of sex, and indeed of every form of our national weakness and decadence, perform a useful work, cutting right through the masks into the very bone and marrow.

I suppose that a number of people reading this will wonder at the inclusion of Clarence Day, Jr., author of "This Simian World." Modest in his seclusion, his quiet work has a permanent quality which places him on a high level among those who are really able to judge.

That freedom of expression, which, since the war, has flooded us with every variety of obscenity, and developed a vocabulary among writers and a form among artists, which has stopped at nothing in its shamelessness, has necessarily influenced whatever the thing is that we call humor, and which assumes such contrasting shapes as "funnies," acidulous essays, horse-play stories,

wise-cracks, columns and incredible extremes of fantastic slang.

The result is that we have had a period of burlesque,
the three chief protagonists of which have been George
Chappell, Corey Ford, and Donald Ogden Stewart.

Of these the chief offender is Corey Ford, who beginning with *Life* when I was Editor of that journal,
rapidly developed a vein of his own, and, becoming associated with *Vanity Fair,* found his opportunity. His
first hit in book form was made with "Salt Water
Taffy," a burlesque of that adventurous lady, Joan
Lowell. Later this was followed by a burlesque of Willard Huntington Wright, who, under the pseudonym of
S. S. Van Dine, started the epidemic of thrillers by
writing "The Benson Murder Case," following it with
the "Green Murder Case" and others. These astonishing detective best sellers lent themselves to ridicule, and
young Ford made the most of his opportunity in his
"The John Riddell Murder Case," by John Riddell (a
name he had been using in *Vanity Fair*) and illustrated
by that amazing artist Covarrubias.

George Chappell, an architect besides being an author, made his first essay into burlesque in 1921, when,
under the name of Walter E. Traprock, he issued "The
Cruise of the Kawa." This was followed by "My
Northern Exposure." Capt. Traprock rapidly became
notorious, and Mr. Chappell, who had been aided and
abetted by that playful genius Don Marquis, went about
lecturing as Traprock.

These successful take-offs on polar exploration were
followed by one on traveling in the Sahara Desert, and
then "Through the Alimentary Canal with Gun and

Camera," with interior decorations by artist A. Soglow.

As for Don Stewart, nothing better in parody has been done than his "Parody Outline of American History," his "Father William," or his "Crazy Fool," a wild mixture of the most fantastic irony, which it is quite impossible to classify, except to say that it is excessively funny for those able to rise to its nonsensical delight.

In fact, each of these three writers, in his own manner, is a highly valuable addition to our antiseptic guardians.

These men are pleasant enough about it. There may lurk in their work a latent savagery, but never bitter, except possibly the criticism that has been made of Mr. Corey, that he hits too hard. That is absurd. Intelligent members of wholesome and cultivated families (for example, read the literature of the celebrated Adams family) are often much more free with one another. Anything is friendly which has no other motive behind it but the comic, if it stops short of murder.

It may be asked now, What of H. L. Mencken and Sinclair Lewis? Are they humorists or satirists or burlesquers; that is to say, do they come in here? The answer is faintly yes and louder no.

Widely separated in technic, they have both lashed out fairly well at their country; but the charge against them on the humorous score is that, if not exactly unpleasant (and both are that), they are certainly not pleasant. There is in Mencken no comedy. His temperament is so personally affectionate that he has had to get a release by lambasting everybody, and has done it as one might say, to the queen's taste. It is entirely

unimportant whether he has been right or wrong, and
he has even, if only occasionally, been accused of being
right. Possessed of an inherent genius for invective
and a concealed conscience, it is almost impossible to
overestimate the service he has done us. In the last
resort there is no such thing as right or wrong, but
there is such a thing as degradation of national sentiment, and this Mencken has pilloried; the evangelist,
the sob-sister, the sob-brother, in fact all of the lay
figures of sentimentality, have been his fair mark. I
cannot see very well what we would have done without
him. The point about him is that he has put the country on the defensive, and that is highly important. But
he is not a humorist, for—if it can be defined at all—
humor is an aroma, it is good-natured. Comedy, it is
true, is occasionally brutal, but this is because of its in-
advertence. A. B. Frost, one of our best comic artists
of a preceding generation, made the most comic calves
cavorting in fields. That is comedy, which is joy, abandoned joy. Charlie Chaplin is our true comedian, even
if his custard pies are mildly brutal. Life itself is
brutal, and any attempt to depict it in terms of comedy
must also be so.

Sinclair Lewis is thus brutal and shameless, both of
which are essential to certain forms of high talent, if
not genius. Practically all the big literary artists have
been shameless. You have to be big to be shameless
and get away with it. Sinclair Lewis probably has the
worst taste of any writer in America, but if he had ever
attempted to control either that or his exposure of himself as Babbitt and Elmer Gantry (for he is both) they
would have been straw men instead of national charac-

ters. He has indeed created one comic character, which is a very rare accomplishment. Mark Twain created two, Hawthorne created one, Montague Glass created two, and there are Amos 'n' Andy.

Who else? Calvin Coolidge came very near creating a comic character in himself, and may do so yet, if he keeps on writing. Charlie Chaplin, distinctly yes. Don Marquis came near it in "The Old Soak," and nearer possibly in "archy the cockroach," but they both lack the final touch. There are a number of them, pictorially speaking—Foxy Grandpa, The Hallroom Boys, Mutt and Jeff and many others. But there is a fictitious reality about them, because of their more or less fixed anatomy.

And that has been the difficulty with so many humorists, who, lacking the projective, creative genius to produce living character, have fallen back upon their own personalities. Artemus Ward is the classic example. He was never anything else than Artemus Ward; extremely funny in his day, but still Artemus. Mark Twain rose above this by sheer genius; so we have his Huck Finn and Tom Sawyer, two of our best comic characters, besides being real boys.

Bill Nye never rose above it. Today Bob Benchley, certainly our most accomplished side-splitter, uses his own personality to great advantage; and that accurately amusing artist, Gluyas Williams, helps him greatly to put himself over. If you have not the dramatic, or whatever you choose to call it, story-telling, character-projecting gift, then the rule is, among humorists, "Be yourself." Bob Benchley's latest book, "The Treasurer's Report," which ends with this, one of the first and best of his pieces, is, however, much more than just a burlesque of his own personality, as comic as this has become through G. W.

As one of the essential qualities of humor is that it shall be humorous, and as this quality depends largely on the element of surprise, it follows that it is very difficult to read any long humorous book without becoming jaded. In short, the only way to read any humorous book is by fits. Yet there is something about Benchley's stuff like a bubbling fountain, that one can be continuously sprayed with and this without losing heart.

Don Herold, who, since the war has been very active with his "Bigger and Better," "There Ought to be a Law," "Our Companionate Marriage," and others, is not so good, possibly because he is a good enough artist to draw his own caricatures of himself, his work being so intensely and fantastically individual as to become tiresome. Here one is quite at an *impasse,* for you simply cannot tell why some things are funnier to you than others. Don Herold is an extraordinary humorist, but possibly it is because he lacks indignation; his affections possibly are too universal, and not, as I have indicated in the case of Henry Mencken, confined to his friends and not to his country.

To be either a good humorist or a good satirist, you must have indignation. It is unimportant whether it be moral indignation or not. Immoral indignation is just as good for your purpose. You can be just as indignant with two virtuous people happily married, as you can with two erotic people not married at all. Nothing matters but your quality of indignation.

Possibly this is the reason why there are no woman humorists in our American Academy of Humor. When women become indignant they scratch and bite; with them, it doesn't run out into anything constructively entertaining. The real satirist or burlesquer keeps his temper. Still more than this, he eventually becomes impersonally personal. He takes his victim as a type of something worth holding up to scorn. He loves his victim, singular as this may seem, and why not? Think of what the Babbitts and Elmer Gantrys have done for Sinc Lewis?

But women, being, as one might say, all sex, cannot segregate their indignation long enough to make it useful as a form of entertainment for themselves. Broadly speaking, I suppose that Nina Wilcox Putnam, who has written some amusing pieces about herself in the *Saturday Evening Post,* comes nearest to being a female humorist, in the masculine tradition of Bill Nye and Benchley. Yet she lacks what Falstaff had and she hasn't. I have pointed out elsewhere the extreme excellences of the writings—both prose and poetry—of Dorothy Parker. As a genial humorist she is almost a total loss. As a writer she is a total gain for everybody. Since the early chapters of this book were issued, one of those rare books, namely, "Laments for the Living," has come from her—impossible to describe and subjectively entrancing.

In her "Gentlemen Prefer Blondes"—which, by the way, languished in the editorial rooms of *Harper's Bazar* for ever so long, not being thought well enough of to print—Anita Loos achieved more popularity than she deserved, and this because of the title. Not that it isn't good, but here again you have to make reservations. It is doubtful if she could have written it without the influence of Ring Lardner, plainly evident.

As for Ring Lardner, it does seem still to be true on all counts that he is our best modern humorist. He has written the best humorous stories, the best satire, the best—shall I call it plain?—humor. Some of his friends tried to ruin him by making a highbrow of him. He has survived that. As for the drama, his "June Moon," along with that other real humorist, George S. Kaufman, is a masterpiece, no matter how little he did of it. Nothing funnier in plays has been produced here. For personality humor, his account of himself, "The Story of a Wonder Man," remains the high water mark.

In this my book, which has all the defects of its qualities, it should be evident that the entire field cannot well be covered, nor is this necessary, the object being not to provide an encyclopedia, but to indicate in a general way who are our principal humorists, and—for those who wish to explore the subject in its more intricate details—where further information can be discovered.

It may thus be convenient to classify them under the heads of:

Burlesque Writers.	Broadcasters.
Short Story Writers.	Soil Humorists.
Columnists.	Verse Makers.
Raconteurs.	Comedians.
Playwrights.	Caricature Artists.
Satirists.	Comic Artists.

Cartoonists.

It is obvious that space will not permit me to go into a detailed review of these merrymakers, and besides, this is wholly unnecessary. I shall merely indicate some of the best of them.

The word burlesque covers a number of meanings, from close imitation to broad farce. Aside from those writers already mentioned, there is a group of writers who produce what may be termed farce comedies in novel form, which, generally with a main character and a somewhat grotesque love theme, gives them the opportunity to give a story interest to an otherwise bald and inconclusive take-off.

Thus collaborators like S. J. Perelmann and Q. J. Reynolds present their "Parlor, Bedlam and Bath," and Carroll and Garrett Graham present "Queer People," followed by Whitey, in which a modernistic and wholly irresponsible "hero" diverts us by his alcoholic and other riotous revelry. These books—and a number of others of which they, possibly, are the best—are screamingly funny if read in the right mood, and show positive genius in the art of ephemeral fun. The fact that they are recklessly sexy does not particularly matter. Indeed, their object, if there is any object beyond letting off steam, is to hold sex up to ridicule (note "Is Sex Necessary?" by J. Thurber and E. B. White) and there is little in them to stir our appetites.

Similarly the short story writers use this medium, but in a much more miniature manner. Octavus Roy Cohen has thus, in the *Saturday Evening Post*, produced a series of extremely laughable comedy-satire sketches of the Southern negro, and similarly, William Hazlitt Upson in his earthworm tractor stories, has used this mechanical device as a humorous theme, with great success. Perhaps the most consistently interesting author of short stories is Richard Connell, his first book, "The Sin of Monsieur Pettipon" (1922), and his last one, "Ironies" (1930), showing his capacity to maintain a high level. There are a number of others but it is probable that, after all, none equals Ring Lardner.

So far as the columnists are concerned, this field has had a wide development since the first edition of this book. I still think as already stated, that F. P. A. is the best of them; but E. J. Phillips of the *Sun,* and Edward Hope of the *Herald-Tribune,* New York, are both excellent. Raconteurs like Walter Winchell, who have an almost supernatural cleverness for producing wise-cracks, reap big rewards in money. It is a very rare accomplishment to produce daily laughs with unfailing wit, and their superficial quality need not obscure our sense of genius behind the typewriter or the dictaphone. Will Rogers and Walter Winchell represent two different angles of an amazing gift which—speaking for the whole people, for these flashes are widely syndicated—"helps a lot." Eddie Cantor, the Marx Brothers, Charlie Chaplin, Winchell and Rogers, Sam Hellman, Nunnally Johnson, the other columnists not here mentioned, extending across the country, the comic artists—all these represent various kinds of talent all proceeding from the racial fountain of mirth, and if they should all stop doing what they do, God help the country. As for Frank Sullivan, he has come near creating one character, and at his best he is wholly irresistible.

The verse makers are necessarily more limited in their form, but with many of them (as with Don Marquis) verse is only one of their mediums. Samuel Hoffenstein with his "Poems in Praise of Practically Nothing," Baird Leonard with her "Simple Confession," Stoddard King with his "Raspberry Tree," Newman Levy with his "Saturday to Monday," and Ogden Nash with his "Hard Lines"—these and more, show a great advance in the technic of verse writing over former periods. One of the most accomplished writers of metrical satire is revealed in "The Great Enlightenment," by Lee Wilson Dodd. A masterpiece of burlesque of the old sob ballads is the work of Clarence H. Knapp, in his "I'm Sorry if I Have Offended." Still another (mostly prose, however) is "Frankie and Johnny," by John Huston.

Parenthetically, what I have termed the *New Yorker* School of Satire, developed around that audacious journal, giving a group of writers and artists the opportunity, not only to ridicule their present environment—thus applying a suitable antiseptic to so many social stuffed shirts—but, owing to our rapidity of living and the fact that we have thus outgrown former periods, to burlesque these periods. The best of this burlesque is seen in Josie Turner's "Elsie Dinsmore," in which that saintly adolescent is reincarnated with unerring modernistic insight.

By far the most consistent pictorial satire of a past period, however, appeared in *Life*, the work of that gifted artist, R. V. Culter, who, gone from us, leaves such a gap. His "The Gay Nineties," for sheer delight and true restraint and fidelity to the originals, has not been equaled in this country.

Our comic artists and cartoonists belong in another book, so we must pass over the intensely penetrating grotesques of Milt Gross, the vividly innocent reconstructions of John Held, Jr., the awful and delightful devastations of Peter Arno, Percy Crosby's delightful Skippy, and alas! so many others.

On the whole, the true spirit of comedy is more widely and more effectively revealed by our artists than by our writers; but, because a picture is over with almost immediately after it is looked at, and because words, in their assemblages, are more permanent, it does seem as if the real importance of our comic artists is not understood. And this is true also, of course, of our comic actors. Charlie Chaplin, ceasing to act, becomes merely a delightful memory; whereas, the works of Ade and Lardner, Benchley, Corey Ford, Don Marquis, and so on, are preserved for us, a perpetual solace, an ever present help in time of depression.